ADVANCED REPORTING
Beyond News Events

Gerry Keir
Honolulu Advertiser

Maxwell McCombs
University of Texas at Austin

Donald L. Shaw
University of North Carolina at Chapel Hill

Longman
New York & London

Executive Editor: Gordon T. R. Anderson
Production Editor: Pamela Nelson
Text Art: Nina Tallarico
Production Supervisor: Eduardo Castillo

Advanced Reporting

Longman Inc.
95 Church Street
White Plains, N.Y. 10601

Associated companies:
Longman Group Ltd., London
Longman Cheshire Pty., Melbourne
Longman Paul Pty., Auckland
Copp Clark Pitman, Toronto
Pitman Publishing Inc., Boston

Library of Congress Cataloging-in-Publication Data

Keir, Gerry.
  Advanced reporting.

  (Longman series in public communication)
  1. Reporters and reporting. I. McCombs, Maxwell E.
II. Shaw, Donald Lewis. III. Title. IV. Series.
PN4781.K38 1986   070.4'3   85-24105
ISBN 0-582-28477-5

86 87 88 89 9 8 7 6 5 4 3 2 1

Contents

v

Part III
DOCUMENTS AND RECORDS

Preface

History has always challenged journalists to match their news gathering skills with the changing nature of events they cover. When Nellie Bly in the nineteenth century faked insanity to report on the New York asylums, she produced stories that traditional records and interviews could not yield. Nellie became a participant journalist. She became part of the event.

Nineteenth-century reporters also discovered that a good interview, if smoothly written, equals a good story. Muckrake journalists Lincoln Steffens and Ida M. Tarbell learned that exceptional interviews could produce journalism of great power and, in the case of Steffens, even high literary achievement. These journalists of nearly a century ago stepped up the power of their reporting techniques in order to probe the news of the day more deeply.

Steffens and Tarbell, among others, also examined public and private records. Like journalists today, they found these documents revealing and often at variance with public pronouncements. Records are revealing, if reporters are willing to find and read them.

These early reportorial experiences form the backbone of newsroom tradition today. But reporters need to expand these traditions to meet the challenge of contemporary events. For example, political leaders commonly make use of survey data to devise campaign strategies and even to determine whether or not to run. Reporters must understand how to evaluate survey data and, beyond that, how to conduct surveys themselves.

Surveys really represent the stepped-up power of single interviews. Through surveys, reporters can check assertions that the public supports or does not support war in Central America or that the public will or will not support greater taxes for local schools. Politicians and many others routinely argue that the public supports these positions. That's good politics. Interviews with these leaders are not likely to uncover a different view, but you may discover something different with your own survey.

Reporters need to understand survey research in their own self-defense, if nothing else. Reporters with little knowledge of sampling, question bias, or survey timing will be at the mercy of those who conduct a survey and who have a point of view to present. Too often, reporters cannot match skills with those presenting survey information and so just pass along the information. Responsible journalists possess skills to evaluate information, not just to write it up well.

The ability to step up the power of using documents enables reporters to produce many other kinds of evidence about particular communities. For example, tax records enable reporters to see whether local taxes are disproportionately paid by the poor. Court records can provide ways to determine whether justice is meted out fairly to blacks and whites. Police records can provide ways to determine areas where it is unsafe to walk—not always dark, out-of-the-way places. Documents can provide insights that interviews or surveys cannot.

Nellie Bly was ahead of her time in many ways. Reporters who find simple observation of limited use can sometimes "set up an experiment" to find out how things really work. Does a black reporter pretending to look for a home get the same treatment at local real estate offices as a white reporter? What about seeking a bank loan? Interviews cannot tell you, nor can documents. To find the answers to these questions, you have to heighten your power of observation.

Reporters are both writers and observers. Most of the public thinks of reporters as writers; journalists take great pride in their writing and work at it constantly, as they should. But most importantly, reporters are observers. They must be able to match news gathering skills with the challenge of changing events. If asking a few persons is not enough, they must be able to enlarge the survey. If a single or a few documents are not enough, they may want to conduct a content analysis and compare documents over time. On occasion, reporters may want to test a hypothesis about how things really are by conducting an experiment.

Imagine, for example, a situation in which the mayor says: "The public wants a street built between Elm and Oak Streets as a convenient connector to reach the new bypass." That is a good interview story. But you check documents, finding that the mayor owns land through which the new street would pass. That is a good document story. Next you conduct a survey and find that only 22 percent of the community favor such a street, while 46 percent oppose it and the rest are undecided. That is a good survey story. You check more documents and find that three members of the city council also own property on the proposed new street. So you extend your search and discover that council members and, on occasion, the mayor have profited several times before by street construction projects. In fact, no new street has recently been constructed without some profit to these city officials. A content analysis of still more documents reveals that certain construction companies are overly represented, companies incidentally in which the city officials have an interest. The story deepens.

You can see that the story is now far more interesting and important than the mayor's simple assertion: "The public wants a street. . . ." If you are not prepared to examine this assertion fully, you may mislead the public. Sometimes being prepared means stepping up the power of the trusted techniques of simple observation, interviews, and documents to include participant observation, surveys, and content analysis. This book is not about the routine stories that do not require this increased power. It is about those times when events do require it. Or should!

The origins of this book lie in Gerry Keir's visit to Syracuse early in 1983. Taking a leave of absence as city editor of the *Honolulu Advertiser*, Gerry was a visiting scholar in the John Ben Snow Program of Advanced Study in Newspaper Research. At that time Maxwell McCombs was the John Ben Snow Professor of Newspaper Research at Syracuse University. Joining them in this enterprise was McCombs's longtime research and writing partner, Donald Shaw, professor of journalism at the University of North Carolina at Chapel Hill.

Key to making this partnership successful was the energetic and creative work of Lynne Manuel, John Ben Snow research secretary. All three authors and the readers of this book owe Lynne a great debt of gratitude for her skills in word processing, designing, and organizing the many tasks necessary to produce a book.

Thanks also are due to Ed Caudill, an experienced Ohio journalist who was Don Shaw's graduate student at Chapel Hill and now teaches at the University of Tennessee at Knoxville, and to the numerous research assistants and secretaries in the Communication Research Center who helped bring this volume into existence. The authors would also like to thank Donald A. Bird of Long Island University for suggesting several excellent examples of investigative journalism and UNC Professor William Chamberlin for reviewing certain legal portions of the manuscript.

We hope this working partnership between newsroom and campus will intrigue the new generation of journalists now in college.

ADVANCED REPORTING

Part I
PERSPECTIVE ON REPORTING

CHAPTER 1
What's News?

News is anything that makes a reader say, "Gee whiz!"
Arthur McEwan, *San Francisco Chronicle*

News is anything you find out today that you didn't know before.
Turner Catledge, *New York Times*

When a dog bites a man, that is not news; but when a man bites a dog, that is news.
John B. Bogart, *New York Sun*

People have been trying to define *news* for a long time. Journalism texts on the subject could fill a bookcase. On key points, there is consensus:

> The more timely, the more news value. Yesterday's city council meeting is a newsier story than last month's.
> The closer to home, the newsier. A bus crash in Johnson City is a far better yarn for the *Johnson City Times* than a bus crash in Mexico City.
> The more consequence to more people's lives, the newsier. A change in the property tax rate affecting every Johnson City homeowner gets better play than a change in the excise tax for widget manufacturers.
> Names make news. Research has shown that people are drawn more to human interest stories than to other kinds. The human interest factor can be your next-door neighbor or a Hollywood celebrity.
> The unusual is news. Man bites dog.

Beyond these areas of consensus, it's tough to get agreement, even among practiced journalists, on just what news is. The most common response might be, "I may not be able to define news, but I know it when I see it." In *The Fourth Branch of Government*, Douglass Cater's book on the power of the Washington press corps to shape events in the nation's capital, news is described this way:

> News is a vaguely definable commodity recognized more by instinct perhaps than by copybook maxims. One of the perennial sources of astonishment for the nonprofessional is to attend a congressional committee hearing and witness the row upon row of reporters seated at the press tables as they lift their pencils and lay them down with almost ballet corps precision while the flow of testimony moves along.

These decisions about what is and is not news determine the daily information diet we receive from the media about everything around us. Choices made by thousands of news reporters and ed-

Figure 1.1   View of a typical city room (*The Honolulu Advertiser*).

itors determine what makes the news. *You*, as a journalist, make the news. At individual newspapers and television stations, news is what the reporters and wire services cover. The decisions may come down from on high when an editor, publisher, or city editor assigns reporters to cover an event, or they may come from the bottom when you as a beat reporter can choose which among competing events or topics you will cover.

NEWS EVENTS

For a long time, the definition of *news* has included one other important attribute: the *news event*. Most news is event centered. Some events are automatic news producers, such as the daily stock market, presidential press conferences, the World Series. For the most part, this is indisputable—journalists describing the world must provide accounts of the newsworthy events that take place in it.

The Washington bureau of a wire service maintains a list of important congressional and agency hearings and decides which to cover each day. Also on the list will be the day's roster of press conferences by presidents, visiting kings, senators, lobbyists, and foreign diplomats. At the local level, the newsroom of a newspaper or broadcast station has a daily calendar of its own would-be news events to pursue. Instead of congressional hearings, a news event might be the city council. Instead of the Supreme Court, it might be the arraignment of an accused Johnson City bank robber. Instead of a presidential news conference, it might be the mayor cutting a ribbon.

The court reporter looks at judges' calendars for Tuesday, picks out what to cover in his or her eight-hour shift, and seeks help from the city desk or news director for the remaining newsworthy trials that would otherwise go uncovered. The assignment editor picks and chooses from among local hearings, speeches, meetings, press conferences, and other staged news events. Some get covered; others do not. Adam Hochschild, editor and columnist for the investigative journal *Mother Jones*, put it this way:

> American reporters are like tourists in Disneyland. In various places around the amusement park, visitors will recall, there are little yellow signs that read, in essence: "This is a suggested picture taking spot."

Dutiful vacationers stand and click away, then troop on to the next sign.

The press does the same. The vast bulk of what newspaper correspondents write, and of what television reporters declaim in their resonant baritones, is news marked by the equivalent of one of those yellow signs. A sign that says, in effect: "This is a suggested news story."

The signs, of course, mark what governments, corporations, or elected officials consider newsworthy.

This sort of decision making constitutes the bulk of news judgments. One result is that surface developments usually keep reporters busy, not important social trends or pressures beneath the surface. The "why" of events often receives only minor attention.

Eric Sevareid, former CBS commentator, has called this sort of event-oriented coverage "the daily needle shower of unrelated facts." Hasty and superficial event-oriented news fails to give people a context in which to understand bewildering changes in the world. "Without that background, people are simply bombarded by so-called 'facts' which frighten them into an apathy in which they feel powerless and all the world's problems seem insoluble," said Donald Trelford, editor of *The Observer of London*.

"The most pernicious journalistic convention is the notion that a thing is not newsworthy until it becomes an event; that is, until something happens," said Donald McDonald, former head of Marquette University's College of Journalism. "Two things follow from this: First, significant phenomena that are not events (e.g., situations, trends, conditions) go largely unreported; second, often the context which can make even an event meaningful is either not reported or reported inadequately."

Television gave a new twist to this convention. It became essential to get film (now we use tape) to fill up the news broadcasts. It was unthinkable that the viewer should be subjected to a half hour (22 minutes, after commercials) of the anchorperson's and the reporters' talking heads. We needed action. As a result, TV news became not what happened that day but, as former newsman/press secretary Frank Mankiewicz said, "what happened in front of a camera . . . well, no, what happened in front of *our* camera."

As with newspapers, TV news is event centered. It's easy to film an antiabortion march. It's tougher to come to grips with subtle shadings of community public opinion on abortion issues.

It's easy to film press conferences where the mayor and county executive argue about whether to build a new garbage-powered plant that turns steam into electricity. It's a little harder to find out how the public at large really feels about the plant, or to discover how a similar plant three states away has affected air pollution, electricity costs, and the municipal trash-collecting budget.

It's easy to send a reporter and photographer/cameraperson to the Wednesday Rotary Club luncheon to hear the city prosecutor say judges haven't been tough enough on prostitutes. It's more time consuming to find out what actually happened over the last year to Johnson City's prostitutes after they got to court.

It's simpler to cover a civil rights riot than to do preliminary digging and reporting before the riot occurs, to pinpoint the frustrations and anger that may cause riots, or to become a sort of journalistic "distant early warning system," alerting a community to its problems before they become news events. As reporter-turned-precision-journalist (and now professor) Philip Meyer noted, "*If* a man biting a dog is news, a man thinking about biting a dog is a potential scoop."

BEYOND NEWS EVENTS

Mike O'Neill, former editor of the *New York Daily News*, said:

> We need to put more emphasis on what I call preventive journalism—deliberately searching for the underlying social currents that threaten future danger so that public policy can be more intelligently mobilized.

The tougher assignments increasingly are being tackled by today's journalists, at least the ones fortunate enough to work for media that have gone beyond just covering news events as defined by other people—press conferences, hearings, speeches, reports being issued, or sign-waving protesters. These journalists are trying to make their own definitions of what is news. This is not to say that any news medium should suddenly stop covering school board meetings, politicians' speeches, and fires. Important events should and always will be the main staple in the daily news diet. As a reporter you will cover them throughout your career. Readers and TV audiences want and need them.

Philip Schlesinger called news "the exercise of power over the interpretation of reality." Journalists exercise this power by deciding what to cover and how. But if the coverage is chiefly of preplanned events designed in part or in whole to capture media attention, then journalists have abdicated a great deal of their power to the planners of news events, in other words, to those with political or economic power. Shoe clerks who call press conferences don't get covered, but mayors, governors, and corporation presidents do. Those who argue that journalists are holding up a mirror to the world fail to recognize that newsmakers are often a small group of elite personalities who can summon journalistic attention and decide exactly what the mirror focuses on.

Knee-jerk coverage of press conferences and heavy reliance on government and private industry public-information officers turns over to would-be sources nearly exclusive control over news dissemination. Historian Daniel J. Boorstin decried a system that "produces always more 'packaged' news, more pseudo-events. . . . To secure 'news coverage' for an event, . . . one must issue, in proper form, a 'release.'"

Sociologist Herbert Gans, who spent a lot of time in television and magazine newsrooms researching his book *Deciding What's News*, pointed out that the product of this sort of news event journalism is a "top-down" perspective in the media. High officials speak; other high officials react; journalists write. By contrast, getting away from an event-centered perspective allows journalists to view the world from the "bottom-up," a grassroots view of the world in which, after all, most of us reside.

Instead of always focusing on pronouncements from on high— government budgets, tax rates, public programs, and so forth—you must occasionally aim the journalistic mirror at the *effects* these programs have on your community. Do government programs really benefit the people they theoretically are designed to help? Or do they create new victims? What does input from Capitol Hill produce in output on Main Street? This approach requires you to make a conscious effort to focus on segments of society unable or unwilling to create news events.

The op-ed pages in newspapers provide access for points of view different from the papers' own editorial policies. What kinds of news could be generated if city desks and broadcast news departments worked harder to provide access to the newsmaking machinery for segments of society outside the traditional groups that create news events?

One mayor is easier to interview than are 25,000 average citizens. However, one product of this reoriented philosophy of news is better feedback to the people at the top, who often are insulated by the trappings of office from the people they represent. In fact, you can—through a survey—interview a representative sample of the 25,000.

More and more editors and news directors are seeing that a preoccupation with events leaves reporters with too little time and too few resources to pursue the leads these events can give about deeper social, political, and economic trends in their communities. If you master the techniques discussed here for going beyond event-centered journalism, you'll do a better job for both your audience and your own career. A demonstrated ability to find and relate the larger currents in society will mark you as a journalist with breadth and insight and will earn you better assignments.

INVESTIGATIVE REPORTING

At many small or medium-sized newsrooms, the job of nonevent journalism is often left to one or two *investigative reporters*. They tend to be experienced journalists who have shown a facility for systematic inquiry, for finding nuggets of information among piles of documents, for milking sources of otherwise confidential information.

Yet all reporters are investigators. You routinely will sift through the information available about an event, a person, a situation, and try to lay out the most prominent, pertinent, relevant facts in an orderly way that allows a reader or viewer to have a coherent picture of the world.

The shift to a nonevent orientation requires a different mindset and, coincidentally, some courage and persistence. As a beat reporter, you must allocate your time and energy differently. You must be willing to skip a city council hearing because you think it is more worthwhile to go through a file of records in the building department. The problem is that your newspaper and television competitors are probably at the news event. They'll have a "hearing" story; you won't (for a while, at least).

Try explaining that to some old-school editors and news directors. And don't kid yourself—the pressures are there, even for reporters considered to be the cream of the crop. James Doyle, who covered for the *Washington Star-News* the 1972 presidential campaign of George McGovern, told Timothy Crouse for his book *The Boys on the Bus*:

> I find it hard not to write . . . It's a very hard thing to do—to say, it's not worth it today, so I won't file. You always say, "But Jesus, Bill Greider's gonna write today and he'll be on page one and the editors will think that Greider found a good thing to write today for the *Post* and Doyle didn't write anything for our paper." You always worry about that.

But what if it's the tenth time the candidate has given the same speech? What if the hearing is the fourth city council rehash of some obscure zoning bill? What if your search through the building department's files—long and painstaking as it may turn out to be—leads you to a story saying that zoning doesn't matter much anyway because the building department is granting permits that violate the zoning? In that case, it turns out that skipping the hearing was worth it.

Bob Cummings of the *Maine Sunday Telegram* covered a long-running dispute over a dam that would flood forest land in the process of providing more hydroelectric power to his state. His approach to the story?

> I try to avoid the day-to-day coverage. A good, thorough story is worth more, and is more valuable to the reader than covering each development as it happens. The reader doesn't care week to week, so I try to do stories that tell where the overall issue is going.

Suppose you want to practice this kind of journalism. Will you have a chance? At many newspapers and local television stations, the answer may still be, "No, kid, go cover the press conference." But in many newsrooms you can expect considerable leeway in deciding how to spend time on a beat.

USING YOUR FREEDOM

In 1982 three Michigan State University researchers interviewed 489 reporters and editors in 9 cities around the country. They found that 7 out of 10 of the reporters agreed with the proposition, "[I have] extensive freedom to plan and organize my work." If you have the freedom, you can opt not to cover the marginal events on your beat and instead pursue a more promising idea for a nonevent-centered story. That story may help explain your community better than would one more tale from a public hearing.

A reporter's freedom to cover nonevent news will vary from paper to paper and TV station to TV station depending on the philosophy of the editor or news director in charge. But every reporter will have some discretionary time. You shouldn't spend all of that time sitting with other reporters at media events when you could be productive elsewhere.

Crouse's *Boys on the Bus* describes how being wedded to news events began to bug many of the better presidential campaign reporters more than a decade ago. These reporters felt hemmed in by the old formulas of classic objective journalism, which dictated that each story had to start with a hard news lead based on some phony event that the candidate's staff had staged.

J. Edward Murray, a former president of the American Society of Newspaper Editors, says the process of deciding "what is news" is the daily asking and answering of this question: "What is really significant, really interesting, really useful, and really new for the readers of my newspaper?" Unfortunately, he goes on to say, far too many journalists answer that question by using

> outworn definitions of news. . . . First, is it a recent event or development? Second, is it catastrophic, confrontational, aberrational, negative, violent, lurid, glamorous, or otherwise entertaining? Third, does it involve quick, episodic, once-over-easy politics, economic, law enforcement, or human-interest novelty of any kind? Unfortunately, all of this . . . is guaranteed to miss much of the important serious news.

Just this sort of focus on too much wire service news has given rise to complaints from Third World countries that the only thing the American press is interested in from overseas is "coups and earthquakes." American reporters overseas seldom file stories on the slow progress being made in education, agricultural productivity, health, and sanitation; on reducing child mortality, increasing longevity, or liberating women. This complaint could well be echoed by American audiences looking for a different perspective on their communities.

If such a change in philosophy were applied to local news coverage, it would come closer to giving readers a more accurate picture of the life of their communities. Here's how Frank Batten of Landmark Communications put it:

> Warts and problems are at the root of the news, but they are not all the news. Even against the tide of modern life, people, and institutions make progress. We should be generous in coverage of achievement; our pages should reflect the grit, devotion, and durability of the human spirit.

Certainly, journalists need to react to and report about the events around them. But you also should expend time and energy to recognize emerging trends and to write the sorts of stories that will cause the community itself to react to your work. In short, if you occasionally risk missing "what happened" at a marginal news event, you have the opportunity to use your time and talent to become the only journalist around to report "What's really happening" or, better yet, "What's going to happen."

REFERENCES

Boorstin, Daniel. *The Image*. New York: Harper & Row, 1961.

Cater, Douglass. *The Fourth Branch of Government*. Boston: Houghton Mifflin, 1959.

Crouse, Timothy. *The Boys on the Bus*. New York: Random House, 1973.

Gans, Herbert. *Deciding What's News*. New York: Pantheon, 1974.

Hage, George S., Everette E. Dennis, Arnold S. Ismach, and Stephen Hartgen. *New Strategies for Public Affairs Reporting: Investigation, Interpretation, and Research*. 2d. ed. Englewood Cliffs, NJ: Prentice-Hall, 1983.

McCombs, Maxwell, Donald Lewis Shaw, and David Grey. *Handbook of Reporting Methods*. Boston: Houghton Mifflin, 1976.

McDonald, Donald. "Is Objectivity Possible?" *The Center Magazine*, IV:5 (Sept./Oct. 1971), pp. 29–42.

Murray, Edward J. "Quality News vs. Junk News." University of Hawaii, Honolulu: Carol Burnett Fund Lecture on Ethics in Journalism, March 8, 1984.

Sigal, Leon. *Reporters and Officials: The Organization and Politics of Newsmaking*. Lexington, MA: D.C. Heath, 1973.

Tuchman, Gaye. *Making News: A Study in the Construction of Reality*. New York: Free Press, 1978.

CHAPTER 2

Vantage Points

Obviously, writing skills are essential for both print and broadcast journalists. But so is another set of skills—observation. Even the best writers, if they are poor observers, have little to say, no matter how cleverly they say it. To a considerable extent, creativity in journalism lies in the ability to make acute observations of what is happening in the world, even in its most ordinary and obscure corners. Mike Royko and Jimmy Breslin are superb writers, but they also are superb observers of Chicago transit buses, Manhattan taverns, and dozens of other settings known by ordinary people. Their ability to highlight familiar experiences is what makes them good communicators.

A reporter who is a good writer but a poor observer is like an artist with keen technical skills who has little to put on canvas. The result is pictures of poor quality. In short, good journalism demands two distinct sets of talents and skills—observation and writing. Although the job title *reporter* might seem to emphasize the latter task, presenting the report, it also assumes there is something to report, that some time has been spent observing what is going on. After all, journalism is an empirical activity—you have to gather facts before you can report them.

Some of the common, rudimentary techniques of observation are learned early by all journalists and journalism students. Short interviews, the rewriting of press releases, and the use of background documents such as reports and minutes of meetings, are staples of journalistic observation.

With these techniques and the routine information they typically provide, the journalist is essentially a bureaucrat, much like the bureaucrats at county courthouses and insurance company of-fices who push their way through piles of information each day. While most journalists hold a stereotype of their own occupation that is strikingly different from their stereotype of bureaucrats in government and private industry, nevertheless, newsrooms and their staffs have many of the same characteristics as these other bureaucracies. It is due to the bureaucratic routinization of much of the work that it is possible to produce the daily newspaper or evening newscast day after day on a tight schedule.

Why be concerned with all this? Why not just write and report and let the social scientists worry about the underlying character-istics of bureaucracies and their tasks? If you accept journalism as a trade, as nothing more than another set of routine skills, then there is no reason to read on. But the distinguishing mark of a profession, and of professional education, is that it moves beyond rote proce-dures and traditional practice. The purpose of education is to stim-ulate analytic thinking, not just to teach technical skills. An edu-cated professional is a person who has reflected about his or her work and has some sensitivity about what it all means, why things are done the way they are, and, most important, in what other ways they can be done.

ROUTINE SHORTCUTS

As soon as you strive for this overview of professional journalism and turn your attention to the task of observation, the realization emerges that journalists' daily observations of the world rely upon a great many routine shortcuts.

Press conferences, handouts, press releases, and routinely pre-pared minutes and proceedings from meetings of every sort head the hierarchy of sources that reporters rely upon as routine infor-mation sources. Even on major newspapers, such as the *New York Times* and the *Washington Post* with their large reporting staffs and emphasis on journalistic enterprise, these routine shortcuts are ex-tensively employed. Leon Sigal's detailed analysis of these large newspapers in *Reporters and Officials* found that *enterprise re-porting*—such as the use of interviews, direct observations, or library research—accounted for less than a third of their staff-produced news stories. Most of the news originates with informa-tion prepared by others.

The shortcoming, if not danger, of this kind of reactive reporting is obvious: News media become passive conduits for the views and objectives of others. All the rhetoric about serving the people and the special role of the news media in a democratic society becomes very empty.

Even when the most benevolent of sources are used, yet another problem arises—heavy reliance on a few techniques of collecting information. For decades, social scientists have been concerned with the inherent structural biases in information that is based on a single observation technique. Every means of observing people and communities has distinct limitations. Information based on a number of different techniques, a kind of *triangulation* on reality, is inherently a better picture of the world than information gathered from only one type of source. Preoccupation with one or two techniques of reporting is the hallmark of a trade, not a profession. Use of a variety of observation techniques is the hallmark of a creative professional.

To evaluate how good our techniques are for observing what is happening in the local community, consider these two criteria:

Factual adequacy, meaning accuracy, precision, and completeness of the facts.

Efficiency, meaning both the initial cost of collecting any facts at all about an event or topic, plus the cost of gathering additional facts to increase the scope of the picture.

Under the pressure of deadlines, which seldom are more than a few days away and more frequently are just a few hours or minutes away, news organizations have emphasized the second criterion, *efficiency*. The routine sources of observation—press conferences, releases, and documents—are efficient methods of gleaning at least the highlights and most salient features of daily events. Furthermore, because these techniques are restricted largely to observations of official sources to whom the facts can be attributed, there is at least a passing score on the criterion of *factual adequacy*.

However, as we shall see repeatedly in subsequent chapters of this book, the factual adequacy of the news that is collected through these routine procedures, or any small set of observation techniques for that matter, is quite limited. A true professional understands and employs a full *strategy* of journalistic observation, not just the rote application of a few, commonly employed *tactics*.

INFORMANTS AS SOURCES

Although the term *informants* may seem to imply sinister and unethical behavior, a moment's reflection reveals that this phrase really describes in a general way various techniques of observation commonly used by journalists. There need be nothing underhanded in the use of informants. In journalism they are usually called *sources.*.

The term *informant* has one advantage over the traditional jargon in that it makes explicit that our facts are secondhand. Relatively little news is directly observed by reporters. First, there are not that many reporters. Second, the occurrence of major elements of the news is not neatly scheduled. So, for much of the grist of the daily news—fires, accidents, crimes, and deaths—you rely on an informant, either someone who was there to observe the event or, more commonly, someone whose official duties involve collecting facts about what has now become the focus of a news story. Sometimes you collect these facts by interviewing informants; other times you read informants' reports. In any event, traditional journalistic practice has two major characteristics:

> Journalistic observations of what is happening are *indirect*, relying upon the reports of informants who, as witnesses or officials, are in a position to possess some of the facts about what happened.
>
> Journalistic observations of what is happening are *episodic*, usually limited to the reporting of a single event occurring in the past few hours.

SYSTEMATIC OBSERVATION

As noted in Chapter 1, journalists' observations need not be limited to single events. It is also important to report situations broader than those comprising the news events of the past 24 hours. Although a great deal of political reporting, for example, is narrowly focused on the political events and hoopla of the day, there is need to push beyond these ritualistic, sometimes superficial, events to get at the real meaning of a political campaign and how it affects voters.

One approach has been for journalists to turn more and more to polls and survey research as instruments for observing and understanding the political news of the day. In the abstract, there is little difference between the traditional interviewing of politicians and campaign managers, and interviewing a sample of voters in a poll. In both instances, you rely upon informants to tell what is happening and why. But in using sources such as campaign managers, you are relying upon a few people with major vested interests in both the outcome of the election and the content of your news story.

Individual voters, too, may feel some vested interest in the outcome of the election, although for many it is a matter (unfortunately) of rather peripheral concern. In any event, the vested interests of hundreds of voters interviewed in a general population survey will balance out far more evenly than the strong interests of a few political sources. The important point here is this: Unlike relying on a few sources conveniently at hand, the use of polls and surveys yields *systematic* observations about general voter sentiment.

Although predicting the winner in advance of election day still remains the major purpose of many surveys conducted by journalists, this systematic means of observing the community opens the door to numerous other news stories that are difficult, if not impossible, to report from an episodic news event perspective.

In the 1960s city after city burst into flames and rioting, with no advance warning from routine news reports about these neighborhoods. It was a classic example of Walter Lippmann's definition of news as an aspect of society that has obtruded itself. Only when events and problems reach the attention of major social institutions, such as the police, fire department, or city council, do they commonly become news and receive broad public attention. It is at locations such as these, where problems do routinely surface, that news organizations establish beats.

However, many social problems with explosive potential do not lead to this kind of episodic reporting. In many cases, such as the urban riots of the 1960s, public involvement in these problems does not capture the attention of reporters until the problem has risen to a crisis level. Hunger, child abuse, employment discrimination, and numerous other topics of social concern appearing in the news of recent years existed long before the news media put them on the national agenda.

Even when such social problems become part of the daily agenda of our social institutions, they may not be recognized by the

Crowd Counts

A recurring and thorny problem for journalists is figuring out how many people are in attendance at a parade, a rally, a protest march, or any place where people gather without turnstiles present.

Even where there are turnstiles, crowd counts can be suspect. One famous account of a game in a struggling new football league noted that either the announced crowd had been inflated or most of the audience "must have come disguised as empty seats."

But what about the hero's parade in New York City, or the anti-abortion march at a state capitol, or the antiwar rally on the Mall in Washington? Just how do you tell how many folks are present?

One frequent way to pass the buck is to ask some official. Richard Nixon's press secretary assured reporters that at least 700,000 people came out to see the president one day in Atlanta. Many reporters used the number. But Jim Perry of the *National Observer* obtained information from the city about block sizes, length of the parade route, and the like. He concluded: "In an act of charity I'm willing to say that 75,000 people turned out to welcome Richard Nixon to Atlanta."

Herbert A. Jacobs, formerly on the journalism faculty at the University of California, Berkeley, has done research on crowd size and developed a formula by measuring frequent rally sites and using photographs to make actual counts of people.

He suggests pacing off the length and width of a crowd and multiplying to find the area in square feet, then dividing by a density figure. Densities usually range from 6.5 to 8.5 square feet per person, with an average of 7. Jacobs says this will get you a number within 20 or 25 percent of an actual headcount.

From material excerpted and reprinted from the COLUMBIA JOURNALISM REVIEW, Spring 1967 ©.

journalist on the beat. Police reports, for example, typically are episodic accounts of crime. Most news organizations monitor these events and report at least some of them, but few news organizations routinely monitor crime as a social problem. In short, the normal workings of social agencies and the episodic reporting of their activity emphasize individual behavior, not the aggregation of human activity and behavior that defines a social trend or a social problem. For the most part, the police, the courts, and journalists deal with individuals and their activities, not social problems.

In the last decade or so, however, journalists have recognized the need to systematically observe social trends in their communities. For example, journalists seek to determine how teachers, students, and parents view public education, and to examine what the changing character of central cities and suburbia means to the people who live and do business there. To report dozens of such stories, news organizations use survey research and the systematic interviewing of a sample of representative informants. Each individual reports only his or her own behavior, perception, or opinion of the topic at hand. But put together, these reports provide an accurate portrait of the community.

People are not the only sources available to reporters. Documents can be invaluable also—sometimes more so than people. Persons being interviewed, whether as traditional sources or as respondents in a survey, are aware of their role as informants and may consciously or unconsciously shade their responses. On the other hand, most documents used by journalists were not prepared for the journalist's use but, typically, were prepared for some other purpose, and the reporter's perusal of them is incidental. This is not to say that documents are not "biased" in the way they record information, but usually the biases of documents are quite different from the biases of human informants. In Chapter 10, where a variety of techniques for extracting information from documents are discussed, the point is made that documents can be systematically observed in much the same manner as voters or other members of the general public.

If we diagram the major points made so far about journalists' observations of their communities, the picture we get looks something like the top row of Figure 2.1 (see p. 20), where traditional, routine techniques of episodic observation (listed on the left) have been supplemented by the systematic observation techniques (listed on the right). All the techniques listed in the top row are indirect observations of the news, based on the use of informants.

	Episodic	Systematic
-Indirect	I Interviews Reports and Documents	II Polls and Surveys Content Analysis Social Indicators
Direct	III Sports Events Public Meetings Eyewitness Accounts	IV Participant Observation Field Experiments

Figure 2.1   Types of observations made by journalists.

DIRECT OBSERVATION

Clearly, instances occur where journalists directly observe news events. Many events covered by news media are scheduled in advance, so if a reporter is available, he or she can directly observe a city council meeting, a court trial, planning board hearing, or civic club speech. Of course, often there simply are not enough reporters to go around, so these events end up being covered on the basis of indirect observation.

There is one category of news where direct observation is the norm—sports. The press box is the working arena for the sports reporter, who views the performance of the local baseball club, high school football team, or college basketball team through his or her own eyes. The technique of direct observation employed to report sports—as compared to techniques of indirect observation used in reporting government news—also results in some major differences between the styles of writing and reporting found in these two kinds of stories. Occasionally, the style of reporting typical of sports is applied to other types of public affairs news in the form of "I was there" features or color stories. Often these are sidebars to the main report of a news event, and they deepen public understanding of complex events.

Direct observation of an event or situation, whether it is a baseball game, city council meeting, or the ravages of a hurricane, is depicted in the second row in Figure 2.1. Box III in this row includes the kinds of episodic reporting just mentioned. This row also includes a fourth box in the bottom right-hand corner of the figure labeled *participant observation*. This type of reporting, combining direct observation with a systematic approach to the subject, has been used in journalism and social science for a century.

A *New York Times* reporter moved into an upper West Side neighborhood for several months to gather information on what life is like in Manhattan. Journalist Hunter S. Thompson spent more than a year riding at various times with the Hell's Angels motorcycle gang. A *Chicago Tribune* investigative reporter took a job as an ambulance driver to gain information for his Pulitizer-prize-winning series on abuses in private ambulance service.

Much of the information desired and needed by reporters for in-depth treatment of such topics simply is not available through routine interviews, documents, and other customary sources. It is necessary to be "inside" some situations in order to understand and to report them. This is where the technique of participant observation is powerful and revealing. The reporter can directly and systematically observe what is occurring—in part, through the eyes of an insider because he or she *is* an insider, temporarily. Chapter 13 explores this approach to observation and reporting.

DESCRIPTIONS AND EXPLANATIONS

Discussion of participant observation, or any other method of observing people outlined in Figure 2.1, must consider the purpose of all this reporting. Certainly, the purpose is more than the immediate, bureaucratic one of filing a story prior to deadline and filling up space or time.

Simple answers to the questions of "Why?" and "For what purpose?" are provided by the traditional event orientation of the press and the use of news values to identify the most important features of those events. From that perspective, the purpose of journalism is to *describe* the major news events of the day. But, increasingly, as Chapter 1 argued, journalists define their task to include some *explanation* for news events. For this reason they turn to survey research, content analysis, participant observation, and a variety of other observation techniques. Developed over decades of social science research and practical journalistic experience, these techniques provide both the basic data for describing some situations in our communities and the procedures for analyzing this information so we can explain why things are the way they are.

Although the participant observer, for example, has a useful vantage point for compiling descriptions of how ghetto neighborhoods, mental wards, or high schools go about their daily routines, the real strength of participant observation is the opportunity to penetrate beneath daily routines and to understand the reasons behind the behavior observed. Through participant observation and other observational techniques one can pursue detailed hypotheses that explain the "why" of surface behaviors.

Hypotheses might sound out of place in a discussion of news reporting, but they are not limited to science and its observations of the world. In journalism our hypotheses frequently are labeled *story lines* or *themes*. You sometimes just call them *hunches*. In any event, they guide your thinking and observations. Neither in science nor in journalism is it really possible to gaze in a thoroughly neutral and comprehensive way on the world around you. As philosopher of science Carl Hempel once remarked, those who aren't looking for anything in particular, seldom find anything in particular. Neither scientists nor journalists can afford the luxury of very many empty searches.

Hypotheses guide our observations and collection of facts. They also help us structure our facts. The purpose of journalism is not simply to report *facts per se*. World almanacs and various other statistical reference works do that. The purpose of journalism is to provide *information*. Although you may not think much about it, reporters must always organize their facts into stories built around some theme or hypothesis. One way of thinking about the lead of a news story is to think of it as an hypothesis that is to be supported with a variety of facts organized into coherent information about an event or situation.

THREE MAJOR STEPS

It is possible to sum up the process of observation in journalism as consisting of three major steps:

Observing
Interpreting
Reporting

Out of all the events it is possible to observe, one can select only a few for attention. The great utility of news values, the event orientation of the press, and the substantive hypotheses of the social sciences is that they reduce this first step—observing—to manageable proportions. Otherwise, journalists each day would find themselves facing the buzzing, blooming confusion of an unorganized world. These values, perspectives, and hypotheses do more than guide our observations. They also help us to interpret them, to convert raw facts into organized information. How odd it is, remarked Albert Einstein, that not everyone can see that every observation must be for or against some hypothesis. Finally, the information gained through observation must be styled in the traditional format of a news story and presented to an audience. Preparing you for these steps is the purpose of this book on news reporting.

REFERENCES

Babbie, Earl. *The Practice of Social Research.* 3d ed. Belmont, CA: Wadsworth Publishing, 1983.

Breslin, Jimmy. *The World of Jimmy Breslin.* New York: Viking, 1967.

Breslin, Jimmy. *How the Good Guys Finally Won.* New York: Viking, 1975.

Donaghy, William C. *The Interview: Skills and Applications.* Glenview, IL: Scott, Foresman and Co., 1984.

Hempel, Carl G. *Fundamentals of Concept Formation in Empirical Science.* Chicago: University of Chicago Press, 1952.

Jacobs, Herbert A. "To count a crowd." *Columbia Journalism Review,* VI:1 (Spring 1967), pp. 37–40.

Lippmann, Walter. *Liberty and the News.* New York: Harcourt, Brace and Howe, 1920.

Lippmann, Walter. *Public Opinion.* New York: Macmillan, 1960 (originally published 1922).

Lippmann, Walter. *A preface to Politics.* Ann Arbor, MI: University of Michigan Press, 1962 (originally published 1914).

Royko, Mike. *Boss.* New York: Dutton, 1971.

Royko, Mike. *Like I was sayin'.* . . . New York: Dutton, 1984.

Sigal, Leon. *Reporters and Officials: The Organization and Politics of Newsmaking*. Lexington, MA: D.C. Heath, 1973.

Stempel, Guido H. III, and Bruce H. Westley, eds. *Research Methods in Mass Communication*. Englewood Cliffs, NJ: Prentice-Hall, 1981.

Thompson, Hunter. *Hell's Angels: A Strange and Terrible Saga*. New York: Random House, 1967.

Thompson, Hunter. *The Curse of Lono*. New York: Bantam Books, 1983.

CHAPTER 3
Strategy and Tactics

Reporters need to have tactical competence in a wide variety of observation techniques, but tactical competence without a strategic game plan is shortsighted. Famed Alabama football coach Bear Bryant was a superb tactician. He trained teams whose tactical execution of the wishbone was flawless. Time after time the ball was smoothly handed off to gain additional yardage. But Bear Bryant didn't get his name in the record book as the winner of more football games in his career than any other college coach simply because his players could execute plays well. Good tactical execution is necessary, but there must be a game plan also, an overall strategy that dictates the variety of plays to be used through the entire game. The Bear trained good tacticians (actually his numerous assistants trained the tacticians) but it was his brilliance as a strategist that built the record.

Every profession—football, journalism, or whatever—involves tactical skills. That's what a large portion of the training for the profession entails. Indeed, in some colleges and universities the training for journalists is totally tactical and rote. But the creative journalist or editor who wants to achieve something more than the successful execution of a few plays—translation: Get some bylines and win a few awards—needs a game plan. You need a strategy as well as tactical competence.

There is no single strategy that will work for every community or newsroom. Creating a game plan for covering a local community, or a region or the nation, for that matter, demands insight and imagination. Not every editor, news director, or reporter will feel comfortable with the same game plan. You must devise you own plan.

Unfortunately, the game plan required for good journalism is considerably more complex than the game plan required to win a football game or even an entire season. The geography to be covered is considerably larger than 100 yards, and the duration of the game plan considerably longer than 60 minutes. However, there is one striking similarity—winning strategies in both journalism and football are composed of dozens of tactical moves. A single play or drive doesn't, by itself, win a football game. A single story or series of stories doesn't constitute complete coverage of a community.

There is at least one other similarity as well—success requires a variety of plays. That is why Chapter 2 spent so much time developing an overview of the various types of observation, and why this book presents the tactical details of numerous reporting techniques. Our picture of the local community is constructed from many tiny pieces. When the pieces are put together with a strategy in mind, the picture is more satisfying both to journalists and their audiences.

A full picture of any community includes a number of major elements:

> People
> Organizations
> Activities
> Geography
> Natural resources and assets
> Created resources and assets

Each strategist will approach these differently. You can expand the list, merge some of these categories, or change the emphasis placed on these elements. And, of course, each journalist will come up with his or her own creative interpretation of how the tactical execution of each strategic element should be carried out day-by-day.

SAMPLE STRATEGIC APPROACHES

To give you something of a taste for just how different various strategic approaches can be, briefly examine the three books described here. Each presents a reasonably comprehensive and systematic approach to its subject, but their perspectives are quite different.

These are only three books. An afternoon spent in any good university library can easily triple that number. Or you can just sit down with a pad and start thinking about your own strategic plan.

The Nine Nations of North America by Joel Garreau. "This all started as a kind of private craziness," explains Joel Garreau, an editor on the *Washington Post*. But, then, that's as good a place as any for a news reporting strategy to originate! And that was precisely Garreau's purpose—to come up with a broad theme and set of concepts that help reporters see and understand the patterns in the news.

Garreau's perspective is based on a rich view of North American regionalism, nine regions in all, stretching beyond the boundaries of the United States to encompass Canada, the Caribbean Basin, and part of northern Mexico.

> It is Nine Nations. Each has its capital and its distinctive web of power and influence. A few are allies, but many are adversaries. Several have readily acknowledged national poets, and many have characteristic dialects and mannerisms. Some are close to being raw frontiers; others have four centuries of history. Each has a peculiar economy; each commands a certain emotional allegiance from its citizens. These nations look different, feel different, and sound different from each other, and few of their boundaries match the political lines drawn on current maps. Some are clearly divided topographically by mountains, deserts, and rivers. Others are separated by architecture, music, language, and ways of making a living. Each nation has its own list of desires. Each nation knows how it plans to get what it needs from whoever's got it.
>
> Most important, each nation has a distinct prism through which it views the world.*

This concept of "Nine Nations" explains, for example, the controversy over national energy policy in both the United States and Canada. Energy importers in New England, Quebec, and the Canadian Maritime provinces are counterbalanced by the energy exporters of Alberta, Alaska, Texas, and Louisiana. Numerous policies on the distribution of federal funds to state and local governments pit the Frostbelt against the Sunbelt. On more mundane matters, it's bratwurst versus tacos. In short, almost every topic in the news, from the most important problems facing North America to regional variations in lifestyle, can be creatively analyzed and explained from this regional perspective. This is a strategic view which, even if applied in only a single region, yields endless tactical variations.

The Use of Time edited by Alexander Szalai.* In this volume's 868 pages detailing how people budget their time in a dozen nations across the world, from Belgium to Bulgaria and from the U.S. to the USSR, one chapter in particular, "Everyday Life in Twelve Countries," is especially stimulating. The massive detail in this single chapter on how much time people devote to 37 major activities in their lives probably is enough to keep most journalists' imaginations whirling for a very long time.

The economy of this perspective as the basis of a reporting strategy is absolutely striking. If you want to grasp the essentials of what is happening in your community, what better way exists for doing this than to examine how people spend their time? Although there are some obvious constraints on using these data to formulate a game plan—more time typically is devoted to sleeping then to religious activities regardless of the qualitative importance attached to each category of activity—it is, nevertheless, a useful starting point in devising a reporting strategy. For instance, when television saturated America three decades ago, millions of Americans, adults and children, rearranged their days and their use of time to accommodate this new entertainment medium. Now that cable is available to millions of households and increases the options of television viewing, what recent changes have Americans made in the use of their time?

Changing lifestyles have dramatically changed the way people spend their leisure time. What does your news organization have to say to all those people participating in a wide variety of sports? Have you evaluated new lifestyles in terms of how much time is devoted to activities ranging from gourmet cooking and wine tasting to home computers and do-it-yourself household projects? A profile of how people in your community use their leisure time is a game plan for expanded, creative news coverage.

Journalists interested in how people use their time also should consult *Social Indicators III*, a 1980 U.S. Department of Commerce report with 645 pages of detail on use of time, plus a dozen other major topics that reflect both the quantitative and qualitative aspects of people's daily lives.

* The Hague: Mouton Publishers, 1973.

Studying Your Community by Roland L. Warren.* This is about as close to a step-by-step, how-to-do-it manual as you will find on the library shelf for drawing up a strategic reporting plan. It contains everything from basic chapters on a community's economic life, government, politics, and law enforcement to chapters on such recent concerns as urban planning, provision for special groups, and family problems.

Each of the 16 chapters in this book provides an overview of its topic and lists key questions that need to be answered in each community. If you make any dent at all in answering those hundreds and hundreds of questions, your strategic plan easily will reach the end of this century. For example, the chapter on providing for special groups in the community posits 146 specific questions that any good journalist would ask. A bibliography of background reading and statistics also is provided in each chapter. These obviously need updating, but the basic perspective of this book and its specific leads remain timely.

Each of these books—and there are dozens more, plus the one you should write—expands the scope of news reporting. Each stretches the journalistic imagination beyond routine news beats, press conferences, and handouts. Just as Chapter 2 emphasized the existence of four very distinct ways of observing what is happening in our communities, the present discussion emphasizes the need for a comprehensive plan or strategy to guide the application of those tactical tools. Without a game plan, you are no different than a small boy with a new hatchet wandering about and hacking everything in sight—just for the thrill of using a new toy. In particular, the stress here on strategic thinking and having a game plan guides the application of systematic modes of observation. A comprehensive game plan, however, will use the full array of available reporting techniques.

GAME PLAN BY-PRODUCTS

Several interesting by-products result from the construction of a strategic plan. The first of these is a substantial influence—albeit only partially visible in the short run—on the evolving nature of

* New York: Free Press, 1965.

news. Although journalists and this book tend to speak glibly of *news* and *news values* (everyone has an intuitive feel for what is meant even in the absence of a formal definition, right?) these are not Platonic ideals, absolutes against which specific instances can be compared. There is no journalistic equivalent of the Bureau of Weights and Measures or the Greenwich Observatory.

The nature of news, the behavioral definition of news as the information that journalists communicate to their audiences, is constantly evolving. Everyone is aware that language changes over time, that the symbols with which we communicate are in constant evolution. *Sloth* and *trollop* are out, for example, and *rock star* and *hacker* are in. The very appearance of new words and phrases suggests new foci of attention as do new and evolving definitions of news, which shift even more rapidly than do our overall vocabulary and style of expression.

The first substantial body of journalism in the United States, the colonial press of the eighteenth century, looked more like today's *Wall Street Journal* than like the *Charlotte Observer* or other contemporary general circulation dailies. The implicit game plan of the colonial press had a strong commercial perspective. In the 1830s the convergence of new technology, social change, and new

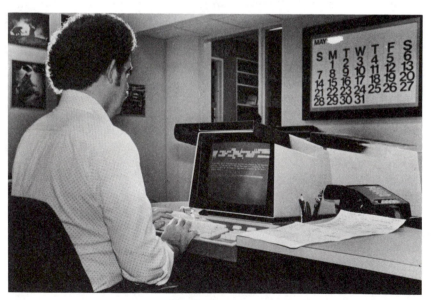

Figure 3.1   Reporter and VDT (*The Honolulu Advertiser*).

entrepreneurial game plans produced the "penny press," a new style of journalism with lively news values. Half a century later, "yellow journalism" exemplified yet another evolution of news values. And on it goes.

The history of journalism, told in terms of what kind of news copy was produced, is a history of movement and change as new practitioners and new generations have applied their talents. Change will occur, with or without planning, but when a reporter, editor, or news organization explicitly analyzes and plans, creative change will occur at a more steady pace. Everyone knows the anecdote about random behavior: Place enough monkeys in front of enough typewriters and eventually they will produce all the world's great literature. But placing a few good men and women in front of a few typewriters or word processors will produce significantly better results.

There is another, more immediate by-product of strategic planning. It creates ways to evaluate current coverage and to deploy reporters and resources to cover sources of news. It doesn't matter what the perspective of your game plan is, or how simple or complex it is—every game plan says something about the people, activities, and sources in your coverage area.

For example, many years ago some social scientists conducted a poll in the Maryland suburbs of Washington, D.C.. They asked people: "Who are the leaders here in your community?" The responses to this question were compared with a simple content analysis of the news sources cited in the Maryland news section of the *Washington Post*. Like most newspapers, the *Post* relies heavily upon "official" sources, especially those in government. But these political leaders and government officials were perceived as only a tiny part of the community leadership by the general public. Clergy, for example, cited in the poll as a significant segment of the community's leadership, almost never are used as news sources. In this instance the method of evaluation was a simple map of community leadership. The implications of strategic planning for credible, comprehensive coverage are obvious.

Or take "ascertainment" surveys, which used to be mandatory for all broadcasters and are still continued by some. A major purpose of these surveys is to ascertain what the general public perceives to be the most important problems facing the community. If you don't have access to a local ascertainment survey, the Gallup Poll asks an almost identical question, "What is the most important problem facing America today?", in a national survey once or twice every year. Take one or both of these survey research sources and compare your news coverage with the answers to the survey questions. Is your news organization providing relevant, timely news about the salient issues of the day?

Setting up a scorecard, however, does not require a survey, not even a single poll question. It can be done with far simpler and more readily available resources—such as the telephone directory, a resource that even the most budget-conscious newsroom can use.

Did you ever read the Yellow Pages as a portrait of your community? The number of listings, or simply the amount of space, for each category in the Yellow Pages identifies the relative importance of various occupations and activities in the community. It doesn't take much imagination, just a bit of time, to devise a scorecard from these listings both for the evaluation of current coverage and for planning new coverage.

Once you become aware of this idea of setting up scorecards for keeping track of news coverage, you will start to see them everywhere!

REFERENCES

Bauer, Raymond A., ed. *Social Indicators*. Cambridge, MA: M.I.T. Press, 1966.

Garreau, Joel. *The Nine Nations of North America*. New York: Avon, 1981.

A Researcher's Guide to the 1980 Census. Ithaca, NY: American Demographics, 1981.

Szalai, Alexander, ed. *The Use of Time*. The Hague, Mouton, 1973.

Warren, Roland L. *Studying Your Community*. New York: Russell Sage Foundation, 1955.

CHAPTER 4
News and Ethics

The press is a human institution and no human institution ever conforms precisely to a consistent ethical or philosophical theory.

Nelson A. Crawford, *The Ethics of Journalism*

When we enter the area of journalistic ethics, we pass into a swampland of philosophical speculation whose eerie mists of judgment hang low over a boggy terrain. In spite of the unsure footing and poor visibility, there is no reason not to make the journey.

John C. Merrill, *The Imperative of Freedom*

What is ethical on the *Daily Bugle* is unethical on the *Daily Clarinet*.

Richard Harwood, former managing editor, *Washington Post*

Some journalists think the ethics codes of their profession date from the soul-searching of the post-Watergate era. It's true that a good deal of attention was focused on the topic then, but some leaders of American journalism were thinking lofty thoughts about ethical precepts many decades ago.

In 1910, the Kansas Editorial Association adopted a code of ethics dealing with advertising, circulation, and news. It defined news as the "impartial report of the activities of mind, men, and matter which do not offend the moral sensibilities of the more enlightened people."

Various other state editors' groups adopted codes of their own. In 1923 the American Society of Newspaper Editors (ASNE) passed its first "Canons of Journalism." It contained such guidance as "Freedom of the press is to be guarded as a vital right of mankind" and "By every consideration of good faith a newspaper is constrained to be truthful." It was nice prose and unquestionably ethical but, as Gene Gilmore and Robert Root wrote in 1971, when the ASNE code was nearly a half century old, "few working newsmen could quote a single canon."

In the flurry of ethical debate during the 1970s, new codes abounded. Sigma Delta Chi adopted a new "Code of Ethics" in 1973. ASNE updated its ethical standards and approved a new "Statement of Principles" in 1975. Still, journalists have not reached a true consensus about the subject of ethics, journalism, and how the twain shall meet. Are formal, written rules a good way to promote ethical standards? The proliferation of codes is proof that many journalists think so.

Some, however, such as James C. Thomson Jr., curator of the Nieman fellowships program at Harvard, have questioned whether journalistic ethics should be

> Set forth in some code like a Boy Scout oath or a catechism? The answer is certainly no. The ambiguities of journalism are too endemic and too ineradicable. . . . In the end there seems to me no possible code, no firm guideline, for the ethical conduct of a journalist other than the craft's age-old bywords, "fairness," and "accuracy"—to which I would also add emphatically "compassion."

Many of the codes of journalistic ethics in the 1980s go beyond the platitudes of the earlier efforts and attempts to give the working reporter and editor specific guidance and standards. Following are some of the ethical issues dealt with in today's codes.

FREEBIES

Is there such a thing as a free lunch for a reporter? "There is hardly a reporter alive who, at one time or another, has not eaten a meal supplied by a news source . . . only a naive newsmaker would assume that reporters can be bought with a free lunch," wrote journalism professor Meyer L. Stein. Well, if not a free lunch, can you buy a reporter with a case of wine at Christmas time? Free tickets to the circus when it comes to town? How about a free "inaugural flight" to some resort to celebrate the fact that an airline has started up a new route? "Junketing is widely viewed as a threat to objectivity, but is widely practiced nonetheless," observed the *Wall Street Journal* 15 years ago.

Can you buy (or at least rent) a reporter with a free "evaluation kit" of cameras and photographic equipment? Some 300 reporters and photographers showed up at an Eastman Kodak press conference in 1976 where such "kits" were handed out. "If a picture is worth a thousand words," asked the *Columbia Journalism Review*, "how much is a camera worth?"

When does the free lunch become so big that it constitutes a bribe with the expectation, realistic or otherwise, that the reporter will come across with a story (or at least a more favorable story than would otherwise be the case)?

The Sigma Delta Chi code says that "nothing of value should be accepted" because "gifts, favors, free travel, special treatment, or privileges can compromise the integrity of journalists and their employers." What, exactly, does "nothing of value" mean? The 1973 *Milwaukee Journal* code permits "gifts of insignificant value— a calendar, pencil, key chain, or such . . . if it would be awkward to refuse." Other gifts (specifically including liquor) must be declined or returned or, if impractical, donated by the company to charity.

How about a sportswriter covering a game or a reviewer covering a play? Many papers continue to accept free tickets or free admission for such working journalists, but do not allow the sports promoter or play producer to hand out additional free tickets to others in the newsroom who want to attend.

At the *Milwaukee Journal*, a free lunch or dinner paid for by a potential news source is allowed "if the event is related to news coverage or if it is valuable for background. 'Freeload' affairs that have little or nothing to do with news coverage should be avoided." Overall, not only the *Journal*—but many other papers as well— now prefer that reporters avoid any suspicion of bribery by picking up the check (within the limits imposed by the paper's expense-account policy, of course).

CONFLICTS OF INTEREST

Can I cover the election and write speeches for the mayor, too? No, you can't—not any more—even though many reporters used to earn money on the side doing public relations work for candidates or others that they also wrote about. The *Wall Street Journal* reported in 1967 that "on some papers, courthouse reporters have been appointed by courts as estate appraisers" and that a labor reporter on a big daily had held a public relations job with a major railroad.

At many papers, top-level management people, who tend to be older and to come from a different tradition than younger reporters, do become involved in outside activities frowned upon by younger reporters. Some papers feel the conflict is less problematical if it involves people far removed from actual news coverage. An editor or publisher might be on a corporate board of directors, for example, whereas a business reporter could not serve on a board and also write about the corporation.

The *Knoxville News-Sentinel* in 1983 fired a reporter who had been elected to a nonpartisan school board seat in a suburban town where her son went to school but which she did not cover as a reporter. The reporter and the Newspaper Guild fought the dismissal and a rival Knoxville newspaper questioned how the *News-Sentinel* could fire the reporter while the paper's own editor sat on a city advisory parking authority. (Later, the reporter was rehired.)

Many papers and journalists still are trying to balance these two, sometimes mutually exclusive, goals: How do you get involved so that you don't become an isolated, elitist journalist, while at the same time avoiding conflicts of interest in which your community ties get in the way of doing your journalistic job?

Very few of the formal ethics codes have been able to do more than quote generalities on this subject. The Associated Press Managing Editors (APME) code states that reporters should avoid "involvement in such things as politics, community affairs, demonstrations, and social causes that could cause a conflict of interest, or the appearance of such conflict." Sigma Delta Chi says "involvement in such things as politics, community affairs, demonstrations, and social causes that could cause a conflict of interest, or the appearance of such a conflict, should be avoided."

Aren't some outside ties harmless? Loren Ghiglione, editor and publisher of the *Southbridge Evening News* in Massachusetts, thought so when he agreed to serve on a YMCA board of managers in his town.

"I soon discovered it [the Y] was faced with the apparent misappropriation of funds by an employee. That was news," Ghiglione recalled. He quit the board and his paper reported on a big insurance settlement brought about by the apparent misappropriation. "I learned a lesson: Any involvement with community organizations, however harmless on the surface, compromises the integrity of the paper."

In an attempt to deal with the possibility that outside activities and their income may conflict with a journalist's job, the *Chicago Tribune* in 1983 instituted a policy requiring annual financial disclosure statements from all professional employees, including reporters. But how far can a newspaper try to monitor its employees? Can your employer make rules about what your spouse can do?

The *Seattle Times* found itself in just such a quandary. The managing editor's wife was named press secretary to the mayor. The *Times* moved to transfer the managing editor out of the newsroom, because its code prohibited employees from being involved in editorial decisionmaking about people related "by blood or marriage." The problem was solved when his wife gave up her press secretary's job so that her husband could keep his. But James F. McDaniel, managing editor of the *Memphis Commercial Appeal*, is troubled that a newspaper would "try to control somebody's spouse."

COOPERATING WITH GOVERNMENT AND POLICE

For the most part, news media espouse the general goal of remaining aloof from government and law enforcement. As a reporter, you get information from them, of course, in the process of covering the news, but should you furnish information to help these agencies do their jobs?

According to one theory, cops should be cops and reporters should be reporters. A reporter's job is to report the news, not to cover it up or to structure it to help the police. Whenever a reporter strikes a deal with a mayor or police chief or prosecutor, he or she opens the door to charges of collusion. Sources will stop bringing in tips if they think the reporter will turn around and run to the FBI with them. A source will not trust you to keep a pledge of confidentiality if you are too close to the enforcers. The media cannot cover demonstrations and rallies by antiestablishment types if the demonstrators believe the press will turn film and negatives over to the grand jury the next week.

There are exceptions to this theory, however. In 1983, a Toronto-area millionaire was kidnapped. Threats were made that he would be killed if police were told. Journalists found out about the case, but three papers and four broadcast outlets kept the lid on the story for three days at the request of the police chief. The victim was freed and the story told.

Also in 1983, the wife of a former El Salvadoran diplomat was kidnapped. The FBI asked the wire services and certain newspapers in several cities to hold off publicizing this event because the kidnappers threatened to kill the victim if anything was made public. All the news outlets complied. The woman was rescued three days later. Former UPI executive H. L. Stevenson, who went along with the FBI in this instance, says the wire service in general tries to "guard against some requests that are not really valid." UPI considers the following points in deciding whether to go along with a law enforcement request to hold up a story: Is the victim in danger? Is UPI satisfied with the explanation given? What are other news organizations doing?

Consider a more common example. Sometimes people call up newsrooms threatening to commit suicide. When this happens, most editors try to get enough information to allow police to intervene and stop the act.

Another example occurred after the series of "Tylenol murders" in 1982, when *Chicago Tribune* columnist Bob Greene was approached by the FBI and asked for help. Someone—yet unknown—had poisoned several bottles of Tylenol. Greene responded by saying he was part of "a reporting generation taught to get queasy at the idea of journalists working hand-in-hand with law-enforcement agencies." But when an FBI expert told Greene and his editor that mass murderers sometimes become curious "once they [are] made to think of the victim in human terms," Greene agreed to help. Although until then, the parents of a fatally poisoned 12-year-old girl had avoided the press, at the FBI's request, they agreed to be interviewed by Greene. He wrote a column saying, "If you are the Tylenol killer, some of this may matter to you . . . you may be harboring just the vaguest curiosity about the people on the other end of your plan."

The column was a heart-tugger, but didn't work as "bait" for the murderer. Several months later, Greene wrote a magazine article about the episode. "It is one thing to say that a reporter should never cooperate with a law-enforcement agency; it is quite another, when seven people have been poisoned to death in the area where you live, to say that no, you will not help."

The ultimate extension of this idea, it might be argued, is the role of the press in wartime. Until the Vietnam era, it had generally been the case that the press was "on our side." But as Nieman curator Thomson pointed out, that era "weakened and finally destroyed the unspoken alliance between journalists and the government. . . . Good citizens eventually gave way to good journalists, even in semi-wartime."

SELF-CENSORSHIP

If printing it is only going to cause more trouble, should I keep it out of the paper? In Iowa, somebody was painting swastikas on synagogues. As soon as one incident was reported, another followed. One radio news director in the area told his staff, "It is apparent that our reporting of these events is actually encouraging them to happen. Therefore, our policy as of now is to report no more stories about swastikas being painted on synagogues unless some entirely new angle develops." Was he right or wrong?

In Honolulu, editors took somewhat the same position about a rash of small school fires apparently set by young vandals. Other media, using the same approach, have decided to forgo reporting of routine bomb threats and ensuing building evacuations, including evacuations of schools around final exam time caused by telephoned threats from kids who hadn't studied the night before.

The issue of self-censorship can be considered in the broader context of what journalism professor J. K. Hvistendahl calls *microethics* versus *macroethics*: "Are the news media responsible for the effects of what they publish, or just for getting the information to readers or listeners fairly and accurately?" The microethicist argues that you always publish the facts because, as Hvistendahl puts it, "in the long run humanity will benefit, the truth will be told without fear or favor. . . . Beyond that, they disavow responsibility for the effect of what they write." According to the microethicist, philosophy makes a journalist into a censor and "in a true democracy, no person or group, including reporters and editors, has the right to dictate what is in the best interest of others." On the other side, the macroethicists say that "if the effects of an act are more negative than positive for humanity as a whole, the act is considered unethical." The macroethicist believes that when you can predict that reporting an event "will change the nature of the event, by intensifying it, or causing it to be repeated, caution is in order."

This issue crops up at all levels, from the highest to the lowest. The *Honolulu Advertiser* once decided as an experiment to stop publishing news stories warning people about obscene phone callers disguising themselves as doctors and researchers. This decision was based on the theory that if the callers didn't read about themselves in the paper, they might not get so much of a kick out of making such calls and would thus stop doing it. The callers didn't stop. The paper later went back to its original policy of informing the readers about bogus sex surveys.

WRITING CONTESTS

Everybody wants to win a Pulitzer, but would you write a story for the Home Appliance Manufacturers Association prize? In 1973, *Editor & Publisher* listed 107 nationwide journalism contests, more than two thirds of them sponsored by nonjournalistic interests. A decade later the same magazine listed 254 annual contests, plus several dozen more regional and state contests. The most lucrative jackpots offered more than $100,000 in prizes.

Health-minded journalists can win contests for stories about nursing homes, heart disease, epilepsy, high blood pressure, nutrition, alcoholism, muscular dystrophy, multiple sclerosis, or the mentally retarded. Sportswriters can get a plaque, trophy, or check for articles about bowling, horse racing, golf, skiing, boating, and auto racing. The American Meat Institute gives an award for food news, and your chances probably aren't good for winning it with an article touting vegetarianism.

On the business side, American Express Canada offers $6000 plus trips for articles "that encourage people to travel to Canada." Articles promoting travel to Mexico qualify for $2750 from the Mexican Tourist Council. It's not hard to guess the topic for which the Pacific Area Travel Association gives prizes. The firefighters union offers $5000 for accounts about firefighters; the National Coal Association, $2000 for "stories and commentary about the U.S. coal industry"; the Atomic Industrial Forum, $2000 for news about peaceful use of nuclear energy. One oft-cited example is the cigar industry's photography prize for published pictures of cigar smokers.

The media that win these contests like to bask in the glory. But there are contests and there are contests. Many news media in the 1980s are being selective about the ones in which they will participate. "Why are all those people offering all that money to recognize outstanding newspaper work?" asked the Associated Press Managing Editors (APME) Professional Standards Committee. "Are they sincerely interested in raising our level of professionalism? Probably not. . . . More likely, the hope is that such contests will stimulate stories about certain things—hi-fis, swimming pools, etc."

An APME-sponsored study in 1974 found that 9 out of 10 newspapers enter contests and 8 out of 10 have managed to win something. Eventually, the APME added a provision to its own code of ethics saying "stories should not be written or edited primarily for the purpose of winning awards and prizes. Blatantly commercial journalism contests, or others that reflect unfavorably on the newspaper or the profession, should be avoided."

Many editors agree. "No self-respecting journalist should participate in special-interest contests sponsored by trade associations and commercial firms to promote their professions or products. It's frightening to see how many respected newspapers allow themselves to be used . . . in return for a brass plaque," said Joe Smyth of the *Delaware State News*. Another editor called commercial contests "a not-so-subtle form of payola."

"Can anyone doubt that the thrust of all this effort and cash [from contest sponsors] is to buy favorable news and feature space?" asks Bill Smart, editor of the *Deseret News* in Salt Lake City.

The *Philadelphia Inquirer*, which has won many major journalism awards, has tried to be selective in submitting entries. Its guidelines for determing which contests to enter "seek to avoid the possibility that the newspaper or its staff will be exploited by the companies or organizations that run journalism contests primarily to benefit themselves." The following are the major points of the *Inquirer* contest guidelines: No entries to contests "named for the sponsoring company" (such as the Champion Media Awards for Economic Understanding, named for Champion International Corporation), because that helps the sponsor "gain commercial advantage," no entries to contests that "serve the special interest" of the sponsors (e.g., real estate brokers, home builders, title insurance companies), and no contests where entry fees exceed $10; the *Inquirer* enters only contests where judges are independent.

The *Milwaukee Journal* evaluates each contest and avoids any sponsored by corporations or pressure groups, unless judging is controlled by "an intervening and disinterested party." The *Seattle Times* got even more specific, drawing up a list of "acceptable" and "unacceptable" contests. Among the no-nos are contests sponsored by the National Society of Professional Engineers, the Atomic Industrial Forum, and Planned Parenthood. Said Watson Sims of the *Home News* in New Brunswick, New Jersey:

> Contest-ism is a malady which can become a loathsome disease if untreated. At the highest level of the Pulitzer prizes, it can lead some editors to think in terms of professional prestige rather than reader service. At the lowest level, it can lead reporters to think of even less noble purposes than professional prestige. In either case, the reader is the loser.

PRIVACY

What happens when the public's right to know collides with the individual's right to be let alone? The concept of a right of privacy first surfaced in a *Harvard Law Review* article in 1890 coauthored by Louis Brandeis, later to sit on the U.S. Supreme Court. The article said "solitude and privacy have become more essential to the individual" in a complex world. By the 1920s, the American Society of Newspaper Editors was urging that newspapers "not invade private rights or feelings without sure warrant of public right as distinguished from public curiosity."

Both the debate and the legal underpinning for the newly enunciated right of privacy continue to develop in the 1980s. Was Rep. Wilbur Mills's right of privacy invaded when the news media reported that the tipsy congressman and his stripper girlfriend went for a midnight dip in the Washington Tidal Basin? Most reporters agree Mills forfeited any right of privacy on that one. Charles Seib, former ombudsman for the *Washington Post*, wondered later, however, about how the news media would handle a congressman who had a mistress "with whom he quietly spends about as much of the people's time as some of his colleagues spend at the poker table or on the golf course. . . . A rule of thumb sometimes used is that the misconduct must demonstrably affect a public man's performance of his job before it should be reported."

But what of private figures thrown into the public limelight by circumstance, such as rape victims? Most media don't print their names, although there is no legal reason why they can't. The prohibition against naming rape victims, one of the oldest and most widespread practices of self-censorship in the news media, has generated a lot of recent debate.

Chuck Hauser, executive director of the *Providence Journal-Bulletin,* wondered if suppressing the names of rape victims "reinforces and perpetuates the idea . . . that a rape victim has reason to anonymously hide her shame?" One editor who participated in a study of the issue by Carol Oukrop of Kansas State University wondered whether "our not using the names of the victims merely postpones the day when there will be no stigma at all. Implicit in our not using the names is the subtle suggestion that there is some sort of shame in being a victim." James Ragsdale, who edits the *New Bedford Standard-Times,* says this perception is still real and that newspapers must recognize that the community makes a "distinction between a woman who alleges she was forcibly raped and a woman who alleges she was held up at knifepoint." Most papers still keep rape victims' names out of print because as William B. Ketter, editor of the *Quincy Patriot-Ledger,* explained, "publishing the name of a victim might well discourage other women from coming forward and pursuing sex crime cases in court."

The rule against naming rape victims has its detractors also. Stephen R. Coffey, a defense attorney from Albany, New York, questions the fairness of naming the alleged rapist before a trial, yet concealing the name of the woman who brought the charge. "The basic assumption, when you think about it, is that the guy is guilty."

However, the policy about rape victims' names is becoming increasingly less of an anomaly. Journalists are reexamining their tendency to print or broadcast everything they can find out. The rule against naming crime victims is being broadened to include more than sex crime cases. A 1983 White House task force recommended that addresses and phone numbers of crime victims routinely be kept secret. "Victims and witnesses share a common, often justified apprehension that they and members of their family will be threatened or harassed as a result of their testimony against violent criminals," said the President's Task Force on Victims of Crime.

A 1983 study by the Associated Press Managing Editors asked 100 editors about a hypothetical robbery. Less than one quarter would fully identify the victims. Seven years earlier, a similar APME study of editors found that half of them would have fully identified the two women who were held up.

Nowadays, the question is not merely one of taste, but a matter of law. The Hawaii State Constitution now has a provision in its bill of rights guaranteeing a right of privacy. This right has been cited in court cases elsewhere. What, exactly, is the right of privacy? The law is changing, but Michael Giudicessi, a lawyer for the *Des Moines Register and Tribune*, says there are four problem areas in which news media and privacy can collide: publication of private embarrassing facts (unless newsworthy or consented to); casting a person in a false light (say, using an unrelated photo with a story); intrusion into a person's seclusion by trespass; and unauthorized use of a person's name, likeness, or unique skill in an advertisement.

Seib says the whole issue of privacy is causing "considerable agonizing in newsrooms and editorial offices." As a guideline, he suggests that journalists post a small sign next to their desks "bearing the word *compassion* as an antidote to the superficially attractive idea that everything that is true is publishable."

CONFIDENTIAL SOURCES

How can I know when somebody else's "usually reliable source" is reliable? This question gets publicly debated by nonjournalists more than any of the other items so far discussed. Meyer Stein summarizes the reporter's dilemma: "The reporter's job is to get the news. He would rather use the source's name because it makes the story more believable, but sometimes he has to compromise or walk off empty-handed." The Associated Press Managing Editors Code of Ethics states that "news sources should be disclosed unless there is clear reason not to do so. When it is necessary to protect the confidentiality of a source, the reason should be explained."

Certain questions about source confidentiality arise: What is the source's motivation? How might that motivation color the information given? "When journalists are presented with secret information about issues of great import, they become, in a very real sense, agents for the surreptitious source," observes media critic Edward Jay Epstein. "Even if the disclosure is supported by authoritative documents, the journalist cannot know whether the information has been altered, edited, or selected out of context."

Epstein cites as an example the famous 1971 Jack Anderson story that quoted Henry Kissinger as saying in a secret meeting that the publicly neutral U.S. should "tilt" toward Pakistan in the Indian–Pakistani war. It later developed that a Navy yeoman working as a White House stenographer leaked the minutes to Anderson at the behest of the Joint Chiefs of Staff, ostensibly to undermine Kissinger's authority. "Anderson was used as an instrument in a power struggle he probably was unaware of," said Epstein.

Another ethical question related to protecting sources arises when anonymous sources are allowed to make charges and criticisms about nonanonymous people. The U.S. Constitution gives defendants in criminal cases the right to confront their accusers. Should the accuser be allowed to hide behind a cloak of anonymity in a charge repeated by the mass media? Is it fair to the person charged or to the reader/listener when a source fails to give information that will help them judge the reliability of the charge?

Confidential sources will always be with us—at least journalists hope they will, for without them many stories would go unreported. But it is important to be aware of the impact that material of this sort may have on the overall correspondence between a story and the real truth it purports to describe.

The preceding discussion has been about news ethics only. There is also the legal side. Refusal to disclose a source may cause you to lose a libel suit or get thrown in jail. This is a possibility to consider when you accept information the source of which you cannot attribute in a story.

ETHICS AND THE CONTEXT OF NEWS

All of the ethical points just discussed are important considerations for individual reporters' behavior. What we have not yet discussed, however, is the macroethical question of the news itself, which was put quite succinctly in 1947 by the Commission on Freedom of the Press, headed by Robert M. Hutchins of the University of Chicago: "The press must give a truthful, comprehensive, and intelligent account of the day's events in a context which gives them meaning. . . . The press must project a representative picture of the constituent groups in the society."

These sentences summarize the "givens" of journalism—first, that its product must be *truthful*. At a minimum, that involves factual accuracy. More than that, however, it must be *comprehensive*, which implies that it looks at the facts from more than one angle. It implies using some of the techniques described in this book to try to see into a situation from as many viewpoints as possible. Putting facts *in context* requires that you strive to make your news accounts contain more than just a slice of reality from a single interview or even from one person's perspective on an event. The philosophy of journalism and the techniques described in this book will help you to provide that context. This approach will give you confidence that the heartwarming, human examples so necessary to good writing are in fact grounded in reality. The "man-in-the-street" interview always gives quotes and anecdotes. The use of sample surveys or systematic documents research or some of the other methods described in this book will tell you whether the anecdotal material represents something typical or just individual quirk and whim.

These techniques help you to acquire the "representative picture of the constituent groups in the society" that the Hutchins Commission prized. This way of practicing journalism will take you away from a 100 percent reliance on the world of officialdom—the world of the press conference, the news release, and the staged media event.

Lee Hills, a former editor of the *Detroit Free Press* and later an executive of the Knight-Ridder newspaper chain, notes:

> Our definition of news is pathetically simple: An overt act takes place at a particular point in time and we assess the act's significance. If it measures up, it's news. But someone has got to *do something*—fight a war, hold a press conference, punch a policeman—before we'll accept it as news. . . .
>
> Do we report our readers' attitudes—bring their thoughts out into the market place for others to consider, provide the thinkers themselves some notion of how many other people feel the same way—and provide news that relates directly to these concerns?
>
> The answer is no; in large measure, we do not.

Hills called the use of sample surveys (see Chapters 6 and 7) "the machinery to report the changing public mind," a way to provide "a new dimension of information that our communities must have."

Use of the various observation techniques described in this book goes beyond the traditional requirement for objectivity—"Get both sides of the story." Many stories have more than two sides, and obtaining quotes from spokespersons in two camps does not necessarily allow you or your audience to judge the truth. Back in the 1920s, the South Dakota Press Association Code of Ethics said it well: "Accuracy is not only to be an absence of misstatement, but the orderly presence of *all the pertinent truths.*" The Sigma Delta Chi Code of Ethics states that "photographs and telecasts should give an accurate picture of an event and not highlight a minor incident out of context." The use of the systematic techniques advocated in this book will help you as a journalist to apply this standard of fact gathering to the word pictures you paint in stories. These techniques can give you a better idea of what the context of a story is.

Looking at the world in this way will help you gather all the pertinent information it is reasonably possible to obtain about a community event, trend, or personality. Given normal deadline constraints, you cannot, of course, go through this book chapter by chapter and apply each technique to each situation. What this book asks of you is only that you be aware of these tools and use them where appropriate to put together your "truthful, comprehensive, and intelligent account of the day's events in a context which gives them meaning."

REFERENCES

Bernstein, Carl, and Bob Woodward. *All the President's Men.* New York: Simon & Schuster, 1976.

Brady, John J. *The Craft of Interviewing.* Cincinnati: Writer's Digest, 1976.

Christians, Clifford G., Kim B. Rotzoll, and Mark Fackler. *Media Ethics: Cases and Moral Reasoning.* White Plains, NY: Longman, 1983.

Cochnar, Robert J. "Is the Awards Game . . . getting out of hand?" *The Bulletin of the American Society of Newspaper Editors* (February 1984): 3–5.

Commission on Freedom of the Press. *A Free and Responsible Press.* Chicago: University of Chicago Press, 1947.

Crawford, Nelson A. *The Ethics of Journalism.* New York: Alfred A. Knopf, 1924.

Epstein, Edward Jay. *News From Nowhere: Television and the News.* New York: Random House, 1973.

Gerald, Edward J. *The Social Responsibility of the Press.* Minneapolis: University of Minnesota Press, 1963.

Gilmore, Gene, and Robert Root. *Modern Newspaper Editing.* San Francisco: Glendessary Press, 1971.

Greene, Bob. "Trying to Trap the Tylenol Killer: A Columnist's Conscience." *The Bulletin of the American Society of Newspaper Editors* (March 1983): 20–22.

Harwood, Richard. "Newspaper Ethics: The Confusion over Conflict of Interest." *Quill*, 59, no. 7 (July 1971).

Hocking, William E. *Freedom of the Press: A Framework of Principle.* Chicago: University of Chicago Press, 1947.

Hohenberg, John. *The Professional Journalist: A Guide to the Practices and Principles of the News Media.* 4th ed. New York: Holt, Rinehart and Winston, 1978.

Hvistendahl, J. K. "An Ethical Dilemma Over Self-Generating News." *Grassroots Editor*, 14, no. 5 (Sept./Oct. 1973): 3–6.

Merrill, John C. *The Imperative of Freedom: A Philosophy of Journalistic Autonomy.* New York: Hastings House Publishers, 1974.

Meyer, Philip. *Editors, Publishers and Newspaper Ethics.* Washington, D.C.: American Society of Newspaper Editors, 1983.

Rivers, William L., and Wilbur Schramm. *Responsibility in Mass Communication,* rev. ed. New York: Harper & Row, 1969.

Schmuhl, Robert, ed. *The Responsibilities of Journalism.* Notre Dame, IN: Notre Dame Press, 1984.

Woodward, Bob, and Carl Bernstein. *The Final Days.* New York: Simon & Schuster, 1976.

Part II
INTERVIEWS

CHAPTER 5
Personal Interviews

Reporter from the Daily Thunderstorm: I've come to interview you. . . .

Mark Twain: What do you do it with?

Reporter: . . . It ought to be done with a club in some cases; but customarily it consists in the interviewer asking questions and the interviewee answering them. It is all the rage now. . . .

Q. How old are you?

A. Nineteen, in June.

Q. Indeed. I would have taken you to be thirty-five or six. Where were you born?

A. In Missouri.

Q. When did you begin to write?

A. In 1836.

Q. Why, how could that be, if you are only nineteen now?

A. I don't know. It does seem curious, somehow.

Q. It does, indeed. Whom do you consider the most remarkable man you ever met?

A. Aaron Burr.

Q. But you never could have met Aaron Burr, if you are only nineteen years—

A. Now, if you know more about me than I do, what do you ask me for?

Mark Twain, "An Encounter with an Interviewer"

Fortunately for journalists, most interview subjects aren't quite that hard to tackle. Unfortunately, however, few interview subjects are able to infuse a question-and-answer session with any wit at all. A good deal of this book is spent arguing for the use of a variety of noninterview techniques to gather the news, but the interview remains a key technique in the reporter's repertoire. The message of this chapter can be simply stated:

> Know when an interview is appropriate.
> Know how to do one correctly.

The first advice about approaching an interview is to know when it isn't the right thing to do. Interviews, for instance, usually are not the best way to gather factual information, but they are an excellent technique for getting opinions. For facts, you're better off looking at the record—the written record. People often forget or misrepresent or incorrectly recall names, dates, figures. Don't use an interview when you can get factual information more quickly and reliably somewhere else.

A second important warning about the interview situation is to remember that you and your subject don't share the same goals. As journalist Thomas Morgan put it: "I want the truth; *they* want to be beautiful." Remember that even a source who attempts to be honest or candid is at least subconsciously measuring his or her words, knowing they will be in print or on the air. A source has a point of view that will color the content and tone of the information you get from the interview.

Having said all of this, here are some guidelines for making an interview as useful, complete, and valid as possible.

GETTING THE INTERVIEW

Beginning journalists often are afraid to approach people for an interview, especially prominent people in "high" places. Yet the simple, direct approach is often the best way. In 1950, Arthur Krock, Washington bureau chief of the *New York Times*, got an exclusive interview with Harry S Truman that made the rest of the press corps apoplectic. How did he score his beat? By asking President Truman for the interview at a dinner party! Harrison Salisbury, also of the *Times*, recalled that author George Bernard Shaw "didn't give many interviews." Nonetheless, he continued, "One of our reporters just went down to that little house he had in Hertfordshire and walked in on him one day and got a hell of a good story."

Moral: If you don't ask, you'll never get an interview. Don't assume, even about the most prominent people, that the answer will be no before you have asked. Of course, it helps if you can say you're from the *New York Times*, but don't despair if you need an interview for the *Daily Bugle*. Ask.

Generally—almost invariably with prominent people—you need to make arrangements in advance. The late Isaac Marcosson, a prominent journalist in the early 20th century, interviewed Presidents Woodrow Wilson and Theodore Roosevelt, British Prime Minister David Lloyd George, Russian revolutionary Alexander Kerensky, actress Ethel Barrymore, writer Mark Twain, and tycoon J. Pierpont Morgan. Marcosson offered this advice:

> Interviewing outstanding personalities is in the last analysis merely a piece of glorified salesmanship. . . . Just as the salesman must eventually convince his prospect that he needs and is able to buy the product under discussion, so must the interviewer persuade any world figure that an interpretation of personality or a wide publication of his utterances is vital or opportune to the moment and the cause in which he is enlisted.

The job of salesmanship can be difficult when would-be sources have reason to believe you are investigating something unpleasant about them. But even then, you can make the pitch that any story will be more more fair and accurate if it has their point of view in it.

Occasionally, catching people unprepared will work—as it did with George Bernard Shaw. Working on their Watergate stories, *Washington Post* reporter team Bob Woodward and Carl Bernstein often found that catching people off guard was the best approach, so they would go and knock on people's doors at home in the evening with no advance warning. "Nine times out of ten, people wouldn't let us in the door," said Bernstein. "But sometimes it worked. The theory was that there were a lot of people who worked in places where the last thing in the world they would want was a visit from somebody named Woodward or Bernstein. And if you call them on the phone they're gonna say no. . . . But instead you show up at their homes and show that you're well-dressed and civilized. . . ."

When you catch people off guard before they have a chance to erect their defenses and hedge their answers, you often can obtain honest, straightforward replies. The practice is more defensible when dealing with public figures who are accustomed to reporters' queries than it is when interviewing private persons who are thrust into the limelight by an event. Many believe that nonpublic figures should be asked to give their *informed consent* before the interviewer begins his or her questions.

BE PREPARED

If an unprepared subject is "the dream of any interviewer," the unprepared interviewer is the bane of the subject's existence. On occasion, however, a reporter will be thrown into an interview situation with no time to get ready. For example, a city editor might say, "Bulwinkle, Dr. Ernest Grinchfink, the famed world expert on geonuclear sociographics, is in the conference room for his interview and the science writer just called in sick with the flu. Go interview him." The best you can do in a situation like this is to wing it. Honesty is probably the best policy up front, coupled with a devout wish that Grinchfink is able to explain geonuclear sociographics without jargon and without prompting from you.

Usually, however, you'll have time to prepare yourself properly. Learn as much about the person and situation as time permits. Don't ask a U.S. senator how long he's been in politics, what party he belongs to, what committee he sits on. You waste interview time gathering information you can more easily obtain elsewhere and you give the subject the impression that you haven't done your homework. Use your newspaper's library or the public library. A source who feels you are unprepared or not knowledgeable will often feel free to "snow" you—to give only vague, ambiguous, or half-true answers. If you are unaware of the subject's background, you won't be able to detect inconsistencies or half-truths, and you may miss some real news when it comes along.

Try to put yourself in your audience's position. Ask yourself what readers or viewers would ask this person if they could. Having enough questions on varied topics prepared in advance can help move even the most floundering interview along.

TIPS FOR INTERVIEW PREPARATION

1. *Type or write out your questions in advance to make sure you cover all the topics you want to cover.* However, don't be rigid. If an interview heads down a promising path not covered by your questions, don't rein in the subject and force him or her back on course to a question on your list. Often the unanticipated angles produce the most newsworthy results.

2. *General versus specific questions.* Usually, specific questions produce more usable materials for journalists than do abstract or hypothetical inquiries. Although the general question often provokes a useless answer filled with platitudes, some reporters, such as freelancer Edward Linn, do like to prepare some broad questions. If you ask only questions that are specific and narrow, you risk putting your subject in a straitjacket of your making. Toss in a few broad "softballs," too, and you may obtain some serendipitous responses. Change the pace occasionally as you go.

In *The Craft of Interviewing* John J. Brady offers some good advice: "Generally, if your subject is at home with words and ideas, lead him out with an open, general question. If he is ill at ease, make him comfortable with a question about the concrete, the easily explained."

3. *Avoid "leading" questions that are so pointed they steer the subject into a predetermined answer.*

4. *Ask just one question at a time.* Avoid "double-barreled" queries. They generally produce only single-barreled answers and much confusion as well.

5. *Don't make speeches.* Avoid overlong questions.

The following excerpt from one of President Kennedy's news conferences illustrates points 4 and 5:

> Mr. President, I have a two-prong question on the NATO nuclear force. First, can you tell us how goes the Merchant Mission? [Livingston Merchant was envoy to NATO.] Secondly, in view of the lack of enthusiasm, if we can believe the press, reflects a certain amount of public opinion in Europe as to the Polaris armed surface force because of its alleged greater vulnerability as compared to the atomic

submarine. Why haven't the proposals for a conventionally powered submarine force been put forth, a proposal which would not apparently annoy Congress as much as an atomic submarine and would cost about half as much as the atomic submarine?

6. *Remember who is being interviewed.* "I went to one of the restaurants in town one day and Joe Alsop was in a booth with·a source," recalled writer Gay Talese. "And the joke at the end of our lunch was—the source never opened his mouth. Alsop simply talked to him all the time." As a reporter, guide the interview and keep it from rambling, but don't monopolize the conversation yourself.

7. *Use a clean-up question to sweep up the loose ends when you finish.* "Is there anything about this subject that is important that I haven't asked you about?"

TELEPHONE VERSUS FACE-TO-FACE INTERVIEWS

If there is time, you invariably are better off doing a face-to-face interview than attempting one over the phone. It is easier to establish rapport, and you are better able to draw cues from the expressions and moods of an interview subject. Feature interviews or sessions dealing with complex scientific or statistical matter are virtually impossible over the phone. In the case of a feature interview, you get no sense from a phone call of color, setting, personal quirks, or habits.

Long treatises have been written about "nonverbal communications"—the twitchings, body movements, facial expressions, and other subconscious clues to attitudes that people give when they talk with one another. You don't need to read the academic literature on the subject to know intuitively when someone sitting across from you is uncomfortable with the question or the questioner, when your subject hasn't properly understood the thrust of your questioning, or when a subject is nervous. In a study of news story accuracy in three California papers, Fred C. Berry Jr. found that "personal interviews produced about 1½ times as many accurate stories as telephone interviews."

Pocket Guide to the Interview

The ten stages of a typical interview.

1. Define a purpose for the interview.
2. Conduct background research.
3. Request an interview appointment.
4. Plan your strategy.
5. Meet the respondent: Icebreaker conversation.
6. Ask your first serious questions.
7. Proceed to the heart of the interview.
8. Ask "bomb" questions if necessary (potentially sensitive or embarrassing questions).
9. Recover from "bomb" questions.
10. Conclude the interview.

Ken Metzler, NEWSGATHERING, © 1979, p. 135. Reprinted by permission of Prentice-Hall, Inc., Englewood Cliffs, New Jersey.

Finally, phone interviews tend to be shorter because they are not as comfortable to do. A subject will get restless much more quickly and cut you off. That said, however, often you only have time for a phone call as deadline approaches. A call is better than nothing.

ESTABLISHING RAPPORT

You're not going to get much out of an interview if you don't establish some level of rapport at the outset. There is no foolproof system for doing this. Each reporter develops his or her own style over time. Hugh C. Sherwood, in *The Journalistic Interview*, for example, offers the following advice:

If you are to be a good interviewer, you must impress most of the
people you interview as friendly, intelligent, not easily maneu-
vered—and, above all, as a human being who can be talked with as
another human being and not just as a journalist.

Harrison Salisbury of the *New York Times* describes how his technique for establishing rapport has evolved:

In the early days it was much tighter and I had a series of very sharply
defined questions and I was in a great hurry to put them across, bing,
bing, bing. As the years went on I've taken a much more relaxed
technique which I think is more effective, of letting the interview
develop its own pace and establishing a sort of a mood of interchange
before bringing in the sharper questions.

The conversational, soft opening, however, can fall flat too. Associated Press veteran Saul Pett recalled interviewing labor leader
James Hoffa and trying to break the ice by asking, "My wife wants
to know why you always wear white socks." Hoffa replied, quickly,
"Because my feet sweat less in them." No ice broken there.

In the final analysis, although everyone agrees about the worth
of achieving rapport, the absence of it doesn't necessarily doom an
interview. Author Alex Haley once made an appointment to interview American Nazi boss George Lincoln Rockwell for *Playboy*.
When they talked on the phone, Rockwell asked him, "Are you a
Jew?" Haley said no, not bothering to volunteer the fact that he is
black. The interview was set up, Haley arrived, and there was a
good deal of embarrassment all around.

"He [Rockwell] said: 'I see you're black, and I'm going to be
very honest with you right now, that we call your kind "niggers"
and we think you should all be shipped back to Africa,'" Haley
remembered. "And I said: 'Well, sir, I've been called "nigger" before. But this time I'm being paid very well for it, so now you go
right ahead. . . .'" In time, Haley said, "he and I became quite
garrulous together," and later carried on a correspondence.

The Haleys of the world are few and far between. Professional
survey organizations and the news media commonly try to minimize
the chance of this sort of thing happening by making at least a
rudimentary match between interviewer and subject.

Many interviewers suggest establishing rapport before pulling
out your notebook or tape recorder. Others argue that drawing your
note-taking weapon after you have begun chatting can change the
mood in mid-interview, make the subject wary, and destroy any
rapport that you have built up.

Eventually, you must move away from the initial pleasantries. With a talkative source in the mood for just passing the time of day, this can be tough. A reporter once got an appointment to talk to the governor of Hawaii about a specific topic for a specific story. It was the end of the day. The governor was relaxed and talkative. Try as he might, the reporter was unable to direct the governor's attention to what the reporter felt was the matter at hand. Ultimately, after 90 minutes of very pleasant but not very journalistically productive discussion, the governor's secretary came in and reminded the governor of a dinner engagement. Under that pressure of time, the governor switched gears, cut out the small talk, and gave the reporter all he needed—and more—in about 10 minutes.

There are no panaceas for such situations. Few reporters are very good at walking out on rambling governors, especially if the reporter hopes to get an appointment for an interview ever again. For a "beat" reporter, such sessions can foster lasting rapport that goes long beyond that one situation. Cheerfully bantering your way through a chat like that can help the source see you "as another human being and not just as a journalist," as Sherwood suggested. It can pay dividends in the long run.

In nearly every journalistic interview, the journalist seeks to acquire information for publication on a topic of his or her choosing, and eventually must get down to business. At this point, you must decide whether to open with generalities or immediately zero in on what Salisbury called the "very sharply defined questions . . . bing, bing, bing." Different reporters have different ways of doing this. Associated Press reporter Sterling Green said, "I like to land on him with a hard one right from the start and show him that we mean business and get away from the idea that 'This is a puff piece.'" Saul Pett agrees that for "a hard news spot interview, you can't really fool around too much. If it's a personality-type interview, you almost have to."

INTERVIEWER ROLE PLAYING

At times you should continue the friendly rapport throughout an interview. At other times, after initially establishing rapport (or even without establishing rapport, as in clearly confrontational situations), you must change posture and mood. You can choose among roles ranging from "ignorance" through "knowledgeability" to an "I-know-more-than-you-think-I-do" bluster.

Feigning ignorance can elicit useable quotes. You can get explanatory matter in quotable, attributable form. You as the journalist won't have to say something in a story on your own. You get your source to say it.

Often, however, you don't need to "feign" ignorance, because you really are ignorant. Generally, the source knows more about the topic than you do, or you wouldn't be doing the interview. If you don't understand something a source says, stop right there and clear it up. Sooner or later, you have to write the story, and it's hard to bluff through your ignorance at that point. Which would you rather do—expose your ignorance to a source, or try to explain to your city editor or news director that you yourself don't understand the story you just turned in? This does happen. Ask any news executive.

Most interviews go more smoothly when the interviewer has at least a passing knowledge of the subject at hand. Pulitzer-prize-winner Clark Mollenhoff provides some good advice:

> It may occasionally be wise strategy to play ignorant. But it is never an advantage to be ignorant about the facts, the specific terminology, or the relevant law when interviewing a subject.

If you seem a little knowledgeable, the source may be more at ease. Legendary journalist A. J. Liebling once interviewed jockey Eddie Arcaro. "The first question I asked was, 'How many holes longer do you keep your left stirrup than your right?'" Liebling later commented: "That started him talking easily and after an hour, during which I had put in about 12 words, he said, 'I can see that you've been around riders a lot.'"

At the far end of the spectrum is the use of a bluff—encouraging the subject to believe that you know everything anyway so it is best to come clean. In such situations, the source may open up, confirming things that you only suspected, or may not even have guessed at, but about which you haven't known enough to write a solid story.

A story has been told of a *Wall Street Journal* reporter who tried to get a source to admit that he had invested in a particular project. Although the reporter's research indicated that the man invested $77,000, he wasn't sure this was true. The reporter asked, "How did you happen to invest $77,000 in the XYZ project?" The man assumed the reporter knew about it, so he explained. If the reporter had asked "Did you invest?" the man could have denied all. Even if the $77,000 figure was wrong, the source might have answered, "It wasn't $77,000, it was. . . ."

One time, a city's symphony orchestra was preparing to announce the selection of a new conductor from among three candidates. One newspaper's reporters went from source to source in the symphony hierarchy saying, "Why was 'A' considered the best choice?" "A" wasn't, as it turned out. Eventually, however, the paper was able to pin down which of the three men was chosen.

NOTE-TAKING VERSUS NOTHING AT ALL

Eventually, the interviewee's comments must be turned into a story. That means you must keep track of what was said—by taking notes, taping the interview, having a good memory, or some combination of these. Different interviewers have different styles.

Note-Taking

Most reporters take at least some notes during an interview, even when they are simultaneously taping. The notes can refresh your memory for key points when you listen to the tape afterwards. Some form of shorthand or speedwriting is essential if you hope to have fairly complete notes. Many reporters have benefitted from a course in Gregg shorthand, although you must use it fairly frequently or you'll get rusty. Speed in taking notes is necessary if you are to avoid those awkward moments in an interview when the subject has finished talking, but sits in silence waiting for you to finish writing.

Note-taking reassures some subjects that you are interested in what they have to say and are making an effort to get it down accurately, but it makes other subjects nervous because it continually reminds them that their words may wind up in print, and that inhibits them. You need to know *when* to start taking notes. Flipping out your notebook right at the start of an interview scares some subjects. One excuse for bringing it out is to offer a bit of admiration for some observation that your subject has just made—"Say, that's good. I want to be sure I get that down just right."

Many interviewees will watch your note-taking closely for indications of what *you* think is important. When you're not taking notes, it signals them that they're into some bland or irrelevant area. Some subjects get offended when you stop writing; others use this as a clue to change course.

Taking notes can have the unintended side effect of turning off the spigot just when the flow is beginning. A subject who is trying *not* to say anything striking or newsworthy will become alarmed if you begin to rapidly take notes. To avoid making a subject nervous or irritable, some reporters have perfected the technique of asking an innocuous follow-up question after their source has just let fly with some blockbuster quote. They scribble notes on the blockbuster while the source is answering the un-noteworthy follow-up question. (It's important not to overreact when you do get a blockbuster. You should just quietly continue asking questions and taking notes, or perhaps change the subject to something insignificant. Otherwise, your subject may have second thoughts and will beg you not to repeat what he has said, leaving you with a tough decision or an angry interviewee.)

There is some evidence that excessive note-taking diverts the interviewer's attention from the thread of the conversation. You may get details on a lot of trees, but miss the forest. In an effort to write down each word precisely, you may pay too little attention to the broad sweep of things. A study among journalism students on two California campuses by Friedrich Abel surprisingly found that those "who took notes were *more* apt to record a fact wrongly than those who did not take notes." The non-note takers were more likely to leave details out of stories but they got fewer things wrong.

In taking notes, as in asking questions, be prepared to change course and follow a promising lead when it arises. If you are in the middle of transcribing one quote and a better one comes along, abandon the first one. Get the essential part, the key word or phrase that says it all.

Sometimes you want to take notes, but can't. Gail Sheehy describes one such incident in *Hustling*, her book about New York City prostitution:

> We arrived at David's [a pimp's] penthouse in full dress but without a scrap of paper or pencil between us. Every fifteen minutes I had to excuse myself and dash for the bathroom to make notes with an eyebrow pencil on the back of a checkbook.

Relying on Memory

Some writers have been able to train their memories to regurgitate key passages of an interview verbatim after it is over, with no notes to work from. When the late Truman Capote was researching *In Cold Blood*, an account of a vicious multiple murder, he found that many of his prospective sources tensed up when he tried to take notes.

> If you write down or tape what people say, it makes them feel inhibited and self-conscious. It makes them say what they think you *expect* them to say. . . . I taught myself to be my own tape recorder. What I'd do was have a friend talk or read for a set length of time, tape what he was saying, and meanwhile listen to him as intently as I could. Then I'd go write down what he had said as I remembered it, and later compare with what I had with the tape.

Figure 5.1 Back shop makeup editor and news editor put together a front page (*The Honolulu Advertiser*).

At the end of the day's interviewing for the book, Capote would go back to his motel room and transcribe the remembered quotes. Few reporters have mastered the art as well as Capote did, however.

TAPING PHONE CONVERSATIONS

There is no question that taping phone conversations is an effective way to get a verbatim account. There also is no question that this procedure can provide backup if you are later accused of a misquote, or sued. But is it legal? In some states, it's legal to tape phone conversations without the knowledge or approval of the other party; in about a dozen states, it is not. Phone companies in some states have tariffs that mandate the use of a periodic "beep" tone when you tape a telephone conversation, but these tariffs are not the same as law. Jack C. Landau of the Reporter's Committee on Freedom of the Press notes that the federal Omnibus Crime Control Act specifically allows taping if one party of the conversation, namely the person who installed the recorder, approves. He questions whether a state rule in conflict with federal law permitting one-party consent taping can hold up legally.

In some newsrooms, phone conversations between reporter and source are routinely and clandestinely taped. Elsewhere, the practice is banned, or at least requires the approval of senior editors.

Is taping phone conversations ethical? Journalists disagree.

Frederick Taylor, executive director of the *Wall Street Journal*, argues, "If it is okay to take written notes, even in shorthand, certainly it is okay to take notes on a typewriter. And if it is okay to take notes on a typewriter, it is okay to take notes on your CRT. . . . Why does one step further into the electronic age cause such shudders?" Yet the *Wall Street Journal* forbids taping a phone call without permission from the other party, unless the bureau chief and managing editor are notified and give permission. Taylor adds, however, that this hadn't happened in a decade of practice.

"I favor informing interviewees when it [taping of phone interviews] is done," says Jim Hoge, publisher of the *New York Daily News*.

"It's all just notes, a collection of words or bleeps or electronic impulses that a reporter uses to do the job," says Jan Mittelstadt, editor of an Owatonna, Minnesota, paper. "What's the big deal?"

The Useful "Mm-humm"

Researchers who have spent careers studying interview situations have concluded that long questions tend to produce long answers. One such researcher, Joseph Matarrazo, even took that theory to the boundaries of science by investigating the impact on an interview of an "mm-humm."

Lo and behold, it made a difference. Interviewers who asked questions lasting 5–6 seconds typically got responses in the range of 30–40 seconds, but when an interviewer spiced up his interview with "mm-humm's," the answers to the questions got longer—up in the 50–60 second range.

When in doubt, throw in an extra "mm-humm" or two. It will keep your subject talking while you think up the next question.

A. M. Rosenthal, executive editor of the *New York Times*, said, "It doesn't sit well in the stomach to tape someone and not tell them you're doing it. It's not honest. It's not fair. Period." Yet, as of 1983, the *Times* had no antitaping policy.

Gilbert Cranberg, former Des Moines editor and later a University of Iowa journalism professor, pointed out that the American Bar Association forbids taping by attorneys without consent of all parties. "Journalists should not settle for a lesser standard of conduct than lawyers," Cranberg argued.

The *Los Angeles Times, Boston Globe, Philadelphia Inquirer,* and others forbid or restrict secret taping.

So there you have it. Take your choice of arguments. First, you must decide whether secret taping violates any of your own personal ethical standards. If not, find out whether taping violates either a newsroom policy or a state law. Then make up your mind. Of course, this debate concerns taping without telling. Hardly anybody sees a problem with taping, ethical or otherwise, when all parties to a conversation have consented.

MINING FOR GEMS

Interviewing gets to be like pulling teeth when you come across a reluctant witness who is giving you unadorned "yes" and "no" answers or speaking in generalities and platitudes. When this happens, you need to pull tricks from your repertoire to get usable quotes and colorful anecdotes to illustrate the generalities. Especially when you are dealing with a weighty topic, anecdotal material can make the difference between dull writing and sprightly prose.

Some ways to "probe" with an interview subject:

Silence. If you get a short, noninformative answer where a long one was expected, just sit quietly and wait. Your subject should soon get nervous and try to fill the empty space.

Encouragement. "That's interesting." "Good." "Uh-huh." Any short, encouraging phrase will let your subject know that you have been listening, are impressed, and would like to hear more.

Repetition. Repeat the subject's answer in his or her own words. If you've misunderstood, the subject can clear it up. In any event, this technique can inspire elaboration.

Ask for examples. This can generate anecdotes.

"Why?" Get at the reasons behind what the subject has just told you.

Ask longer questions. Researchers have found that longer questions produce longer answers—up to a point, of course, at which the questions become convoluted and unintelligible. This theory has been tested with presidential press conferences, job interviews, doctor–patient interviews, and even communication between astronauts and ground control, and has been consistently confirmed.

HANDLING BOMBSHELLS

Many news interviews eventually require the reporter to ask tough, embarrassing questions. Beginning interviewers sometimes find this the hardest part of the job. Various methods can be used to minimize the discomfort:

Attribute the question to somebody else. Create the impression that it isn't really *your* opinion, but you need to ask anyway because "other people" are saying things. When Barbara Walters interviewed the then Shah of Iran, she said: "Your majesty, there are people who say you are a dictator, a benevolent dictator, perhaps, but a dictator all the same. I know you have heard these criticisms. This is your opportunity to answer them."

Use a nonbeat reporter for a tough interview, so that the beat reporter's rapport with a regular source is not destroyed. A variation of this is to double-team a subject, using a "good cop–bad cop" approach in which one reporter is "sympathetic" to the subject, while the other one bores in with more accusatory, confrontational language.

Ease into it gently. Ken Metzler, in his book *Creative Interviewing*, offers this example of how to talk about rape with a rape victim.

> You would not say 'Tell me about the time you were raped.' You would edge gradually toward the subject. You might discuss crime, violence, safety on the streets, personal safety, and ultimately her own feelings of safety or insecurity. A time will come to inquire about the attack. If you have any feeling for people, you'll sense when the time is right. It may come sooner than you think. . . . To take you off the hook, she may bring it up herself.

Wait until late in the interview. In public opinion polling, it is common to put the more personal items—questions about family income, attitudes about sex, and so forth—at the end of a questionnaire. The same approach works for journalistic interviews. Toward the end of the session, an interviewer should have established rapport and, even if the questions provoke anger or cause the interview to end, you have gathered all the other information you need anyway and stand to lose very little.

Mary Anne Pikrone, who wrote for the *Rochester Times-Union*, recalls interviewing a former nun.

> One of the first things I wondered was, does she date and what does it feel like to be in the arms of a man and be kissed again, after 10 years in the convent? I finally got that question out about two hours into the interview, and by that time we were communicating so well that she answered it without hesitation. Don't be afraid to ask what you're wondering.

After asking the tough questions, throw in a couple of final, easy questions before departing. That will leave the subject in a little better frame of mind and make it easier for you to come back for information later if you need to. Above all, don't chicken out. People can be more forthright than you'd expect, even about such topics as sex, money, or religion.

THE FINAL SCENE

Don't overstay your welcome. If your subject has agreed to give you a 30-minute interview, get ready to leave at the 30-minute mark. Often, you'll be asked to stay anyway. If not, it'll be easier to get a follow-up visit if you have shown that you won't try to monopolize your source's time.

But don't stop listening after you've packed up your notebook and recorder and started to head for home. Many is the time that an interviewer has gotten the best anecdotes and most pointed quotes when the source has relaxed and is making pleasant conversation at the door. Usually, it's better not to restart your recorder or pull out your notebook at this point, but you should pay close attention and then make notes as soon as you depart.

OFF-THE-RECORD

Q. When were you born?
A. Off-the-record?

It seldom gets quite that bad, but the off-the-record syndrome has reached ludicrous proportions in journalistic interviews. Should you accept off-the-record information? Sometimes, you probably should, but usually not. The first hurdle to cross is to define exactly what *off-the-record* means. Journalists themselves disagree on the fine distinctions made between several types of restricted information:

Off-the-Record

This usually means "You can't use it in print, even if you don't use my name." Journalists differ on whether they are allowed by the off-the-record ground rules to search for ways to get at the same information on the record. Alfred Friendly, *Washington Post* managing editor a quarter-century ago, tried to codify all the various ways of hedging on attribution of information. He concluded that off-the-record information means the reporter

> may not use it in anything he writes, even without attribution to the source, however guarded. A violation of a confidence of this kind is considered, and properly, a cardinal newspaper sin. . . . If the source persists in speaking off-the-record and the reporter does not accede, he must leave the gathering.

Friendly contended that the rule *did* allow the reporter to try to get the information from another source, "but without in any way indicating that he has already heard the news . . . from someone else."

One problem can occur: If you do track down the information elsewhere, the source may never believe you, but will just assume you broke an off-the-record confidence. For this reason, many journalists bring an interview to a screeching halt whenever a source says, "Off-the-record," because they prefer not to have their hands tied.

Deep Background

This version of what off-the-record means came into popular prominence in the Woodward-Bernstein Watergate investigations. Here's how their book *All the President's Men* defines a *deep background* agreement with Woodward's favorite source, Deep Throat:

> He [Woodward] would never identify him or his position to anyone. . . . He agreed never to quote the man, even as an anonymous source. Their discussions would be only to confirm information that had been obtained elsewhere and to add some perspective.

In Washington, another version of deep background is the so-called Lindley rule, named after Ernest K. Lindley of *Newsweek*. This allows the reporter to print what he gets, but without any quotation or even a veiled attribution to anyone.

To Mike Feinsilber of Associated Press, the term *background information* means, "I'll agree to talk with you if you agree not to use my name or title." Instead, the writer uses such terms as "an administration source" or "a Pentagon official" or "an aide close to the secretary." But the rules vary. In some cases, background means that no attribution may be given even to the source's organization.

Not for Attribution

This term is similar in meaning to "background." It generally means, "You can use this in print, but don't quote me by name. Don't attribute the information in such a way that I can be identified as the source." This is often the only way to get sensitive information. People in touchy situations won't give you such information if they think the leak can be traced back to them. On the other hand, the device is also a convenient way for the source to grind an axe without being spotted. An unattributed quote doesn't allow the reader or listener to evaluate the credibility of the source or identify what ulterior motives may be present.

Many times, when a source says "off-the-record," what he or she *really* means is that the information is not for attribution—which is a lot less onerous. You should make the ground rules clear. Often, if you dig in your heels and refuse to accept information on an unattributable or off-the-record basis, the source will go ahead and give it to you on the record anyway.

Don't *ever* ask a source, "Is that on the record?" Asking that question virtually guarantees that it won't be. (However, some reporters feel it is only fair to explain to sources who aren't in regular contact with the news media that anything they say is considered on the record. They have an ethical concern about taking advantage of a naive source.)

Some newsrooms have explicit rules requiring reporters to obtain permission from a supervisor before giving any grant of confidentiality. Some editors insist on this because they believe that lazy or sloppy reporters overuse anonymous sources when they ought to be working backward more often, using such sources—if at all—only as tipsters and then verifying the information from documents and other on-the-record sources.

Other editors feel it is unrealistic to expect a reporter to terminate an interview and contact a superior before continuing a conversation on a confidential basis. According to this argument, ultimately the boss must decide whether to print or broadcast information obtained confidentially. Because this provides a final "filtering" of the story before it becomes public, why tie a reporter's hands at the fact-gathering stage?

Sometimes a source tries to impose an ex post facto censorship on an interview by insisting that you show him the story after it is written, but before it is printed or broadcast. Few reporters accede to such requests. However, some feel more comfortable when dealing with complex technical or statistical subjects if they check back with the original source—with the understanding that the source doesn't get to "edit" the story, only to suggest corrections in fact or perspective.

Another common ploy used by sources is to complete the interview and then make a belated "off-the-record" demand because of a concern that something explosive has been said. Few reporters grant such requests, contending that any deals about confidentiality should be struck in advance—after all, the source knows he or she is talking to a reporter and that reporters interview people to get information to publish or broadcast.

Above all, play fair with sources. Cutting corners on the confidentiality rules to get a story generally is an empty victory followed by penalties and regrets afterward. You don't want to be known as a reporter who backstabs sources, because if you gain that kind of reputation soon you won't have any more sources.

THE ETHICS OF "SOURCERY"

"Where I come from in journalism, the magic word is 'attribution.' When I decide to protect a source, I stick to it as a matter of principle. But I don't make such decisions casually," said Peter Bridge, editor of *The Observer* in Kearny, New Jersey. In 1972, Bridge did make such a decision in connection with a story about an alleged bribe to a Newark housing official. Later, Bridge spent three weeks in jail for refusing to testify about his confidential source before a grand jury. But even Bridge says there ought to be tight limits on anonymity: "I'd much prefer to write, and read, articles in which information is connected with an identifiable and identified source. Attributing facts to real people or documents fortifies credibility. Conversely, attribution to 'unidentified sources' detracts from credibility."

Richard Smyser, editor of the *Oak Ridger* in Oak Ridge, Tennessee, says journalists need to distinguish between two types of sources. First, there are the invaluable sources who need to be "cultivated, appreciated, protected." They tend to be lower-level

Guidelines on Use of Sources

1. Try to get sources on the record.
2. Don't rely totally on unnamed sources. Use sources as tips to find someone who will talk on the record or to uncover independent confirmation, such as from records.
3. Distinguish between "leaked facts" and "leaked opinion."
4. Talk to an editor about any promise of confidentiality so the two of you can "share the burden of trust that such a promise carries."
5. Reveal your source to an editor.
6. Do not use such words as "key officials," "well-placed," or "informed" sources. Provide the fullest possible identification, such as "an official in the city manager's office." (Jeff Portnoy, a Honolulu attorney who represents several news media clients, has similar advice from a legal perspective: "Try not to use the word 'source' in a story. Use some other word which means the same thing, but does not carry the same emotional tag.")
7. Don't allow an unnamed source to demean, attack, or vilify a named person or institution except under extraordinary circumstances, and if then, with permission of a senior editor only.

Roanoke Times and World-News

people, "real whistle-blowers. People who are genuinely upset when they see wrongdoing and want to do something to right it, but have themselves, their jobs, their families, to think of, too."

And then, says Smyser, there are

"sourcerers" [who] tend to be big-time folks—presidential aides like [Carter press secretary Jody] Powell; presidential advisers like

Henry Kissinger and Zbigniew Brzezinski; aides to presidential hopefuls during primary campaigns; negotiators—both management and union—at intense bargaining times; members of Congress and their staffs during heated congressional battles. People on the make, mostly.

Do they want the public to know the truth? Do they want to right a wrong. . . . Perhaps, but don't count on it. Mostly "sourcerers" are out to win an election, pass a bill, trash an opponent or make a buck. And if leaking on someone or something might help, they'll do it. And with our help, they do it all too often.

CLEANING UP QUOTES

On the other side, these attacks that are coming on the other side of the aisle, on the defense spending, incidentally, in the figure that we've submitted in the budget, we ourselves and the Defense Department, under the secretary, reduced that budget by $16 billion before it was submitted by taking things out that would have been worthwhile, would have increased our security ability, but which we believe we could do without for a time, and settled on this particular thing.

These words were spoken by President Ronald Reagan at a February 22, 1984, press conference. If even presidents talk this way, think how the verbatim quotes of ordinary people look when you put them in writing. You need to decide, therefore, how much to "clean up" the quotes of your sources in writing a story.

Written sentences tend to have a subject and a verb and to make a single point before they reach a period. When people talk, they intersperse their words with "uh" and "ah" and "you know." They tend to ramble around before stopping for breath. The syntax is garbled, even though the meaning may come through.

What is a reporter to do about this? Novelist George Higgins says, "You can't write the way people actually talk, because it's just too difficult to read. You *are* dealing in a different medium." Many reporters agree that it is better to polish up quotes a bit to help the speaker look literate—so long as (and this is a very important "so long as") the reporter remains faithful to the meaning and intent of the speaker.

When it is too difficult to clean up a quote, don't use quotation marks; use a nonquote that paraphrases and attributes the speaker's words. When you do keep matter in quotation marks, often the use of ellipsis is all that is needed to bring sense and order to the words. Eliminate the ramble; keep the nuggets. When you are finished, put yourself in the speaker's shoes and see if you would be satisfied with the way the sentiments are expressed.

Special problems of "cleaning up quotes" arise when the speaker has a regional accent or a dialect that renders his or her speech ungrammatical. In many cases, especially in feature stores, capturing the rhythm and pace of such speech is an important part of revealing the source's personality. However, a long story filled with southern-accented quotes or Zsa Zsa Gabor-type Hungarian-English gets tough on the reader. Also, the overall effect can seem condescending or patronizing to the speaker. Sometimes, you can use a few illustrative and colorful quotes early in a story to convey the impression, then slide back into standard grammatical English for the rest of the story.

Obscenity presents yet another challenge. If a lawyer curses a judge and gets held in contempt of court for it, you have a tough problem writing the story unless you can convey the sense of what was said. Most news media have rules about what obscenity is allowed and what isn't. When in doubt, consult with an editor to see whether you need to use "_____ ," "expletive deleted," or some other convention to deal with the problem.

BE SKEPTICAL

"In the case of news, we should always await the sacrament of confirmation," Voltaire wrote to the Count d'Argental in 1760. This is still good advice for any reporter using an interview. Don't put something in a story just because you have a quote to that effect. It may be wrong. Your responsibility to your readers doesn't stop at the end of the interview.

Double-check with other people, by referring to documents, by direct observation of a situation, or by any of the other techniques discussed in this book. In short, don't rely on one interview with one person to capture the essence of a situation. Broaden your base of fact-gathering. Interviews can be an important part of this search, but normally should not be the only one.

REFERENCES

Berry, Fred C., Jr. "A Study of Accuracy in Local News Stories in Three Dailies." *Journalism Quarterly*, 44, no. 3 (Autumn 1967): 482–90.

Brian, Denis. *Murderers and Other Friendly People*. New York: McGraw-Hill, 1973.

Capote, Truman. *In Cold Blood: A True Account of a Multiple Murder and Its Consequences*. New York: Random House, 1965.

Donaghy, William C. *The Interview: Skills and Applications*. Glenview, IL: Scott, Foresman and Co., 1984.

Friendly, Alfred. "Attribution of News." In Louis Lyons, ed., *Reporting and Gathering the News*. Cambridge, MA: Belknap Press, 1965.

Hage, George S., Everette E. Dennis, Arnold H. Ismach, and Stephen Hartgen. *New Strategies for Public Affairs Reporting, Investigation, Interpretation, and Research*, 2d ed. Englewood Cliffs, NJ: Prentice-Hall, 1983.

Landau, Jack C. "Tape Record Important Interviews." *Editor and Publisher* (Jan. 21, 1984): 22–23.

Marcosson, Isaac. *Adventures in Interviewing*. New York: John Lane, 1919.

Matarazzo, Joseph D., Morris Weitman, George Saslow, and Arthur N. Weins. "Interviewer Influence on Duration of Interview Speech." *Journal of Verbal Learning and Verbal Behavior*, I (1963): 451–58.

Metzler, Ken. *Creative Interviewing: The Writer's Guide to Gathering Information by Asking Questions*. Englewood Cliffs, NJ: Prentice-Hall, 1977.

Metzler, Ken. *Newsgathering*. Englewood Cliffs, NJ: Prentice-Hall, 1979.

Meyer, Philip. *Precision Journalism: A Reporter's Introduction to Social Science Methods*. 2d ed. Bloomington: Indiana University Press, 1979.

Sheehy, Gail. *Hustling: Prostitution in Our Wide-Open Society*. New York: Dell, 1973.

Sherwood, Hugh C. *The Journalistic Interview*. rev. ed. New York: Harper & Row, 1972.

Smyser, Richard. "Sourcerers Are Bad People." *The Bulletin of the American Society of Newspaper Editors* (Sept. 1983): 20.

Talese, Gay. *The Kingdom and the Power*. New York: World Publishing, 1969.

Talese, Gay. *Honor Thy Father*. New York: World Publishing, 1971.

Webb, Eugene J., and Terry R. Salancik. "The Interview or, The Only Wheel in Town." *Journalism Monographs*, no. 2 (Nov. 1966).

Wolfe, Tom. *The Electric Kool-Aid Acid Test*. New York: Farrar, Straus and Giroux, 1968.

Wolfe, Tom. *Radical Chic and Mau-Mauing the Flak Catchers*. New York: Farrar, Straus and Giroux, 1970.

CHAPTER 6
Using Surveys

Newspapers have long conducted "man-in-the-street" interviews and called them surveys. The idea was simple enough.

The city editor said, "Bulwinkle, go downtown and find out what the man-in-the-street is thinking about the Vietnam war/abortion/rising property taxes/last week's quintuple murder." Off Bulwinkle went. He questioned a little old lady just after she had been helped across the street by a Boy Scout. He questioned a businessman in an office building elevator. If he had enough of an expense account, he splurged and took a taxi ride so he could get some wisdom from the cabbie. (In those days, cab drivers spent much of their time answering questions from newspaper reporters eager to take the pulse of the town. Talking to cab drivers was especially popular among visiting reporters in unfamiliar places. The cabbie who brought Bulwinkle to and from the train station might be the only genuine "local" with whom he'd come in contact. Cab-driver quotes were obligatory.) All along Bulwinkle's route, his trusty photographer would snap mugshots of each interviewee.

In the end, if Bulwinkle was an inventive writer and lucky—lucky enough to find some articulate, quotable people to answer "the question"—the city editor would be satisfied. There would be a cute story about what *The Daily Bugle* found Johnson City's citizens to be thinking, based on Bulwinkle's "survey of residents"—but the premise was fatally flawed. No man-in-the-street project of this sort can give you the foggiest reliable notion about what Johnson City residents are thinking about "the question."

In the jargon of survey research, what Bulwinkle had was a *convenience sample*. The people were convenient to interview— all in the same block of Main Street or the same supermarket parking lot. Usually, however, there were only a handful of them, and Bulwinkle and his editor had no basis for inferring that the sentiments voiced by the interviewees were in any way typical of anyone other than that particular handful of citizens. It is ridiculous to use such a method to draw any conclusions about what proportion of Johnson City's residents support Reagan or legal abortion or tax reform or anything else. It simply is not a representative sample.

The motivations behind the city editor's man-in-the-street assignment were laudable. It got names in the paper and "names make news." Also, it got feedback from citizens about an issue of the moment. This concern about feedback is an important one for journalists. Most of the space in newspapers and the bulk of the time on TV news broadcasts is used to let our leaders speak to the rest of us. Reporters cover a state-of-the-union address in which the president tells us what he thinks, or a state legislative session to listen to lawmakers, or a Rotary Club speech by the city prosecutor. Nobody would suggest that news media not do that. In a democracy it is important for all of us to know what our leaders are doing, thinking, and saying.

The problem is that virtually all of the communication reflected in the news media is one-way communication—from them to us. Our fictional city editor with his man-in-the-street assignment for Bulwinkle was, consciously or not, trying to supply some sort of information channel through which "the people" could speak.

Fortunately, most news media have long since realized that the people interviewed in such a project are not typical or representative. But increased understanding of the hallmarks of reliable surveys hasn't completely driven this type of survey out of the news market.

The *Detroit Free Press* regularly prints a feature called Sound Off. Each day the newspaper prints a question and invites readers to "Call before noon to vote: YES—961-XXXX, NO—961-XXXX." The next day, the percentages of answers are printed, along with a scattering of quotes in support of each position. The *Free Press* asks such questions as, "Does it matter to you if 'Hitler's diaries' are real?" and "Do you think the U. S. Football League will catch on?" In partial recognition of the phoniness of it all, the *Free Press* warns in print that "Sound Off is a non-scientific, reader opinion feature."

Not only newspapers play the game. Many evenings on its six o'clock news, CBS affiliate WTVH in Syracuse runs a "telephone poll," inviting viewers to phone in *yes* or *no* answers to the question of the day. One night in 1983, for instance, the station asked viewers whether they thought Syracuse's police chief should run for mayor. Obviously, it would have been simple to stack the results one way or the other—either the chief's backers or his critics could have had two or three people call in—over and over again—with "votes" for the TV "poll."

SURVEYS: TO BELIEVE OR NOT TO BELIEVE

In the 1980s, the successor of man-in-the-street interviews is the modern public opinion survey, also called a scientific poll. Where public opinion surveys are concerned, many journalists tend to fall into two polarized categories—the nonbelievers and the suckers. Nonbelievers distrust all surveys. They can't buy the notion that Gallup or Harris can talk to 1500 Americans and say that they represent the whole country. On the other end of the spectrum, the suckers will accept any press release with numbers in it, feeling there must be some magic in those integers.

Let's talk about the suckers first. There are right ways and wrong ways to do survey research. There is more than one way to do a survey "right," but there seem to be many more ways to mess up a survey—through either ignorance or malice.

Perhaps the two most common ways to get it wrong are to use

A biased sample of respondents
Sloppy or biased question writing

Chapter 7 will discuss how to get a sample right, and how to see if somebody else's sample is a good one. Right now, let's talk about getting it wrong.

SAMPLING PROBLEMS

The most notorious example of a sample gone astray is the 1936 presidential election poll taken by the then-prestigious *Literary Digest*. The 1936 poll was not the *Digest's* debut into the field. In the 1920s and in 1932, the magazine had developed a record of successfully predicting presidential winnners on the basis of its "straw" polls. It wasn't so much that the *Literary Digest* was always on the money; its errors often were well over 10 percent. But the straw polls always had the right man in the lead. In 1936, the *Digest*'s polling method generated more than two million "votes" and predicted Alf Landon of Kansas would score a 3-to-2 victory over President Franklin D. Roosevelt. As anyone who has ever searched for the name of Landon in a list of presidents knows, the *Digest* missed—and not by just a little. In fact, Roosevelt got 62 percent of the vote and carried 46 of the 48 states.

What happened? Analysis over the years attributes the error to the fact that the *Digest*'s sample was drawn mostly from its own subscriber lists and telephone directories—places where, in the middle of the Depression in 1936, you were apt to find more well-to-do (and Republican) people. Statistician Maurice Bryson says that aspect has been overplayed and, in fact, the key culprit is that the *Digest* relied on voluntary response in its poll. The magazine mailed out 10 million sample ballots, got 2.3 million back, and believed them.

"As everyone ought to know, such samples are practically always biased," Bryson wrote. "The respondents represent only that subset of the population with a relatively intense interest in the subject at hand, and as such constitute in no sense a random sample. In the 1936 election, it seems clear that the majority of anti-Roosevelt voters felt more strongly about the election than did the pro-Roosevelt majority."

The result, based on whatever combination of sampling and response bias, was that the *Digest*'s "electorate" wasn't constructed in such a way that it was likely to reflect the makeup of the actual United States electorate in that year.

CONGRESSIONAL POLL SAMPLES

Professional pollsters these days wouldn't dream of building a sample the way the *Digest* did, but there is one group of would-be pollsters that does it year in and year out—members of the United States Congress. You can hardly escape the ubiquitous congressional questionnaire, mailed at taxpayers' expense to "Postal Pa-

tron" at each address in a congressional district. The example in
the box on pp. 82–83 from Rep. Brian Donnelly, D-Mass., is typical,
although no worse than hundreds of others you might find.

Donnelly is most solicitous:

> Dear Neighbor: . . . The opinions you express in personal meetings,
> correspondence and this annual questionnaire are very helpful to me
> in representing your views in Washington.

If the mailing goes to each address, it escapes one of the *Literary Digest*'s problems. Because rich and poor alike get a questionnaire in the mail, there is not the class bias in distributing the
questionnaires that occurred in the 1930s by mailing them only to
people who subscribed to a literary magazine or had a telephone.

However, beyond this point the procedure falls apart. The
recipient may have the ballot in his or her hand, but in order to be
"counted" in Congressman Donnelly's district referendum, he or
she must

a. Sit down and answer the questions;
b. Tear out the questionnaire, put a stamp on it, and mail it
   in.

Common sense will tell you that these requirements restrict
response to the most politically aware and active segment of Congressman Donnelly's constituency. They are likely to be older,
wealthier, and better educated. They also are more likely to vote,
and that may be all that any member of Congress really is worried
about.

The problem with this kind of poll increases when a member
of Congress gathers up the several hundred or thousand replies to
a questionnaire, instructs an aide to count them, and has a press
secretary generate a news release to the newspapers and TV stations
in the district.

In our example, Congressman Donnelly released the results
of his mail-out "survey" as part of a later newsletter to his constituents. He called the response to the questions "overwhelming" and
said "thousands of residents . . . took the time to answer." Donnelly
did not, however, say how many thousands or what percentage of
return that was.

The *Boston Globe* once reported that a poll by antibusing Con-
gresswoman Louise Day Hicks showed 80 percent of those in her
district agreed with her. Well down in the story, The *Globe* did

One Congressman's Opinion Survey: 1983 Questions and Results

1. What do you think is the most critical economic problem facing our nation today?

Federal spending & deficits	26%
Taxes	14%
Inflation	8%
Unemployment	44%
Interest Rates	8%

2. Do you think Congress should postpone this year's 10% tax cut to help balance the federal budget?

    Yes   46%   No   44%   Not sure   10%

3. Do you think Congress should slow down the growth of military spending to help balance the budget?

    Yes   65%   No   30%   Not sure   5%

4. Do you think Congress should freeze all government spending across the board?

    Yes   40%   No   47%   Not sure   13%

5. Do you think teenagers should work for a lower minimum wage than adults?

    Yes   38%   No   58%   Not sure   4%

6. Do you think Congress should pass legislation to roll back the recent price increases in natural gas?

    Yes   66%   No   22%   Not sure   12%

7. Do you think the government should help create jobs in times of high unemployment?

    Yes   68%   No   23%   Not sure   9%

8. Do you think the federal government should spend more money to improve education in science and mathematics?

    Yes   68%   No   20%   Not sure   12%

9. Do you think Congress should allow clean air laws to be weakened?

    Yes   14%   No   81%   Not sure   5%

10. Do you think the United States and the Soviet Union should impose a mutual and verifiable freeze on nuclear weapons as a first step toward disarmament?

    Yes   82%   No   14%   Not sure   4%

11. Do you think Congress should prevent the IRS from withholding 10% of interest and dividend payments for income taxes?

    Yes   77%   No   18%   Not sure   5%

12. Do you support the Equal Rights Amendment (ERA)?

    Yes   69%   No   27%   Not sure   7%

point out that 200,000 questionnaires were mailed and 23,000 were returned. A 1966 *New York Times* article was headlined "54% in Ohio Poll Assert U.S. Role in War Is Mistake." It turned out that it wasn't a poll of Ohio, only the Thirteenth District in Ohio. The district congressman sent out 130,000 questionnaires, got 4059 responses (a return of less than 4 percent). The 54 percent antiwar sentiment was based on that response. The *Globe* and the *Times* don't report surveys like that today, but many other news media do. They shouldn't.

QUESTION BIAS

Beyond problems with sample rates of return, there is an even more common failing of polling, especially in surveys sponsored by groups with a strong interest in the outcome. That failing is question bias.

Question Wording

Even seemingly subtle changes in question wording can produce major shifts in the results of a survey.

For more than a decade, the Advisory Commission on Intergovernmental Relations has conducted national surveys of public opinion on governments and taxes. In 1981, it conducted separate surveys using slightly different wording on one key question.

The question: "Suppose the budgets of your state and local government have to be curtailed. Which activity would you limit most severely?"

When the list of answers included the term "aid to the needy," less than 10% of the respondents singled it out for curtailment. When the same question substituted "public welfare programs" in the list of answers, 39% selected the category for curtailment.

As congressional questionnaires go, Congressman Donnelly's effort at writing fair-minded questions isn't bad. But consider a few examples:

Do you think Congress should allow clean air laws to be weakened?

You can easily guess how the congressman's constituents would "vote" on that one. Who favors dirty air? Only 14 percent of those responding, as it turned out.

But suppose he had biased the question the other way:

Some people feel our air pollution laws are so restrictive that they force factories to close down unnecessarily and throw people out of work. Do you think Congress should make the laws less restrictive in order to help speed economic recovery and reduce unemployment?

Or consider this more neutral question, from a CBS-*New York Times* poll in 1981:

Would you favor or oppose keeping air pollution laws as tough as they are now, even if some factories might have to close?

In this case, 61 percent favored keeping the laws "as tough as they are now," 29 percent favored weakening the laws, and 10 percent gave no opinion. By presenting the question in a balanced fashion, the CBS-*Times* poll located a significant minority (29%) who felt pollution laws were too tight and were hurting the economy.

Here's another example of problematic question wording from Donnelly's poll:

Do you think Congress should prevent the IRS from withholding 10% of interest and dividend payments for income taxes?

First of all, the question suggests that the Internal Revenue Service came up with the withholding idea on its own and that Congress intended to ride to the taxpayers' rescue. In fact, it was Congress that passed the legislation requiring withholding in the first place, and there was a purpose behind the tax.
What if this were the question instead?

Congress has passed a law requiring the IRS to withhold 10% of interest and dividend payments for income taxes, much as taxes are now withheld from a worker's paycheck. Some people feel this would help catch tax evaders who now avoid paying taxes on their interest and dividends. Others oppose the withholding, saying it would reduce the interest people receive and would be more trouble than it is worth. How do you feel?

Again, the congressman's responses might be considerably different to that question than to the one he actually asked.
Finally, just to show you that members of Congress are not necessarily the worst offenders in writing biased questions, consider this one from a questionnaire mailed out by the Reverend Jerry Falwell's Moral Majority, Inc.:

Do you believe smut peddlers should be protected by the courts and the Congress, so they can openly sell pornographic materials to your children?

When you are doing polling and survey research, it is important that you devote just as much attention to question design as you do to sample design. Although pollsters work on trying to shave

How to Ask a Simple Question

Allen H. Barton's classic tongue-in-cheek guide to asking "embarrassing questions in non-embarrassing ways," as applied to the question, "Did you kill your wife?"

1. The Casual Approach: "Do you happen to have murdered your wife?"
2. The Numbered Card Approach: "Would you please read off the number on this card that corresponds to what became of your wife?" (*Hand card to respondent*)
   1. Natural death
   2. I killed her
   3. Other (what?)
3. The Everybody Approach: "As you know, many people have been killing their wives these days. Do you happen to have killed yours?"
4. The "Other People" Approach:
   a. "Do you know any people who have murdered their wives?"
   b. "How about yourself?" . . .

Excerpted from Allen H. Barton, "Asking the Embarrassing Question," *Public Opinion Quarterly*, 1958

a percentage point or two off statistical errors in designing a sample, badly worded questions can give you results that are very far off the mark.

POLITICAL POLLS

Political surveys, especially the *horse-race polls* forecasting upcoming elections, are the most publicized uses of survey research.

Just about every news medium that publishes any polling at all uses election-year horse-race surveys.

Yet, if the only question asked in a survey is "Who would you vote for?", the poll adds very little to the audience's knowledge of the world that they wouldn't find out eventually anyway. Sooner or later, there will be an election and we'll all know who won. To be truly informative, polls must go beyond the horse-race questions and explore exactly what is going on in the electorate. Survey research allows you to see things through voters' eyes, without the filters of your own preconceptions or the lenses of the political professionals who assess what they believe is happening. Some questions to which a well-designed political poll can elicit answers are the following:

What are the trends? Has Candidate A slipped since the last poll? If so, what has happened in the meantime that might explain why?

How do issues relate to candidates? Sometimes, we assume that because Voter X favors Candidate A, Voter X must agree with the candidate most of the time. But many research projects from coast to coast have shown that this is not necessarily so. People are perfectly capable of holding positions on prominent issues directly contradictory to the stances of the candidates they support.

How are the candidates being perceived? Are people voting for Candidate A because they think he is honest, because they think he is an efficient and competent administrator, because they think he is a warm human being who cares about their problems, or all three? Do voters prize honesty more than competence and efficiency?

In the 1978 election in Florida, for instance, newspapers in Ft. Lauderdale, Jacksonville, Orlando, and St. Petersburg collaborated on a state-wide survey that questioned 1807 voters in depth about gubernatorial candidates Jack Eckerd and Bob Graham. For instance, the survey asked voters which man "is most qualified to be governor," which "has the best understanding of business," which "has the best background in government," and which "has made the better impression in television commercials." Overall, the papers examined perceptions of the two candidates on 12 different personal dimensions.

They found that Graham led on seven of the items—those dealing with experience in government, overall leadership, and familiarity with the problems of ordinary people. Eckerd was judged most knowledgeable about business, best able to expand Florida's economic base, and most likely to limit taxes and spending. Measuring the two men on all of these yardsticks enabled the Florida papers to give their readers a much more thorough picture of the race than simply reporting their "horse-race" standings in the poll would have. (In the end, Graham won, by 56%–44%.)

Who are the undecideds? What kinds of people haven't made up their minds yet, and which candidate seems likely to profit when the undecideds do decide?

Some pollsters simply throw out the undecideds and recalculate the decided vote so that it totals 100 percent. Don't let them get away with it, and don't do it in your own surveys, either. A high undecided vote can mean instability in a political race or in attitudes toward an issue, or it can mean ignorance or apathy. In a political campaign, it also can mean people are afraid for some reason to state their intention. The Gallup Organization has found that "undecideds" can be cut by one third or more in an in-person survey by using a secret-ballot technique in which voters fill out a slip and place it in the interviewer's ballot box or in a sealed envelope instead of just telling the interviewer their preference. (You can't, of course, use this technique in a telephone survey.) In any event, the undecideds mean *something*—so don't just discard them.

Research that focuses on points such as those just discussed performs a real service for your audience that they cannot get elsewhere. Said Douglas McKnight, of San Francisco's KGO-TV: "A vote is a simple declarative sentence. . . . Polls can get the rest of the paragraph."

Invariably, there are people who will say that it's not the business of the news media to get involved in political polling, that journalists can alter the course of an election simply by publishing or broadcasting the results of a poll. Certainly, ethical questions are involved, although the record is far from clear on exactly what impact is made—if any—by public release of poll data.

Some critics say that a poll's publication fosters a *bandwagon effect* that causes voters to leap to the side of the candidate who is ahead. However, research over the years has failed to demonstrate that this happens with any regularity. You can argue at least as persuasively for the existence of an *underdog effect*. This means that a candidate trailing in a pre-election poll may draw a sympathy vote, or that the trailing candidate's workers may apply a little extra effort in the closing days to put the campaign over the top, while the candidate supposedly in the lead sits back, relaxes—and loses.

POLITICS AND POLLS

A wide divergence of opinion exists on the wisdom of public opinion polls in a democracy. Political scientists Richard Scammon and Ben Wattenberg say "accurate and speedy public opinion polling has probably done more to advance the responsiveness of the democratic process than any invention since the secret ballot and the direct primary."

On the other hand, journalist–philosopher Walter Lippmann warned "that whether a plurality of the people sampled in the [Gallup] poll think one way has no bearing upon whether it is sound public policy." Pioneer pollster Elmo Roper said, "It would be a sad day indeed for this country if our statesmen were to follow slavishly the voice of the majority as if it were the voice of God." However, Roper noted that opinion polls can help political leaders and news media understand the nature of opinion and see where they have failed to provide enough information for informed opinion formation.

Winston Churchill decried always using the polls to "take one's temperature. . . . There is only one duty, only one safe course, and that is to try to be right." That begs the question in this day and age. Politicians use polls and believe them. "We have taken the place of political bosses," explains William Hamilton, a well-known pollster for prominent Democrats.

> You don't think somebody in 1920 was not running around to find out what Tammany Hall thought, what this guy in Albany that controlled the upstate vote felt? The candidates are making the same decisions they have always made. They are now using different instruments or different sources of information.

Politicians may use polls wisely—to understand opinion so they can know how to bring it around to believing what is "right," or they may abuse polls—by using a Gallup result to shape their own views in contradiction of what they believe to be right. But polls are going to be used. Can it be wrong for the media to give the public the same information already in the hands of political leaders and their campaign strategists? Or, where a politician may have a distorted idea of how the electorate feels about an issue, what is wrong with a news medium, through responsible reporting of opinion polling, correcting that inaccurate notion?

One Paper's Polling Policy

The better a poll happens to be—the more sensitive its instrumentation, the greater its accuracy and prestige— the more profound is its impact on the political races that poll would monitor. Over the years, *The Globe*'s poll has been a good one and its impact has been pronounced— so pronounced that the poll has long been a source of practical concern for politicians and of ethical concern for *The Globe*.

The problem has not been the poll's accuracy, which has been consistently high; the problem, purely and simply, is the poll's effect: what it does to the political process it seeks to measure; the misconceptions it fosters about *The Globe*'s proper role.

Those twin concerns have led to soul searching within this institution and a decision, effective now, to suspend the traditional practice of measuring the candidates' relative standings prior to election day for publication.

The business of the newspaper is to observe society and to measure and record change as faithfully as possible. Polling can prove an invaluable tool in doing that. Polls, after all, can be and often are the pure stuff of news. They are scientific and objective and by their impersonal nature as credible as mathematics.

But poll results translate into more than just news stories. They can and they do alter the political reality at the precise moment they seek to reflect it.

The candidate caught well behind at the moment the pollster takes his measure finds himself trapped in that position. Sources of funding dry up.

Polls, for all the scientific safeguards, are not infallible. And while *Globe* surveys in the past have almost always proved accurate within the four-point margin of error, some projections have been wide of the mark, and some may have innocently influenced the election outcome.

Voters, assured by a poll they trust that a candidate they favor is certain of victory, may not bother to vote, or may vote for someone else on the assumption that their vote will not influence the results. *The Globe* did not commission a poll immediately prior to the primary election last week, but a pollster did inform Gov. Dukakis that he had a comfortable lead over challenger Edward J. King. Thus assured, the governor may have felt no need to rally his complacent supporters in an 11th hour drive for votes.

The publication of the poll results adds significantly to a newspaper's political power. That power is legitimately exercised in this space, where our opinions and preferences are often openly expressed.

The candidate who wins an editorial endorsement and also finds himself out front in the poll published on the news page is the beneficiary of an unintended bandwagon effect. The candidate who is left unendorsed and labeled a loser in the poll is dealt a heavy blow. It would be understandable if he and his supporters felt doubly victimized.

For these reasons *The Globe* will concentrate not on projecting outcomes but on isolating and explaining issues, while getting closer to the underlying attitudes that shape the public's choice of candidates.

Getting at those concerns is one way to make certain that candidates are addressing what is on the public's mind. It also affords a way to keep in touch with public sentiment without unseemly prying into what many voters hold as an intensely private matter—their preference for specific candidates.

Reprinted courtesy of *The Boston Globe*.

Publication of data from a well-conducted poll allows everyone, not just the political pros, to have a better idea of how opinion is lining up. This ought to be one of the major goals of any news medium—to show its audience how the world is working. Political pundits always have provided their readers with assessments of the progress of a campaign. Before the advent of survey research, they

did it by doing their own sort of "polling." They interviewed leaders from different political camps, perhaps talked to a few "average
citizens," then made a pronouncement. The difference with political polling is that the information comes directly from the voters
and is collected in a systematic, broad-based manner.

EXIT POLLS

One facet of media polling that has come under fire in recent years
is the so-called exit poll popularized by the television networks. In
this procedure, the poll's sponsor places interviewers at a few dozen
precincts chosen so as to mirror a state's political outlook in the
past. Interviewers ask every third or fifth or tenth person leaving
the polls about their actual vote and the reasons behind it. The
results are tabulated throughout the day and used by TV to forecast
the vote outcome, sometimes even before the polls are closed.

Critics have argued that some voters in western states who
had been standing in line at the polls left when they heard broadcast
election analyses forecasting Ronald Reagan's 1980 win and never
did vote in that race or any of the local races on the election ballots.
Despite the lack of statistical evidence to support this theory, in
June 1984, the U.S. House passed a nonbinding resolution asking
news media not to use exit interviews at the polls to characterize
or project results before the polls close.

Clearly, exit polls do enable pollsters to focus right in on the
actual voters, instead of coming up with some turnout "estimate."
Exit polls also get at the reason behind the vote. For instance, in
the 1984 Illinois primary, CBS News polled 1283 voters in 68 precincts around the state and learned that Mondale's victory margin
came largely from older voters, union members, and avowed Democrats. The unemployment problem helped Mondale at the polls,
and he was able to run even with Gary Hart in Hart's normal constituency of younger voters and those with higher incomes.

POLITICAL POLLS—TURNOUT FACTOR

Political polling is not without risk. Eventually, an election will be
held, one candidate will win it, and somebody will compare the
outcome of the election to the numbers in the last published poll.

Such comparisons can help build public confidence in opinion research, or they can plant seeds of doubt about the whole process.

When smart, honest journalists publish a poll, they tell their audience at the outset that they aren't claiming to make a prediction about how the election will turn out. For instance, the *Honolulu Advertiser* has used language such as this with its polling stories:

> Polls aren't perfect, but a carefully done poll can give a good idea of public opinion at the time it is taken . . . No poll is a prediction of what will occur on election day. It is simply a reflection of voter attitudes at the time the poll was taken.

Nonetheless, most pollsters find it irresistible after an election to compare the outcome to their pre-election polls. Also, critics are going to point out any big discrepancy between the final poll and the actual election outcome. If there is a big gap, you, too, should wonder if anything went wrong, because wide swings in opinion are unusual, even in the final days of a hard-fought campaign. By then, nearly everybody has made a decision and major switches don't seem to be common, although they do happen.

There is one factor besides voter-switching, however, that can throw a rather large monkey wrench into things—*turnout*. Figures indicate that only about half of the eligible population in the United States actually votes in a given election. How does a pollster keep his or her sample of citizens as close as possible to the profile of the people who do the voting?

First, try to make sure the pollster talks only to *registered voters*. One way is to draw the sample from a list of registered voters. This may be hard to do or prohibitively expensive because the voter lists usually lack telephone numbers and, to conduct a telephone poll, the pollster needs a number for each name on the list. Thus, another common way to select a sample is to use a preliminary *screening question*—to ask people if they are registered. If they say no, the interviewer terminates the interview with thanks without asking for their vote preference or any of the other questionnaire items.

Second, ask questions about a respondent's *level of interest* or awareness of a campaign. Those questioned by a Gallup interviewer for an election-year poll are asked how much thought they have given to the coming elections, whether they have ever voted in their precinct, how much interest they have in politics, how often they have voted in the past, and whether they plan to vote this year or not. People who score "high" on such questions are, according to a secret Gallup formula, assigned more weight in predicting election outcomes.

It is difficult to admit to a strange interviewer that, no, you aren't following the campaign, couldn't care less who won, and wouldn't vote if they paid you. For this reason, pollsters have tried to devise questions that make it as easy as possible for a respondent to admit to such "uncivic" behavior. Samples:

> Some people are registered to vote. Others either don't like to vote or haven't had a chance to register. Are you registered so that you could vote this year if you wanted to?

> In asking people about elections, we often find that many people can't vote because they aren't registered or were sick or just didn't have the time. How about you, do you think you will vote in the election this November?

As you can see, this last question suggests that it is quite legitimate not to vote, that lots of people don't vote, that not voting isn't equivalent to social leprosy, and that you can safely admit to the interviewer that you don't plan to vote in November.

Making a correction for turnout can bring your poll a lot closer to reality. In 1974, the *Honolulu Advertiser*'s final poll of 1197 voters in a hard-fought Democratic primary for governor came out this way:

> Frank Fasi 29%
> George Ariyoshi 28%
> Tom Gill 27%

However, this poll also included three questions aimed at identifying the most likely voters. The questions dealt with paying attention to politics (*"Would you say you have been fairly interested in the campaign or not very interested?"*), whether voters felt a stake in the election's outcome (*"Would you say that you personally care a good deal about who wins the election for governor . . . or that you don't care very much?"*), and the likelihood of voting (*"Do you expect to vote . . . or do you think something might keep you from voting?"*).

Results of these three questions made it apparent that the *most likely* voters on all three measures—those most personally affected, those who followed politics closely, and those most certain that they

Conventional Wisdom?

Just because the conventional wisdom is conventional doesn't mean it can't be wrong. A sample survey can show you when it is.

Consider this case, highlighted by Philip Meyer, former reporter and news researcher for Knight-Ridder Newspapers and now a professor at the University of North Carolina:

> When the nation's major race riots—in Watts, in Detroit, in Newark, in Washington—took place in the mid-1960s, most of us took it for granted that race relations were getting worse. . . . We know now that it wasn't so. The way we know is that the University of Michigan Survey Research Center, during its election-year studies in 1964 and 1968, asked the same series of questions about racial attitudes among both blacks and whites. It was expected that the 1968 survey would document how much more hostile whites had become toward blacks and blacks toward whites [during the years of the race riots].

Instead, the University of Michigan researchers found that "racial antagonism had decreased . . . whites were more tolerant toward blacks in their attitudes, were more likely to be in physical proximity to blacks, to have blacks as friends and neighbors." The same trend occurred among blacks.

would vote—differed from the overall poll sample. For instance, among the 882 voters polled who said they planned to vote in the Democratic primary (74% of the sample), the governor's race stacked up this way:

George Ariyoshi 31%
Tom Gill 30%
Frank Fasi 29%

Abortion—Pro or Con?

News coverage of the abortion debate in America often consists of stories and pictures of competing "pro-life" and "pro-choice" protest marches. But this sort of coverage, replete with estimated crowd counts of demonstrators on either side of the question, casts little light on the subtle colorations of feeling that make up the mosaic of public opinion on this emotional issue. However, public opinion surveys have tried in different ways to capture shades of opinion. Some examples of the complexity involved:

77 percent agree that "the decision to have an abortion should be left to the woman and her physician." (NBC News-Associated Press poll, 1982).

75 percent oppose "an amendment to the U. S. Constitution which would give Congress the authority to prohibit abortions." (NBC News-Associated Press poll, 1982).

56 percent generally favor the 1973 "U.S. Supreme Court decision making abortions up to three months of pregnancy legal." (Harris Survey, 1981)

55 percent do not think "the government should help a poor woman with her medical bills if she wants an abortion." (CBS News-*New York Times* poll, 1980)

51 percent oppose a proposed federal law "which would declare that human life begins at conception and therefore abortion at any time could be considered a crime of murder." (Gallup Poll, 1981)

49 percent say "abortion is wrong" (NBC News-Associated Press poll, 1982) and the same percentage agree that "to perform an abortion is the equivalent of murder because a fetus's life has been eliminated." (Harris Survey, 1981)

Even these questions, with their widely varying percentage figures, are merely "referendum"-style questions that allow a respondent to vote yes or no to a limited choice.

When the questions get more subtle, the answers vary even more widely. The National Opinion Research Center in 1980 got these answers to a set of abortion-related questions:

88 percent agreed that abortion should be allowed if "the woman's own health is seriously endangered by the pregnancy."

80 percent said abortion should be allowed if the pregnancy is the result of rape or if "there is a strong chance of a serious defect in the baby."

50 percent said abortion should be possible for a pregnant woman "if the family has a low income and cannot afford any more children."

45 percent, however, less than a majority, would allow abortion for a woman who "is married and does not want any more children."

It appears that all abortions are not equal in the minds of many Americans.

The Gallup Poll has tried to go behind the opinions themselves to theorize about what causes a person to have a given stand on abortion. Some of the factors are predictable. For instance, Catholics are more likely than others to hold an antiabortion stance, the official position of their church, but even here there is no unanimity. Gallup found that 22 percent of Catholics say abortion should be "legal under any circumstances," a percentage not markedly different from the percentage among Protestants (23%). Evangelical Christians as a group, both Catholic and Protestant, are even more antiabortion than Catholics overall.

Gallup also concluded that "the public's views [on abortion] depend in considerable measure on their opinions on when life begins." Answers to a question that posed alternative theories on when human life begins revealed that

54 percent say "human life begins at the moment of conception";

17 percent say "human life does not begin until the baby is actually born";

22 percent say life begins at some point in between conception and birth;

The remainder aren't sure or offer no opinion on the matter.

The moral of the story: The relative sizes of demonstration marches don't tell you much about public opinion. Even opinion surveys can give limited or misleading information if they try to boil a complex issue down to one or two questions, although that course is better than counting crowds at a protest rally.

Among the most likely voters, Ariyoshi—not Fasi—was the leader, although still well within the poll's margin of error. This enabled the *Advertiser* to point out a week before election day that "the level of voter turnout may well be the determining factor in the Democratic contest for governor" and that Ariyoshi "seems to have the strongest support in precisely those groups most likely to turn out to vote." In the end, the turnout was 70 percent and the election outcome was as follows:

George Ariyoshi 35%
Frank Fasi 30%
Tom Gill 29%

NONPOLITICAL POLLS

Just because the election-season polls get the bulk of the attention and criticism doesn't mean they are the only kind of survey research that news media can do. Other kinds of questions measuring opinions and attitudes about issues that never appear on a ballot can, in the long run, be more useful. Sooner or later you find out who wins an election, but in the absence of survey research, you may never get accurate readings on attitudes about abortion, the death penalty, or balancing the budget. Here are some examples of topics that news media have examined using survey research:

Minnesotans complain a lot about public education, but they still say schools these days are at least as good as the ones *they* attended. Many even say today's schools are better. (*Minneapolis Tribune*, Minnesota Poll, 1980)

The Iowa Poll shows a landslide conviction in the state that [credit cards] are bad for the economy because people buy things with them that they can't afford. (*Des Moines Sunday Register*, 1980)

The people of Los Angeles are preoccupied with crime—much more so than people in the rest of the country. They have an inordinate fear of it that cuts across socioeconomic boundaries. And they count it as the city's No. 1 problem. Ironically, relatively few have been touched by it. (*Los Angeles Times* Poll, 1981)

Most Americans would like to see the federal government take responsibility for the care of the elderly, according to a nationwide *Newsday* survey, but they do not feel that way about health care. (*Newsday*, New York, 1976)

No amount of prodding by the Greater Richmond Transit Co. can pull many of its nonriders from their cars, a *Times-Dispatch* opinion poll has shown. (*Richmond Times-Dispatch*, 1975)

A majority of Illinois voters approve of registering women for possible military service, but few would want to see women in combat roles. (*Chicago Sun-Times*/WMAQ, 1980)

Hawaii's public school teachers think they're doing a pretty good job. They give the public schools a B-minus grade. . . . The state's high school students don't think quite so highly of their education. They give it a C-plus. . . . Least pleased are the parents, who give Hawaii public education just above the average grade of C. (*Honolulu Advertiser*, Hawaii Poll, 1981)

New York State voters consider themselves overtaxed, but appear unwilling to reduce taxes sharply if such cuts would reduce the level of services provided by state government, according to a *New York Times* poll. (*New York Times*, 1982)

Public support remains strong—67%—for the proposition that organized prayers should be allowed in public schools. (NBC News-Associated Press Poll, 1982)

Focus Groups

About halfway between the quick and easy "man-in-the-street" interview and the not-so-quick and not-so-inexpensive use of sample surveys is another information-gathering technique that can be used profitably by reporters everywhere. It's called the *focus group*.

The idea is to draw a small sample of people from whatever population you're interested in—voters in a city, students in a high school, automobile plant workers, doctors, whatever. You then assemble them in small groups and interview the hell out of them about whatever subject you as a reporter are interested in.

Here's how to go about it:

1. Think carefully about what questions you want answered. Compile a loose guide that addresses the questions in an orderly fashion. This should be used as a map by the interviewers but, unlike sample surveys, the interviewers should feel free to let the focus group participants detour away from the prepared list of questions. The questions should be open-ended, requiring some discussion, not just yes/no answers.

2. Use a telephone book to draw a sample of a few dozen people from your target group and recruit some to be interviewed. Some focus groups give participants a small stipend ($10 or $20), or a gift (a free dinner or bottle of wine). Others find that people are so pleased that somebody is interested in their opinions that they'll do it for free.

3. Set up the groups so you'll have 8 or 10 people per session. More than that doesn't allow everybody a chance to talk. Try to make the groups relatively homogeneous on key variables, such as age, sex, and race. If you're going to discuss race relations, you'll get more honest opinions if you set up the whites and the blacks in separate groups. Younger people tend to be more forthcoming if they're not mixed in with people their parents' age.

4. Use follow-up letters and phone calls to encourage people to keep their original commitments to participate and to remind them of the date and time.

5. Arrange for a comfortable room with a table and chairs. Also arrange for somebody other than the interviewer to unobtrusively run the tape recorder. Coffee and pastry can help set people at ease.

6. Encourage people to introduce themselves, then to speak freely as the interviewer casually guides them through the topics selected. Sessions often last from 90 minutes to two hours, depending on the number of participants and how willing they are to speak up.

7. Transcribe the session later and analyze it. Sometimes the comments can lead you to story ideas or to topics you'll want to follow up in later sample surveys. It can also work in reverse—you may have already taken a sample survey, but the focus groups can give you colorful quotes and anecdotes to illustrate what you found.

By proceeding systematically, you have done a better job at assembling the people you interview than has the haphazard man-in-the-street reporter. Because only a small group of people participate in a focus group, you can't validly generalize from their views, but such groups do give you the voices of real, live people commenting on issues, and they help you to identify issues when you are not sure exactly what you will find or exactly which words people use to describe the issues. Furthermore, because a focus group is an intensive situation, it allows you to ferret out the complexity of opinions that exist "out there," and to gain insight into how people's minds work and what things are important to them, as opposed to the things you think ought to be important. There is more flesh and blood to the results of a focus group than there is to the yes/no answers in most survey research.

WHEN TO PUBLISH A POLL

For local surveys—those conducted by candidates, ad agencies, or other mass media—news media should use a "truth-in-polling" system to ensure that both you and your audience know how the pollster came to his or her conclusions. Did a political candidate pay for the poll that shows him ahead by 15 percent? Did his own supporters make the phone calls, or did he pass out sample ballots at one of his own campaign rallies? It makes a difference, obviously. Polls, like people, are sometimes good and sometimes not.

Some polls are bad because the "pollster" doesn't know what he or she is doing. Some are bad because the interviewers, those doing the actual question asking, are untrained. Some are bad because the sponsor has consciously slanted the poll to produce a desired result.

Only if the pollster provides complete information about methods can a reporter or editor or voter decide whether the end-product is credible. With this kind of full disclosure, you at least can attempt to weed out the obviously sloppy polls. If a pollster doesn't use sound techniques or is unwilling to reveal, in full, the details of his methods, you should decline to print or broadcast the results of the poll.

Below are guidelines you can use in determining whether to publish or broadcast poll results. They can help ensure that your audience has a better chance of not being misled.

Who was interviewed? Is the poll supposed to be representative of all adults in the United States, in one state, or in one city or congressional district? Does it represent all adults or just all voters—or, perhaps, just all those who say they "intend to vote" in the next election? If the poll deals with a primary election, does it represent only registered Republicans or only registered Democrats?

How big was the poll's sample and how was it obtained? Were households identified from comprehensive census or planning-agency maps, from names drawn from a phone book, from a registered voter list, or from the city directory? Or did the interviewer stand on the corner of State and Main Streets and question every third passerby?

Who paid for the poll and what interest do they have in its outcome? Did they find what they wanted to find because of the way the poll was structured?

Who did the actual interviewing? Employees of a full-time, professional company? Part-time help from students working on a class project? Political campaign volunteers?

How were respondents contacted? By telephone? By door-to-door personal interview? By mailed questionnaires?

Exactly when was the interviewing done? Did any prominent news events occur on those dates that might have influenced the

Poll Information

When you publish findings of a survey, you owe it to your audience to give them full information on how and when it was conducted, plus details of the margin of sampling error. Here's how the *Wilkes-Barre Times Leader* in Pennsylvania handles such information in print:

Survey area: The 11th U.S. Congressional District, including all of Luzerne, Columbia, Montour, and Sullivan Counties, plus parts of Carbon, Monroe, and Northumberland Counties.

Survey population: Registered Democrats who said they will certainly/probably vote in the April 10th Democratic Primary.

Number of interviews: 425, including 277 in the Wyoming Valley, drawn in proportion to turnout for the 1982 Democratic Congressional Primary.

Interviewing method: Telephone interviews from households selected using a scientific random probability sampling.

Conducted by: Nine interviewers thoroughly trained and briefed for this project.

Dates conducted: Evenings from Monday, March 26 through Friday, March 30.

Planned and supervised by: Dr. Gary R. Kromer, the *Times Leader*'s Director of Research, a veteran of more than 100 public opinion polls, including over 20 political polls.

Margin of error: Sampling error for 425 interviews is 4.8 percent at the 95 percent confidence level. In other words, were this survey to be conducted in the same manner 100 times, the results of 95 of them would be as reported here, plus or minus 4.8 percent. Other procedures, such as call-backs, were employed to minimize nonsampling error.

Wilkes-Barre Times Leader

outcome? For instance, a Gallup Poll taken just before the Democratic National Convention in 1984 showed Ronald Reagan 14 points ahead of Walter Mondale. A Gallup survey taken on the convention's final two days showed Mondale leading by 2 points, a 16-point swing attributable at least in part to all the news media attention Mondale had been getting at the time of the second poll. Later Mondale dropped behind again. The election confirmed the slide—dramatically.

What were the exact wordings of all questions?

Were any special statistical procedures used to "weight" interviews, or to allocate undecideds?

How many persons actually answered each question? Be suspicious of any reported poll result that adds up to 100 percent but includes no *undecideds* or *don't knows*. It's hard to think of a question that won't get nonanswers from somebody, and the pollster ought to tell you how many there are.

Is the pollster claiming more precision than he has a right to? Polls aren't accurate enough to justify reporting percentages down to decimal points. Unless a poll sample numbers in the tens of thousands of interviews, the size of the sampling error rules out such precision.

A FINAL CAUTION

Even when a poll measures up on all the points in the guidelines, don't embrace poll results to the exclusion of your other informants. Don't abandon your innate journalistic skepticism.

Associated Press polling expert Evans Witt warns that a reporter "should never say what I heard one say after the election in 1980: 'I was out in Pennsylvania for two weeks before the election, and I just couldn't find anyone out there who was a strong Carter supporter. But the polls said it was a close race, so I didn't write what I saw.'"

Polls are fairly good at detecting the direction of opinion, but not so good at measuring the intensity of opinion. A reporter who senses such intensity should not let poll numbers stop him from discussing the matter. "Polls are a tool for gathering information, more complicated and tricky than most methods, but still only a tool, to be used with more familiar ones in every reporter's and editor's kit," says Witt.

REFERENCES

Backstrom, Charles H., and Gerald Hursh. *Survey Research.* 2d. ed. New York: John Wiley, 1981.

Babbie, Earl. *The Practice of Social Research.* 3d ed. Belmont, CA: Wadsworth Publishing, 1983.

Barton, Allen J. "Asking the Embarrassing Question." *Public Opinion Quarterly,* 20, no. 1 (Spring 1958): 67.

Kish, Leslie. *Survey Sampling.* New York: John Wiley, 1965.

Lippmann, Walter. *Liberty and the News.* New York: Harcourt, Brace and Howe, 1920.

Lippmann, Walter. *Public Opinion.* New York: Macmillan, 1960 (originally published 1922).

McCombs, Maxwell. "Sampling Opinions and Behaviors." In Maxwell McCombs, Donald Lewis Shaw, and David Grey, *Handbook of Reporting Methods.* Boston: Houghton Mifflin, 1976, pp. 123–38.

McCombs, Maxwell, and G. Cleveland Wilhoit. "Conducting a Survey." In Maxwell McCombs, Donald Lewis Shaw, and David Grey, *Handbook of Reporting Methods.* Boston: Houghton Mifflin, 1976, pp. 123–38.

Meyer, Philip. *Precision Journalism: A Reporter's Introduction to Social Science Methods.* 2d ed. Bloomington, IN: Indiana University Press, 1979.

Roper, Elmo. *You and Your Leaders: Their Actions and Your Reactions, 1936–1956.* New York: William Morrow, 1957.

Romano, Lois. "Pollsters: The Figures Candidates Count On; Searching for the Winning Combination on the Campaign Trail." *Washington Post* (Jan. 15, 1984): C-1.

Sudman, Seymour. *Applied Sampling.* New York: Academic Press, 1976.

Witt, Evans. "Reporting Polls: The Writer's Job from Stats to Story." *Washington Journalism Review* (April 1984): 19–21.

CHAPTER 7

Good and Bad Surveys

The 95 Percent Confidence Interval: $\overline{X} \pm 1.96\ (s_{\overline{x}})$.

Does this formula make you nervous? Unfortunately, a lot of the word people in journalism become pale and shaky when confronted by numbers.

Don't panic. That's the last formula you'll see in this chapter. But there is no escaping the fact that a considerable amount of mathematics underlies the practice of sampling. The math details the theory on which the practice is based. Without this theory, there is no way to tell how much you should believe a particular set of numbers based on a selected sample of people or documents or anything else.

There is nothing written in stone that says journalists who use numbers need to pass Statistics 898 with flying colors or be able to compute a Chi-square statistic on a calculator, and, in fact, most reporters will never conduct a public opinion sample survey on their own. That job is usually left to the professionals. As a journalist, however, you'll frequently be faced with evaluating the work of other pollsters and deciding how to report it and how much faith to put in the results. This chapter attempts to explain, briefly, the theory that underlines all such polls, and some of the details of methodology that will help you to ask the right questions in analyzing polling data.

You do need to know that one theory, which you can learn if you want to, provides the basis for the fact that Gallup and Harris go out time and again to assess what the country thinks by interviewing no more than 1500 randomly selected Americans.

Start with the premise that you want to know something about reality—how many faulty widgets are produced by a particular factory, the number of red gumdrops in a candy machine, how many convicted drunk drivers lose their licenses, the exact split between Democratic and Republican candidates in an election, or the proportion of people in the United States who are unemployed.

One obvious way of finding the information you want is to count every item. That is called taking a *census*. Every decade the U.S. Census attempts to do just that—count every item (every person) in its reality (the U.S. population). For the 1980 census, 409 offices were opened around the nation, a half-million people were hired, and $1.1 billion was spent—a cost of about $4 for each American counted. Often, a census is impossible or, at least, very impractical. Even the people at the U.S. Census do not claim to have counted every person in the United States. They admit to an undercount of several percent and the undercount is far greater among blacks than among whites.

In many ways, samples can be better than censuses. Raymond A. Bauer, a former president of the American Association for Public Opinion Research, argued two decades ago that data gathered by sampling can be, and generally are, more accurate than data gathered by taking a census. "It is possible to invest more time, effort, and money in each unit in a sample survey," Bauer said.

> This permits more effort on callbacks [follow-up attempts to get an interview when nobody was home the first time or the interview was refused at first] and this increases the possibility of including the stray souls who may slip through the net of total enumeration. Furthermore, it is possible to use more capable and highly trained personnel, and thereby improve the quality of information gathered from each person.

Three factors—time, money, practicality—often lead researchers (and here we include journalists) to seek a typical slice of reality to count, measure, or analyze. Generalizations then are made from the sample to the target population—widgets or voters or drunk drivers or whatever.

The process of obtaining this slice of a particular population is based on a fairly simple idea called *sampling*. What sampling and probability theory say, in essence, is that if you take a typical piece of a large pie and taste it, the result is likely to be representative of the entire pie. When a cook wonders if his or her soup has

Yes, Leilani—There Is a Belief in Santa Claus

Bob Krauss
Honolulu Advertiser columnist

What are the odds that you will hear the magic jingle of sleigh bells tonight and a jolly voice shouting above the rooftops, "Ho, Donner! Yo, Blitzen! Awaaaaaaay"?

It so happens I can tell you within a percentage point.

The *Advertiser*'s respected Hawaii Poll has completed the first computerized survey ever taken in Hawaii to find out how many of us believe in Santa Claus. The results of this poll of 600 of us here in Hawaii just came in.

Are you ready for this?

In spite of high interest rates, stubborn inflation, the economic slump, flash floods and traffic jams, a solid 43 percent of Hawaii residents over 18 have rejected the "bah, humbug!" philosophy.

With clear eyes, sober breaths and judicial judgment, they told the pollsters they believe in Santa Claus.

Another cynical, short-sighted, uninformed 53 percent with questionable reputations and ring around the collar said Santa Claus is merely a figment of the imagination.

From this you can see that numbers are meaningless unless they are interpreted correctly.

That is why Gerry Keir, our city editor, who is in charge of the Hawaii Poll, asked me to go through the figures of our Santa Claus survey and explain to you what they mean.

The first result is very significant.

You see, a similar survey taken last year by the Iowa Poll shows that only 34 percent of Iowans believed in Santa Claus, while 61 percent rejected him. Five percent weren't sure.

This is a clear indication that people in Hawaii are smarter than those in Iowa.

Republicans tend to believe in Santa Claus (47 percent) more than Democrats (40 percent) in Hawaii. The difference is explained when you realize that Republicans also think Reaganomics is still going to work.

The poll shows that more poor people believe in Santa Claus (45 percent of those with incomes below $20,000) than rich people (41 percent of those with incomes above $20,000).

Obviously, there are some things money can't buy.

More married people (45 percent) believe in Santa Claus than singles (37 percent). The worst unbelievers are those who are divorced (35 percent).

This is an important statistic. It demonstrates that people would stay married longer if they believed in Santa Claus.

Moving right along, we find that Santa's credibility is highest among 18- to 24-year-olds—52 percent, a majority.

The biggest cynics are 55 or over. Only 37 percent said they believe in Santa Claus, and the reason given most often in this age group was "I'm too old."

Which proves that wisdom does not increase with age.

Other reasons given by non-believers include:

"There aren't any chimneys in Hawaii. How can Santa come down?"

"He just creates false hopes in people."

"Santa Claus never brought me anything I wanted."

"I'm a realist."

More men (44 percent) said they believe in Santa Claus than did women (41 percent).

Of Hawaii's ethnic groups, more Filipinos (49 percent) believe in Santa Claus than anyone else. Fewer Japanese (40 percent) believe than anybody else.

Finally, Santa Claus believers on the Neighbor Islands (48 percent) outnumber those on Oahu (41 percent) on a per capita basis.

Therefore, people in Hawaii who are most likely to hear sleigh bells tonight are male Filipino residents living on a Neighbor Island who are married, are between

18 and 24 years old, earn less than $20,000 per year and vote Republican.

But what if you are female, divorced, of Japanese descent and a registered Democrat 55 or over and live in Honolulu and earn more than $20,000 a year? Are you condemned to a Christmas without Santa Claus?

Fortunately, there is a statistic which holds out hope even for you.

A clear majority of 51 percent answered a firm "yes" when asked if kids in Hawaii believe in Santa. Those logical, level-headed, straight-thinking respondents include rich and poor, old and young, married, single and divorced of all political affiliations.

So don't despair. All you really need to get a visit from Santa tonight is to be a kid at heart.

enough salt, he or she doesn't eat it all to find out, but stirs it and tastes a spoonful—a sample.

If you have a jar filled with 200,000 marbles and want to know how many are black and how many are white, you could find out exactly by counting them all. But if you just need a very close approximation, you could sample the marbles by mixing them well, picking out, say, 500, and counting them. This sample would come pretty close to representing the actual mix. In fact, there are long statistical formulas to tell you precisely how often it is that you are within 1 percent or 5 percent of the exact total.

If probability theory didn't work, there would be no gambling casinos. Odds and payoffs on throws of the dice or spins of the wheel or turns of the card are figured on the basis of statistical probability.

Probability theory admits there is no way of knowing whether the next coin flip will be heads or tails. However, it says you can be fairly certain that out of 500 flips of a fair coin, you'll get about 250 heads. Or that if you and a friend both throw a fair set of dice 1000 times, it is likely you will both have about the same number of 7s—and the number of 7s can be predicted rather accurately.

Public opinion polling applies the same sort of rules to human populations. Let's say that the United States actually is made up of 50 percent Republican voters and 50 percent Democratic voters, but you don't know that in advance and decide to survey a sample of voters in order to estimate the proportion in it of Republicans and Democrats. Because people aren't as predictable as chicken soup, you wouldn't want to take just one or even a few spoonfuls of opinion. But let's say you draw your sample of voters carefully so that *everybody in the United States has an equal chance to be contacted.* Then you interview several hundred voters.

When are you justified in making generalizations about 100 million American voters, based on what you find in your sample of several hundred? You would only be justified if, first of all, you picked the sample in one of the tested, generally accepted ways.

But, even if you use a sound sampling method, will your estimate come out right on the nose as 50 percent Democrats and 50 percent Republicans? Probably not. (There's even a statistical formula that'll tell you how likely an exact 50–50 split is.) The odds are heavy, however, that you'll get a 51–49 or 52–48 count one way or the other, and this would lead you to conclude that, at the time the poll was taken, the split was nearly even.

No reputable pollster claims perfect accuracy. That's why journalists need to explain in every story about a poll that a *margin of error* exists. (There is a formula for calculating that, too.) For instance, you would say there is only a slight chance that the outcome varies by more than about five percentage points from what you'd get if you had enough time, money, and interviewers to ask *every* voter the same questions you asked your sample of 500.

BIAS AND SAMPLING

A systematic tendency to exclude some kinds of people from a sample—poor people, blacks, or farmers, for example—is called *bias.* If bias is present in a sampling procedure, you lose the ability to generalize from the sample to the population. Furthermore, when a sample selection procedure has a bias built into it, you can't overcome it by taking bigger and bigger samples. That only produces large-scale bias. For a sample to be valid, it must be selected to allow everybody an equal chance of being represented in it.

A second source of bias comes from *nonresponse.* The people who cannot be reached or who decline to take part in a poll are likely to be different from the people successfully interviewed. You can be sure they are different in one way: they were not home when they were called or they turned down the interviewer. The same principle applies to any sample of documents—for example, court records. If you could not get at part of the court files, you cannot know if the ones you didn't sample are different from the ones you did sample.

Any time you introduce an element of human choice into the selection of a sample, you bring into play yet another source of bias. For instance, if you tell an interviewer to choose 20 men and 20 women to interview (this is called *quota sampling*) the interviewer (subconsciously) will be apt to pick people who are easier to get at, who look like they will be cooperative and easy to talk to—but, obviously, who may not be typical of anything in particular. Most often, given the choice, people tend to interview others who are like themselves because they feel comfortable doing it. That makes for comfortable interviewers but bad samples.

To avoid this kind of bias, a survey should use some variation of *random sampling*, in which the choice of whom to interview is dictated by random numbers, not by any person. This can be done by assigning each person in a population a number, then picking numbers at random. Or, most typically for national public opinion surveys, it is done by picking geographic areas at random, then working down randomly stage by stage from county to town to precinct or census tract to block until a particular household and a particular resident in it are chosen—again, purely by a numerical formula that allows the interviewer no choice. Selection of those to be interviewed is made purely by chance factors, by using a modern computerized version of coin flips or dice throws. Chance is impartial. It has no bias for rich or poor, black or white, Republican or Democrat. In a true random sample every member of the population has an equal chance of being drawn.

TYPES OF SURVEYS

Four types of surveys are commonly used these days, each with its advantages and disadvantages.

Voluntary Response

"Clip out this coupon in your Thursday *Daily Bugle* and tell us whether you favor or oppose a new nuclear power plant for West Hogwallow Flats." This is the cheapest way to run a poll: there are no interviewers to pay, no questionnaires to print, no mailing expenses. Also, there are no meaningful results. If you get a valid sample from a survey like this, it can be chalked up to pure luck.

When columnist Ann Landers asked her readers, "If you had it to do over again, would you have children?", 70 percent of those who responded answered No. Some readers fretted about what this attitude might mean for the future of America, so the Long Island newspaper *Newsday* put the same question to a representative nationwide sample of 1373 parents. Of these, 91 percent said "Yes, I would have kids if I could do it over again."

What happened? Apparently, the people who had "had it up to here" with their kids were the ones most motivated to write to Ann Landers and complain. In any event, the avalanche of letters to Landers apparently came nowhere close to approximating the mood of American parents.

Undaunted, Landers went back into the survey business again with the now-infamous question about whether women "would be content to be held close and treated tenderly and forget about 'The Act.'" Of her 90,000 responses, 72 percent voted for cuddling. The Landers column got a lot of news coverage and chuckles. However, it turns out that we need not fear for the future of the human race. Some rather more scientific surveys found sex to be a lot more popular than among Landers's 90,000 respondents.

Another name for voluntary response samples such as the ones by Landers is *self-selected sample*. Whenever you give people the opportunity to exclude themselves, the sample is no longer random. Instead, it is made up of the people most motivated on whatever issue is involved. You get the zealots on either end of the spectrum—the people who are staunchly for or against the issue in question. As one man pointed out to a *Washington Post* reporter: "When people don't have a problem they won't write or complain to Ann Landers."

A common failing of news media is to generalize too much from people who self-select themselves into a news story by showing up at a public hearing. The fact that 19 out of 20 witnesses at the council hearing oppose construction of the new high school doesn't mean that Utopia City as a whole is 95 percent opposed to it. It is possible, of course, that these numbers represent the true breakdown of opinion, but it's more likely that the antischoolers are just more vehement and better organized.

Mail

A mail survey can be a full census, as when a member of Congress sends a questionnaire to each resident of his or her district, or it can be a survey of a smaller sample of any population. Although this method is a little more expensive than a self-selected sample, because it requires printing questionnaires and paying postage, you avoid having to hire, train, supervise, and pay interviewers. However, response rates for mail surveys often run as low as 10–25 percent, meaning you again have a self-selected sample problem, and the people who choose to respond may be very atypical.

Besides the problem of bias due to the differences between respondents and nonrespondents, a mail surveyor also has the problem of losing control of the interview once the questionnaire is mailed out. Who in the household is actually filling out the answers? Has the respondent really understood the questions? Will the respondent answer each question, skipping none?

Mail surveys can be successfully used in some cases, but boosting the response rate to a respectable level is challenging. You must plan for at least a second wave of mailings, and perhaps more, to encourage respondents who didn't respond the first time, or failed to get the first letter, or whatever. These follow-up waves must be handled with care. If you tell people their responses will be confidential, how do you figure out who has not responded and contact them again without identifying those who have responded? This can be done with an envelope code. At any rate, you should be aware that mail surveys almost always involve more than a single trip to the post office to send out the letters, followed by an avalanche of immediate, thorough replies.

There are exceptions. If a newspaper mails questionnaires to elected officials or candidates and promises (threatens?) to print the replies or to publicize lack of them, response may not be bad. Politicians are motivated by a desire to avoid bad publicity. The *Honolulu Advertiser* in 1984 mailed issue-related questionnaires to 148 candidates for the Hawaii legislature and got back 80 percent of them—a very good mail-response rate.

If you do settle on a mail survey, there are a number of ways to improve the response rate:

   Keep the questionnaire short—as few as three to five questions, if possible.

Make questionnaires visually pleasing, simple in format.

Make instructions clear and concise.

Use large type to help those with poor vision.

Sweeten the pot a little. One researcher long ago doubled his response rate by including a 25-cent coin with the mailout. Of course, inflation may have upped the ante. Try offering a trial newspaper subscription or a small gift certificate.

Time mailouts to arrive in the home just before a weekend, when respondents might have more time to complete them.

In the end, consider this advice from sociologist Delbert C. Miller:

> Every researcher who chooses the mail questionnaire should consider himself as a seller in a highly competitive environment in which the majority of respondents will probably not complete and return his questionnaire.

Telephone

This is perhaps the most common type of survey. It costs more than voluntary response or mail surveys, but has a better chance of reaching a sample that gives you results you can believe. According to the 1980 U.S. Census, 95 percent of the households in America now have phones, so you don't run into the same problem the editors of the *Literary Digest* had in 1936, in the middle of the Depression.

Pollsters like to use a room with many phones, so the interviewers can be supervised while they make their calls. It is much more difficult for an interviewer to "fake" an interview when a supervisor is watching in the same room or perhaps even listening in on an extension. Quality control is easiest in this situation.

Some phone sampling methods disenfranchise people with unlisted phone numbers. Studies indicate that, typically, 10–20 percent of the residential phone numbers in most urbanized areas of the country are unlisted, with the figure reaching 26 percent in New York City and Chicago. Furthermore, in all areas, the number of unlisted phones is climbing, not dropping.

Unlisted numbers won't be included in your sample if you just pick numbers from the phone book. One alternative is to start with the phone book and apply some mathematical correction (e.g., add 2 to the last digit of each number you get in your sample from the

What Are the Most Important Issues Local Government Must Deal With?

Using tabular material and graphics can make masses of numbers more understandable to your audience. Here's how the *Wilkes-Barre Times Leader* displayed one number-filled set of findings to help readers grasp them. Use the tables for the numbers, the story for the analysis and explanation. Don't sprinkle number after number through your story text:

	Most important		Three most important
	Nov. 1983	Jan. 1984	Jan.* 1984
Unemployment/jobs	37%	29%	44%
Water problems	0%	19%	28%
High taxes/inequitable taxes	16%	8%	16%
Bad roads/potholes	3%	5%	12%
Attracting new industries	1%	4%	10%
Bad politicians/corruption	11%	3%	8%
Crime/personal security	4%	3%	6%
Quality of children's education	4%	3%	9%
Hunger/poverty/welfare	2%	3%	9%
Better government response to problems	0%	2%	6%
General economic condition	6%	1%	2%
Youth drinking/drugs	3%	1%	2%

(578 interviewed)
* Adds to more than 100% because up to three issues were recorded for each person interviewed

Lack of recreational facilities for youth	0%	....1%	.....3%
Senior citizen's problems	2%	....1%	.....3%
School strikes	2%	....1%	.....3%
Cost of living inflation	1%	....1%	.....3%
Trash/garbage problems	0%	....1%	.....2%
Urban renewal/rebuilding	0%	....1%	.....4%
Lack of adequate housing	0%	....1%	.....2%
Repealing commissioners' pay raise	0%	....1%	.....2%
Snow removal	0%	....1%	.....1%
Health care/health-care costs ..	1%	....0%	.....1%
Other governmental services ..	3%	....1%	.....2%
All other responses	4%	....1%	.....5%
Can't think of any local issues	0%	....7%	.....0%

Wilkes-Barre Times Leader

phone directory). This procedure will yield a lot of nonworking numbers and therefore will take longer, but the method ensures that unlisted numbers will be called in proportion to their share of the phones.

Software for random-digit dialing used by professional survey firms does much of this automatically. It will eliminate phone number ranges not used by the local company and many if not all non-residential numbers. It can even make provision for eliminating the numbers of persons who have been called in the past and threatened a lawsuit if they were called again.

In-Person Interviews

In this kind of survey, interviewers are sent to each predetermined address in the sample to ring the bell and conduct the interview. As you might guess, this is the most expensive method. It takes interviewers more time to get in a car and move around an area even if, as is common, clusters of 3 or 5 or 10 interviews may be planned on a single block or a single street to cut down on travel time.

Traditionally, this has been the method of choice for the best surveys. Response rate has been higher because potential respondents found it more difficult to turn away a living, breathing interviewer on their front step than they did to throw away a mailed questionnaire or to hang up on a disembodied voice on the telephone.

By the early 1980s, however, there was considerable debate in the survey industry over telephone versus in-person interviews. Door-to-door interviewing has suffered because of a fear of crime (people are unwilling to open their doors to a stranger) and because of the increasing numbers of people in high-density apartments or condominiums with tight security where it is impossible for interviewers to get past the lobby. Those factors, coupled with the loss of control inherent in having the interviewers out of sight and hearing of their supervisors, have made some prominent pollsters change their views.

Also, if nobody is home the first time you try in a telephone poll, you can easily call back in an hour or the next night. With door-to-door surveys, it costs time and money to travel a second or third time for *callbacks*, which ought to be a part of any sample design to assure its randomness. Contacting only those people who happen to be home when you first call can produce highly questionable results. People who are home a lot may differ from those who are not.

One advantage of in-person interviews is that they offer the opportunity to present visual or written information to the respondent. Respondents can be asked to react to pictures or lists or graphic formats. They can be given a written copy of a complex answer scale, allowing you to ask more complicated questions than would be possible over the telephone. In pre-election political surveys, pollsters get fewer "undecideds" on a question asking "Who would you vote for?" if they give each respondent a "sample ballot," a card, or sheet of paper to fill out and place in a sealed envelope or ballot box. For some reason, fewer people object to revealing their vote intentions in this way, even though eventually the interviewer will go back to the car, open the envelope, and match up the "sample ballot" with the rest of the questionnaire.

As a practical matter, most in-person interview surveys these days use some variation of *cluster sampling*. What is a cluster sample and why use one? Consider drawing a sample from the phone book. You may pick one name per page. The fact that just one of the phones is on 27th Street, one is in a northern suburb, and one is on a farm poses no problem. The telephone interviewers don't need to go to these places. They just sit in one place and dial. The geographic dispersion is a virtue.

But if you are doing a door-to-door survey, it gets very expensive and time consuming to send an interviewer to 27th Street, then out to the northern suburb (where nobody is home), then out to the farm, for one interview (at best) at each stop. The cost-cutting answer for pollsters is to draw a sample of houses, then use each sampled house as the starting point of a cluster. If they need 500 interviews, they may draw a sample of 100 houses or 100 city blocks, then instruct interviewers to start at the designated house and proceed clockwise until five interviews are obtained. Some statistical analysts suggest that this is not appropriate because you don't know the exact cluster size, that is, the total number of households from which the cluster of five interviews was obtained. As an alternative, you can give the interviewer a set number of housing units from the starting point and tell him to get them all. This tends to clump the interviews together in small groups—or clusters—but it reduces the expense of obtaining each interview. It also tends to slightly increase the statistical margin of error for the survey, but the reduction in cost may mean that the survey is affordable, whereas it wouldn't be if you had to do one interview per place in 500 places around the county.

How many clusters is right? For a sample of 500, you wouldn't believe a poll that used one cluster of 500, and taking 250 clusters of 2 interviews each doesn't markedly reduce costs. Most polls take somewhere between 3 and 8 interviews in each cluster. Gallup chooses about 350 sampling points, then collects about 5 interviews at each stop for a nationwide sample of about 1500, for instance. The Lou Harris Survey generally uses 100 sampling points in a national survey and attempts to collect clusters of 16 interviews at each spot.

CHOOSING A SAMPLE

The way in which the sample is constructed is a crucial part of survey design. The goal, of course, is to be able to generalize from a small sample of 250 or 500 or 1500 to the larger population being studied—whether it is all the adults in America or all the voters in a state or all the 12th-graders in a public school system. The fact that you can generalize at all from the poll is demonstrated by the preceding brief description of the statistical theory of sampling. However, all the statistical formulas depend on the assumption that you have, at the beginning, chosen a *random sample.*

There are many ways to construct a sample that approaches randomness. A key requirement of all of them is that every person in the population (Americans, state voters, 12th-graders, whatever) has an equal chance—or at least a known chance—of being selected for the survey sample. It is almost impossible to achieve perfect randomness when you are sampling people, but certain techniques will help get closer to it.

For instance, with a sample from a telephone book, some percentage of people with phones have unlisted numbers and will be missed unless the pollster corrects for it as described in the box on pp. 122–23.

Personal interviewers can't just ring doorbells during normal weekday working hours, because they will get too many retirees, housewives, unemployed people, and invalids, and too few full-time workers. They must work evenings and weekends. Also, you can't cluster your interviews in one small geographical section of a state and then claim that your poll is able to generalize to the statewide population. The clusters must be spread around.

A phone survey uses the phone book as a basic reference, but what is used for door-to-door polls? How can a pollster assemble a list of all the doors he or she might possibly knock on, so that a decision can be made about exactly which doors to approach? Sources might include city property tax listings, city zoning maps or listings, or public utility master lists of houses that have electric service. Any source that gives a reasonably up-to-date listing of the *universe* to be examined may be used as a *sampling frame.*

SAMPLE SIZE

Once a sampling frame is assembled in this way, how many people should be questioned in the survey? There is no fixed answer to this question. The size of the sample will be dictated by some combination of the following factors:

The amount of money and time available to do the survey.
How much precision is needed in the final results.

How to Draw a Survey Sample from the Phone Book

1. *Determine the sample size*. For this example, let's choose a sample of 250.

2. *Oversample*. You can't expect to complete 250 calls with just 250 phone numbers. Design the sample to produce about twice as many phone numbers as you need, because there will be many not-at-homes, refusals, or disconnected numbers. Thus, our goal here is about 500.

3. *Go to the phone book and count the white pages*. In the Syracuse, New York, phone book, for example, there are 482 white pages. One name from each page will produce a sample of 482 phone numbers, close enough to the target of 500.

4. *Randomly determine the location of the name from each page*. The pages have four columns of names each. Put slips of paper with the numbers 1, 2, 3, and 4 in a hat and pick one out. Let's say we pick out a 2, so we'll use the second column on each page. Now measure the depth of each page with a ruler. In our example, there are 10 inches of names in each column. Put the numbers 0 through 10 on slips of paper in the hat again. If we pick 6, for example, that means the name on each page will be the one closest to the 6-inch mark in the second column.

5. *Go through the phone book, ruler in hand, and write down the phone number on the line closest to the 6-inch mark of the second column on each page*. If that line in the phone book is a nonresidential number, alternately go one line at a time above and below the chosen number until you find a residential phone listing. In the end, you will have 482 phone numbers.

6. *The 482 numbers will all be listed telephones, whereas a good percentage of people in any area have unlisted numbers.* Many surveys try to reach them, too, on the assumption that those who have their numbers listed may be very different from those who don't.

Therefore, to include unlisted numbers in the sample, start from your 482 listed numbers and apply some numerical correction—add two to the last digit of each number, for instance. (Instead of 479-3846, you get 479-3848.) This allows you to reach unlisted numbers as well. Of course, if you do this it also will mean that the phone interviewers will reach a huge number of nonworking numbers and will need considerably more than 482 numbers to wind up with 250 completed phone calls. Perhaps 1000 or 1500 numbers will be required—two or three per phone book page.

A pollster willing to accept results likely to be within 5 percentage points of the "true" value in the overall population can draw a sample of about 400 of the population universe. If the pollster insists on being closer, he or she must talk to more people. Gallup, Harris, and the other national polls generally use samples of about 1500 persons. With a sample that big they can be pretty certain that the results are within 2.5 percentage points of reality—based on sample size alone.

For polls of a city or a state, a more common sample size is 400 to 600 persons (or voters if it's an election-related survey). As the box on p. 124 shows, a sample of 400 yields a margin of error of about 5 percentage points. A sample of 600 reduces the margin to 4 points. It gets tougher to lower the margin after that. You have to go beyond 1000 to get down to the 3-point level.

Sampling error merely refers to the variability inherent in the fact that in a poll you have a slice of reality (a sample) instead of the whole reality (a census of a population). For instance, if you flip a "fair" coin an infinite number of times, you'll get half heads and half tails. If you flip it only 10 times, you may well get a 6–4 or 7–3 split, or even, on occasion, 10 heads and no tails. There are statistical formulas that tell you, with a sample of a certain size, that

Sampling Error at the 95 Percent Level of Confidence for Samples of Various Sizes

Sample Size	Sampling Error*
50	.139
100	.098
150	.080
200	.069
250	.062
300	.056
350	.052
400	.049
450	.046
500	.044
550	.042
600	.040
650	.038
700	.037
750	.036
800	.035
850	.034
900	.033
950	.032
1,000	.031

* Assumes simple random sampling

Here's how to interpret these figures:

Let's say you have a sample of 400, which is not atypical for a citywide or statewide poll. The table lists the sample error at .049, which translates into 4.9 percent "at the 95 percent level of confidence." What does that mean in real words? It means that if you have a simple random sample of 400 persons, you can be 95 percent sure that the figures in your poll are not "off" from the true figures in the whole population by more than 4.9 percentage points.

How would you tell your readers this? What follows is some suggested language to put at the bottom of a poll story:

"Because the results of this poll are based on a sample, they may differ slightly from the results we would get from a complete census—that is, if we contacted all the adults in the state and asked them the same questions. The extent of possible error in a sample survey can be estimated by statistical formulas. In a sample of 400 persons, one can say with 95 percent certainty that the results are within plus or minus 5 percentage points (you can safely round the 4.9 off to 5 in this case) of what they would be if the entire population had been polled. Also, any survey carries within it risks of 'nonsampling' error caused by such factors as people who decline to participate in the poll or who cannot be reached."

your answer is almost certain to be within X percentage points of the true value you would get in that infinite series of flips. The same holds true when sampling people. A sample almost surely will be off by a little by the mere fact that it is a sample. Although it is unlikely that any sample will hit the exact value in the population right on the nose, the formula for sampling error allows you to say, in effect, "I may not be right on the nose, but I know that 95 percent of the time a sample this big will give me an answer within X percent of the nose."

The formulas for random sampling tell you how much error you might expect in a sample of given size just from the problems inherent in sampling itself. There are other sources of error besides the sample itself, however, and these can be even more troubling because there are no statistical formulas for estimating the size of their effect. The most common source is from *nonresponse*—people who fall within the sample but cannot be located (they don't answer their phone or aren't home when an interviewer calls) or refuse to participate. That is why it is important to know the nonresponse or *refusal rate* when you evaluate the results of any survey. If the refusal rate is above 35 percent of those contacted, you should have qualms about the quality of the data. Other sources of nonsampling error include anything else that can possibly go wrong, other than the sample itself—for example, interviewers can skip a question by mistake or record an answer in the wrong column; interviewers can be biased; answers can be punched into a computer incorrectly. Minimizing these errors requires careful planning and double- and triple-checking of the responses.

How much do *nonsampling error* (e.g., nonresponse) and variations in sample design (e.g., clusters) add to the margin of error? Unfortunately, there is no formula for calculating this. To allow for other sources of error, the Gallup polls increase the statistical error margin by nearly half over what the formula gives them.

One way of making an instant check on the bias introduced by nonresponse or other factors is to compare your sample with known information about the population. If half the city's registered voters are male, half the sample (or very close to it) should be male. If 15 percent of the residents are of Hispanic origin, about 15 percent of your sample should be, too. If a poll is too high or too low on demographic factors such as age, income, or education, you as a journalist need to know this beforehand. One way to correct for such imbalances in a sample is by *weighting* the responses to bring the sample back in line with the population. Thus, if a poll has too few men in the sample, the responses of those you do have can be adjusted statistically to count more than do the responses from women.

Most reporters don't get involved in the mechanics of weighting. It is normally done by computer. However, you should be aware that weighting is sometimes needed and you should always ask whether it was done and how far "off" the sample was prior to weighting. Too big a difference between sample and population should cause you to question the poll's procedures.

WHO DOES THE POLLING?

If a newspaper or TV station wants to do its own public opinion survey, who will do the work? Here are the choices, in descending order of cost and ease:

Contract the work out to a professional survey firm. These firms are experienced in drawing samples, drafting questionnaires, coding data once they are obtained, churning out tables from a computer, and analyzing what it all means. They also keep stables of regular interviewers who are trained in proper techniques and who, because of their experience, are better than raw recruits. Profes-

Letting Others Help You

One way for small local polls to take advantage of the expertise of professional pollsters and avoid having to think up foolproof questions is to piggyback on previous work by national polls.

Drawing on these sources allows a local newspaper or TV station to use tested questions and, perhaps even more important, to make valid comparisons of how the people in a city/state/region compare on a given issue with the opinion of a national sample on the same issue.

Here are some places to get information about national polls:

1. For mailed copies of CBS News/*New York Times* Polls, contact CBS News, Election and Survey Unit, 533 W. 57th St., New York, New York 10019 (212-975-3320).

2. Gallup Poll. Many papers already have access to Gallup syndicated material, which routinely contains details of question wording and results. Contact The Gallup Organization, Inc., 53 Bank St., Princeton, New Jersey 08540 (609-924-9600). Also, you can subscribe to The Gallup Report, published monthly, subscription price $75 per year (as of 1985).

3. Harris Survey. Their syndicated stories contain lengthy statistical summaries and the exact question wordings. Much of the Harris survey data is kept on file at the Louis Harris Political Data Center, Institute for Research in Social Science, University of North Carolina, Chapel Hill, North Carolina 27514.

4. The NBC News, Room 1700, 30 Rockefeller Plaza, New York, NY 10020 (212-664-4452) will put you on a mailing list and send copies of regular NBC News-Associated Press polls.

5. The National Network of State Polls, Dr. Patrick Cotter or Dr. Betty B. Hardee, Institute for Social Science Research, University of Alabama, University, Alabama 35486 (205-348-5980). This network is a fairly new group made up mostly of university researchers. They may be able to guide you to well-done research that has been conducted in your own state. They also have been de-

veloping sets of common questions for use by member organizations so that public survey data may be compared across a number of states.

6. The National Opinion Research Center at the University of Chicago has been conducting the General Social Survey for more than a decade. They have published a volume containing the wordings of all the questions they have used—measuring attitudes on topics ranging from abortion to capital punishment, to divorce, to life after death, to race relations, to women's roles. Get the *General Social Surveys, 1972–1984: Cumulative Codebook*.

7. University of Michigan Institute for Social Research, 426 Thompson St., Ann Arbor, Michigan 48109. This institute has been doing national surveys for more than 30 years and has many good, tested questions on politics and other topics. Questions and national sample answers have been compiled in books titled *Measures of Social Psychological Attitudes, Measures of Occupational Attitudes* and *Measures of Political Attitudes*.

8. Roper Public Opinion Research Center, Box U-164, 341 Mansfield Road, Storrs, Connecticut 06268. This is the largest archive of public opinion research in the world and has both Roper poll and Gallup poll data.

9. *Public Opinion* magazine. This bimonthly magazine is a good roundup of data and analysis from current surveys. The "Opinion Roundup" section in each issue gives a lot of data and exact questionnaire wording from many major national surveys. Subscription is $26 a year (1985 price). Write them c/o American Enterprise Institute for Public Policy Research, 1150 Seventeenth St., N.W., Washington, DC 20036 (202-862-5800).

10. *American Public Opinion Index* and *American Public Opinion Data*. These annual volumes, published since 1981 by Opinion Research Service, are a compilation of questions and answers from a variety of national, state, and local opinion polls. The *Index* lists questions in a cross-referenced directory and tells you where to go for details; the *Data* volume provides the findings of polls in the index. These volumes are not cheap; the Index was selling for $125 per year in 1984 and the Data volume

for $100 for each year's data. Contact Opinion Research Service, P.O. Box 70205, Louisville, Kentucky 40270 (502-893-2527).

sional survey firms double-check the work of interviewers afterward to assure high quality. This is called *verification.*

Costs will vary from city to city and from survey to survey because of such factors as size of sample, geographic breadth of the population (polling in a city costs less than statewide polling, which in turn costs less than a national sample), type of survey (telephone costs less than door-to-door; cluster sampling in which you take three or five interviews on one block costs less than simple random sampling with a single interview at each sampling point), and turnaround time (news media generally want the results fast, which may mean overtime for the survey firm).

Before a firm is hired, a news medium should talk to other clients of the firm to see if they have been satisfied. Costs are high, so negotiate the price. Generally, news media can get a lower price than private polling clients because the survey firm will get publicity when the newspaper or TV station reports the results of a poll, and this invariably brings the pollsters more business. After you hire somebody, sit in on interviewer training, listen to a few phone interviews. Any reputable firm should allow this.

Use the resources of a nearby college or university. Professors with background in survey research techniques often do consulting work on the side or are eager for a real-life project to use in a research class. Doing a survey in connection with a class means you may get student interviewers at low or no cost. (However, pay them if you can.) Also, time on university computers costs less than time on a private computer.

When the *Honolulu Advertiser* did a comprehensive study of Honolulu's criminal justice system in 1975, a University of Hawaii professor provided invaluable assistance in research design and paved the way for analyzing all the data from court and police documents on the campus computer. The newspaper obtained stories for less cost, and in return, the professor received information for use in his own research and writing. The project might never have been attempted without the assurance of help from the campus.

Use in-house resources. Many news media have their own survey operations for marketing, advertising, or audience research. The newsroom may be able to piggyback on them, adding several questions for publication or broadcast. These research operations sometimes have their own interviewers and computer capability. Sometimes they will hire part-time interviewers and contract out the data processing. In any event, these people will be experienced at drawing samples, monitoring interviewers' work, and processing the data at the end.

Do it yourself. This is cheaper, but a great deal of time, energy, and expertise is required to do it right. Dozens of details are involved: drafting questionnaires and printing them, drawing a sample, hiring and training interviewers (or arranging for the services of classified phone-room personnel or news clerks), supervising or validating their work, getting the data coded when you are through (often there will be keypunchers in other departments of a newspaper or TV station that can be used for this), and analyzing the results.

Newsrooms or classified advertising rooms do have banks of phones that can be used. You have access to phone books, city directories, and "reverse" phone directories (arranged by phone number) from which to draw samples. Most newspapers nowadays have at least one in-house computer that can do simple data processing, along with a computer program for getting questionnaire answers into machine readable form for processing.

You can do it yourself, but don't underestimate the problems.

QUESTIONNAIRE DRAFTING

If you do decide to conduct an opinion survey, somebody must prepare a questionnaire. Some practical tips:

Don't make it too long. About 10–15 minutes' worth in a telephone interview and perhaps twice that in an in-person setting can be handled without difficulty. Beyond that, unless it's a fascinating topic, respondents get tired or bored, which leads to answers that aren't well considered or may cause the respondent to quit in midstream.

What Did They Ask?

The difficulty of measuring attitudes about a complex topic with a single question is highlighted by a pair of headlines on stories about an Associated Press-NBC News poll in early 1980. Said the *New York Times*: "Poll Finds Public Favors Reprisals if Iran Harms or Tries Hostages." Reported the *Boston Globe*: "Poll: Attack for Revenge Is Opposed."

What does the public think? In this case, the answer was "It depends." It turned out that opinion was subtly structured, depending on the way the questions were asked. As long as the hostages weren't harmed, there should be no military retaliation, 79 percent of those polled said. But 66 percent favored a military solution if the hostages were made to suffer by their Iranian captors.

Look for time-tested questions that you can adapt to your situation or use verbatim. Using the same question previously used in a timely national survey allows comparison of the attitudes of people in your geographical area to those of the nation as a whole.

Avoid biased and emotion-producing words. The pollster should suggest that either alternative of a forced choice is acceptable. The "some people feel this way . . . while others feel that way" design of a question is one good way to do this.

Keep question language simple and direct, using words that have unambiguous meaning. As Eleanor and Nathan Maccoby pointed out, "the word *fair,* for example, may mean either 'equitable' or 'not very good.' The phrase *put up* may mean to nominate a candidate, to stay for the night, to endure an insult, or preserve fruits." A favorite example of Tom Copeland, research director of Copley Newspapers, is "When did you last see your doctor?" "I saw him Wednesday over on the golf course."

Avoid long questions where possible and keep each to a single point. Avoid double-barreled questions. It's hard enough to answer one question at a time.

Consider the respondent's ego and try to cushion it. Ask "Do you happen to know the name of the governor?" rather than "Can you tell me who the governor is?" It minimizes embarrassment.

Try to make clear both sides of a pro–con question. Ask "Do you favor or oppose . . . ?" instead of just "Do you favor . . . ?" The latter wording tends to get more "Yes, I favor . . ." responses. Simply adding "or not" at the end can make it clear that question has at least two possible and equally legitimate answers.

Write a low-key introduction that allows your interviewers to identify the nature of the project (without giving such details as might bias later answers), the sponsor (again, where there is no danger that the sponsor's identity might introduce bias), an assurance of confidentiality, and a promise that the interviewer isn't merely a salesperson in disguise. One example:

> Hello, I'm _____ from XYZ Research, a local opinion polling company. We're conducting a survey for *The Daily Bugle* to find out how parents feel about the local school system. I'm not trying to sell anything. Your phone number was selected at random and all your responses will be kept confidential and added to those of hundreds of others to find out how people feel about these issues.

It is also necessary to have some procedure at the top of the questionnaire for determining exactly who in a given home to interview. One problem is that interviewers are much more apt to find women than men at home. Some of this effect can be minimized by limiting interviewing to evenings (although no later than about 9 P.M.) and weekends. Many questionnaires have a selection system that asks more often for a male respondent or that asks for "the head of your household" as a mechanism to ensure that a proper share of men are included in the sample.

Try to ask the most interesting questions first, to encourage respondents to continue with the interview, rather than turning them off at the start. When you change topics, try to make the transition smooth but let the respondent know you are switching gears: "Here's a different topic," or, "This subject interests a lot of people."

Place any potentially embarrassing questions—such as questions about attitudes toward sex, drugs, and gambling, or information about personal income—at the end, where they won't cause an early termination of the interview. By then, the interviewer will have established rapport with the respondent, who thus is apt to be more cooperative. Even if a respondent cuts things off, you already will have gotten answers to nearly all the questions.

Watch the question order to minimize chances that an earlier question will bias response to a later one. You wouldn't, for instance, ask people "Do you think Governor Windbag is guilty or not guilty of fraud?" and then follow up with a question about which candidate for governor the respondent prefers. This is why it's important for you to ask for copies of the entire questionnaire when you are given polling results for a possible story. You need to know both the wording and the order of the questions to make sure the survey was fair.

Before you put together your final questionnaire, go over the questions one by one and ask yourself exactly what you hope to do with the information. What, really, will it tell you? How will you make use of it in a news story? There are many questions that fall into the "wouldn't it be nice to know if . . ." category, but when you sit down and think about it you can't figure out how to make use of the information even if you get it. Throw out all such questions.

Consult with the data-processing people on designing the layout of the questionnaire so that it will be easier to punch the results into the computer.

Run a pretest of your questionnaire once it is drafted. This step can uncover holes or problems with wording that the drafters overlooked. One legend at the University of Michigan Survey Research Center tells about a pretest of a questionnaire that included the question "What did you do right before you entered the service?" Said one respondent: "Lady, you should ask me what I did *wrong* before I entered the service." The *right* was changed to *just*.

In drafting or selecting questions the major choice to make is between *open-end* and *closed-end* questions.

Open-end Questions

An open-end question simply means the respondent is free to define his or her own terms for answering it. Examples:

"What do you think are the most important problems in West Utopia today?"

"In your opinion, what are the major causes of the violence that sometimes occurs in our public schools here?"

The open-ended question is most useful when you aren't sure what the answers may be and don't want to impose your own set of limits and structures on the responses. If you ask whether crime, inflation, or unemployment is the most important problem in America, you ignore the possibility that people might really think the price of tickets for singer Michael Jackson's tour is most important. An open-ended question lets people say whatever is in *their* minds, instead of responding to multiple-choice answers of the pollsters' choosing.

The disadvantages of open-ended questions are the difficulties in recording them and sorting the answers afterwards. First, the interviewer must get the response down on paper at the time the respondent gives it. Few survey interviewers take shorthand; the best you can hope for is that they get on paper the gist of the key words of the answer. There is no doubt some precision is lost at this stage. Second, when the questionnaires get back to the office, someone needs to discern a pattern and develop a scheme for sorting the answers into categories. This takes time and can result in arbitrary decisions. Then, coders go through the answers one by one and actually do the sorting—placing each answer in a category. This introduces a possible source of error and bias, because studies have shown there is never 100 percent agreement among people who do coding. What one coder might put in an "economic problems" category, another might view as an "inflation" answer. Furthermore, the coding may vary from what the respondent *really* had in mind.

The time and effort to do all this translates into higher costs for a survey, but there are times when an open-ended approach is the only fair way to get at a set of attitudes and beliefs.

Closed-end Questions

More common in survey research are closed-end questions, in which all the answer categories are defined in advance.

"Do you approve or disapprove of the job being done by President Reagan?"

"Do you think parents who send their children to private schools should get a tax break for the tuition they pay, or don't you think so?"

"If the election were held today, would you vote for Abraham Lincoln or Stephen Douglas?"

The answer categories are easily understood by respondent and interviewer alike. The coding is easy once the survey is finished. Time and cost are minimal.

The disadvantages are that this sort of *forced-choice* question may sometimes put a respondent into a box that he or she doesn't really belong in. What if somebody approves of Reagan's foreign policy, but not his domestic economic plan? What if you think low-income parents should get a tax break for private school tuition, but not upper-income people?

Closed-end questions must be worded so the answer categories are *exhaustive* (covering all possible answers) and *exclusive* (so that each answer falls in one category, but not any others). Often, human opinions on complex issues just don't work that way. That is why, on a particularly complex issue, it is best not to rely on a single question—especially a single closed-end question—as the sole indicator of opinion. When reading poll results, keep these factors in mind.

Even using only closed-end questions, a survey can bore in on an issue from more than one side. A 1983 poll by The Roper Organization sought attitudes about President Reagan first by asking for overall attitudes and then by a series of follow-up questions that asked for approval or disapproval of Reagan on the following issues: "Cutting back government spending," "Increasing military and defense spending," "His ability to make the government work efficiently," "Style and tone of government," "Handling of the economy," "Handling of foreign relations," "Kinds of people he surrounds himself with," "His position on deregulating natural gas," "Relaxing environmental controls."

INTERVIEWER TRAINING

If you decide to oversee a survey yourself and are going to hire your own interviewers or use staff members for the interviewing, they must be trained first. This can be particularly crucial if journalists themselves are doing any survey interviewing. The tools of the journalists' trade for interviewing can spell disaster for a public opinion survey. Journalists are used to making small talk with the people they interview, sometimes arguing with them, letting an

Fear of Major Crime Far Outweighs the Reality

Crime in Minnesota is partly a state of mind.

Fear and worry—particularly among old people and women in the state's biggest cities—far outweigh people's own run-ins with major crime, according to the *Tribune*'s Minnesota Poll.

The chance of such run-ins last year, according to the state Bureau of Criminal Apprehension, was one in 21 for Minnesotans, one in 17 for city dwellers.

But look at these poll results:

Two of three Minnesotans worry frequently or sometimes about burglars breaking into their homes, even though just one in four say their homes ever have been burglarized.

Nearly half the state's women worry at least sometimes about getting raped or sexually assaulted. But only 6 percent of all Minnesotans—men and women alike—say they've ever been mugged or assaulted.

More than one in four adults say there is an area within a mile of home where they would be afraid to walk alone at night. But only 2 percent say their neighborhood is dangerous enough to make them think seriously about bailing out. And more than nine of ten say they feel safe and secure in their homes at night.

One of five Minnesota adults worries frequently or sometimes about getting held up by an armed robber. But only 2 percent have ever had that happen to them.

The poll was taken by telephone among 1,207 adults last December. . . .

Minnesota Poll. Copyright 1982 *Minneapolis Tribune*

interview flow in whatever direction the subject reasonably takes it. All of these things destroy the controlled setting of the survey interview. Here are some tips for conducting survey interviews:

Be neutral and noncommittal. A pollster doesn't want the interviewer's opinions, he wants the respondent's. Make sure the interviewer understands there are no "right" or "wrong" answers to questions. The interviewer's view on any subject should not become known during the interview. Take what is given and write it down.

Charles Backstrom and Gerald Hursh give this advice to interviewers in their book, *Survey Research:*

> Merely soak up information like a sponge without giving any of it back. Your job is to record that information, regardless of whether you think it good, bad, indifferent, boring, or exciting. Don't, by word or reaction, indicate surprise, pleasure, or disapproval at any answer. Even a slight intake of breath will cue a respondent that you have reacted.

This can be especially important when an interviewer is instructed to *probe* for additional detail in an answer. A probe can help to fill out an incomplete, vague, or irrelevant answer. But the probe should not direct the respondent in one direction or another. Say something neutral: "Uh huh, I see." That may encourage further discussion. Other options: "What do you mean?" "Why is that?" "Anything else?"

Tone of voice is crucial. The interviewer should not let the respondent feel he or she is endorsing or arguing with anything said.

All questions must be asked exactly as worded on the questionnaire. Any rephrasing may change the meaning and impact of the entire question and make it worthless.

Ask all questions. Don't skip any unless the questionnaire instructs you to.

Don't change the order of questions.

Don't explain the questions or try to define their terms. If a respondent asks what a particular question means, the interviewer should say: "I really can't say, just consider whatever it means to you." The interviewer may repeat the question—again, exactly as worded—if necessary.

Be familiar with the questionnaire. In some questionnaires, there may be some questions or sections asked only if the respondent answers in a particular fashion to a previous question. For instance, the poll might ask whether the respondent favors capital punishment for some serious crimes. For those who answer *yes,* the poll might want to pin down the issue further by asking about specific crimes—murder of a police officer, murder for hire, rape, and so forth—and whether the respondent favors the death penalty for each. For respondents who answer *no* to the first question, the interviewer would skip over the follow-ups and go on to the next topic. Watch this especially carefully when the first few questionnaires are turned in to make sure the interviewer isn't asking the wrong questions of the wrong people.

Stick to the answer categories given. If a particular question is looking for a choice of "excellent, good, fair, or poor" and the respondent says, "O.K.," the interviewer must not assume it means "fair." Ask for a choice from the categories listed.

When finished, the interviewer should review his or her work quickly while the respondent is still present or still on the phone. Then, if the interviewer has missed a question, it can be asked. After completing an interview, the interviewer should go through and edit it—double-check what's written down, correct errors and omissions.

One good tool for training is *role playing.* Have one interviewer go through the questionnaire with a second (perhaps more experienced) one playing the respondent and trying to gum up the works so everyone can learn ways out of rough spots.

Who makes the best interviewers? Traditionally, the field has been dominated by women, especially housewives working part-time. For door-to-door interviewing, they often still are the best bet. Philip Meyer, in his book *Precision Journalism,* suggests that "females of intermediate age have an easier time gaining access and presenting themselves in a nonthreatening manner that enhances rapport." In other words, people (especially women respondents) are more apt to let another woman in the door because they feel less likely to be mugged. The double-barreled problem at the other side of the equation, however, is how to get women interviewers to agree to go door-to-door in high crime areas and how to ensure their safety.

Make clear to each interviewer that a percentage of his or her work will be checked after completion and before payment is made. Then do it. Call up a sample of the people interviewed (most questionnaires conclude by having the interviewer determine the respondent's name and phone number, if not already known, "in case my office needs to verify that I have talked to you"). When you check back, thank the alleged respondent for cooperating and say that you want to double-check a couple of things from the interview. Then re-ask a question or two of the type where the answer isn't apt to change much (age or years of education) to see if the answers match with what's on the questionnaire. The first clue will be if the person answering the phone says "There's no Charlie here" or if Charlie says he never was interviewed. If a cheater is discovered among the interviewers, discard all of that person's completed questionnaires and replace them with more interviews. Generally, it doesn't happen often, if interviewers have been forewarned that results will be spot checked as they come in.

FINAL NOTE

Because they go beyond the traditional interview with a single news source, surveys enable journalists to interview representative samples of their community on key topics of the day. Chapter 5 offers guidance for plumbing the depths of a single source. Chapters 6 and 7 offer guidelines for expanding the scope of reporting through carefully constructed questionnaires and fairly drawn samples. The guidance in these two chapters is useful for evaluating the ever-increasing volume of survey research offered by news sources as well as for fielding surveys under the full control of the newsroom.

REFERENCES

Krauss, Bob. "Yes, Leilani—there is a belief in Santa Claus." *Honolulu Advertiser* (Dec. 24, 1981): A-1.

Maccoby, Eleanor E., and Nathan Maccoby. "The Interview: A Tool of Social Science." In Gardner Lindzey and Elliot Aronson, eds., *Handbook of Social Psychology*. Reading, MA: Addison-Westley Publishing, 1968.

Miller, Delbert C. *Handbook of Research Design and Social Measurement*. 4th ed. White Plains, N.Y.: Longman, 1983.

Part III
DOCUMENTS AND RECORDS

CHAPTER 8
Covering Beats

> Remember, beat reporting is a lot like gardening. Both require you to be in the field every day, cultivating. And in both, the amount of the harvest is directly proportional to the amount of labor invested.
>
> Brian S. Brooks, George Kennedy,
> Daryl R. Moen, and Don Ranly
> *News Reporting and Writing*

The reporter was covering a legislative hearing on money matters.

The speaker, a respected business lobbyist, gave lengthy testimony about government finance and the sale of general obligation bonds. The testimony ended. The legislators asked a few questions. The meeting adjourned.

The reporter, fresh from college, approached the smooth-talking witness. "What," he asked (tentatively), "is a general obligation bond?" (Do you know? You'll need to if you cover government.)

The reporter's admission of ignorance wasn't quite as embarrassing as it might have been because the reporter was new, the subject matter a little arcane, the lobbyist friendly and willing to help. But the incident illustrates an important point about covering any beat to which you may be assigned—the need to learn a little about the landscape where the news stories lie buried.

Some of this learning can take place in college, where, for the most part, journalism students are encouraged to take a broad-ranging curriculum. Useful fields are government finance, the judicial system, political science courses emphasizing government structure and functions, primer courses in criminal law, and rudimentary accounting. But that can't be the end of a beat reporter's education.

GETTING STARTED ON A BEAT

Let's take a city hall beat, for example. How do you find out how a particular city government works? A good place to start is the city's charter, a municipal version of a constitution. It will tell you who the elected officials are and how often they must run. It will lay out the organizational chart for the city's executive branch, explain the budgeting process and the city's taxing powers. You can learn from the charter how the city council goes about introducing and passing legislation, whether the police are allowed to work for the mayor's reelection campaign, and who gets to appoint the members of the zoning board or liquor commission. The charter also may tell you what kind of information government officials must file about their outside jobs and income. In short, a charter is an instruction book describing how the gears and pulleys work in the government machine.

Another source is your news organization's library, where you can skim through clippings to learn about key officials and the current status of recent controversies. The clippings also can furnish conversational openers to use when you meet the key sources on your beat—you may discover that one went to the same college you did, another likes to fish, a third is a former local sports hero. These little tidbits can make you appear competent and interested when you finally get around to meeting these people in the flesh.

Another helper can be your predecessor on the beat. He or she can steer you to good sources (and away from unreliable ones) and help you cope with the mechanical details: how to get advance copies of council agendas, how the building permit files are organized, where to find the coffee machine.

DEVELOPING CONTACTS

Beat reporting isn't only a matter of formal interviews, press conferences, and official public meetings. As a matter of fact, those settings aren't really particularly good for developing the kind of rapport that separates a hack from a professional beat reporter.

The key is the regular contact, the attempt to become part of the furniture, part of the scene on your beat, so potential sources don't think, "Oh, no, here comes a reporter; I'd better be guarded in what I say." This is easy to suggest, but how do you do it?

First, be pleasant and cordial whenever and wherever you come in contact with anybody on your beat. The police reporter runs into officers in the police station restrooms. The government reporter runs across the mayor in the hallway at City Hall. You meet a secretary to a high official at the supermarket. In situations like these take the opportunity for small talk and pleasantries. Discuss your kids' school problems, the weather, the local baseball team. It won't produce a story—right away—but people tend to be less guarded if they are accustomed to seeing you as just another human being, not as an adversary around whom they should clam up.

Always get to know the secretaries to key executives and treat them with civility. A secretary who is on your side can provide you with regular access to an executive even when the boss is not readily available to others. If, on deadline, you really need to reach the mayor or the governor or the police chief, a helpful secretary can let your phone call through or give you a number at the country club.

In contrast, a reporter who specializes in brusque treatment for secretaries—on the theory that they aren't important enough to be nice to—will often pay for it later. Secretaries can be formidable roadblocks if they set their minds to it.

Mid-level civil servants also are good sources to cultivate. They have job security and often know more about what is really going on than does a political appointee at the top who just got there and may be gone in four years.

Spend time talking to people on your beat about your beat. Your first step should be to familiarize yourself with the formal structure. What does the organizational chart say about the chain of command? Who reports to whom? What are the formalities of getting legislation passed? Who has the power (on paper, at least)?

Then, when you understand the theory, spend time finding out how practice differs. Where does the real power lie? Often, somebody in a tiny office with an obscure-sounding title, such as "secretary to the zoning board," will wield the most clout. How? Why? Does he or she know where the skeletons are hidden? Or is it just that this person knows what people want and how to grease the skids to get it? Often, this kind of clout traces back to the power of the purse strings. (Finding out who really controls the flow of appropriations and the structure of the budget can be a key to unlocking any beat, as we'll discuss later in this chapter. The power to spend is crucial, especially in a government agency.)

For instance, common sense will tell you that a house speaker or senate president should be the most powerful person in a legislature. However, the real power may lie with a majority leader, who is too busy controlling patronage and the flow of legislation to bother with the minutiae of being presiding officer, or with a finance committee chairman, who gets to put the numbers in all the slots on the budget, overriding the work done in dozens of other committees, or, in a city government, with the person who dominates a zoning commission or liquor licensing board. The point is not to let titles fool you.

The only way to get this kind of information is to talk to people on your beat. Be sure not to neglect the "outs," people who are not in the power structure. Talk to members of the minority party. Talk to lobbyists. Talk to other reporters who have been there for awhile.

In the executive branch of government, look for people who have discretion over the use of dollars. Often, there will be large loopholes in competitive bidding laws that permit contracts to be given to big campaign contributors. Look for the people who control the granting of such contracts for building and road design, architectural services, and outside consultants. Then find out what ties exist between these people and the political apparatus.

When such a contracting officer is also raising money on the side for a politician, you can be sure that he or she wields significant power. This person can appeal to architects, designers, and consultants for political contributions, secure in the knowledge that he or she can come back a year later and offer them government work in return. Beyond a doubt, this is an effective combination for fundraising!

TACTICS ON THE BEAT

Collect Home Phone Numbers

Try to get them for all the key people on your beat. There will be times in the evenings and on weekends or holidays when you really need to get hold of the mayor or the police chief or the prosecutor or corporate executive for information or comment.

These are just the kind of people who tend to have unlisted phone numbers because they don't wish to be bothered by reporters or the public. Wait until a time when the person you want to reach will suffer because you couldn't get a comment from him or her on a critical story. Then approach that person and point out that you could have used his or her side of the story if only you had had a phone number.

When you have an unlisted number, keep it to yourself. Don't share it with everyone in the newsroom, and don't abuse it. Bother people at home on evenings and on weekends only when absolutely necessary.

Look for Motives and Causes

At the 1972 Democratic National Convention, frontrunner George McGovern's forces lost a key procedural vote. One pundit claimed it was a sign his strength was slackening. It turned out that McGovern's organizers were using a complex facet of the parliamentary rules, deliberately losing one vote in order to assure victory on a more important one later.

If something incongruous happens, don't assume it's a coincidence. More often, there is a cause behind it. Look for the strategy, the motive.

As longtime Northwestern University professor Curtis D. MacDougall said in *Interpretative Reporting,*

> Nothing just happens. A wave of intolerance has a cause. So has a revival movement, excessive hero worship, a bullish stock market, an increase in superstition, or any fad, fashion, craze or mass movement. . . . At any rate, there is always an explanation for how we "got that way."

Always look for the explanation—coincidence and random events are the exception, not the rule.

Learn the Politics

All journalists should engage in politics watching. Every organization has its own politics, from city halls to police departments to corporations to college campuses to the smallest, most obscure group.

A prominent businessman who had once served as majority leader of his state's house of representatives got "out of politics," but later served a term on the state university's board of regents. He once told a reporter: "I never knew what politics was until I got into the middle of things on campus."

Bureaucracies have people in them. People have power goals and personal differences, and personal differences translate into politics within the bureaucracy. On any beat, try to find the interpersonal tensions and how they affect the bureaucracy's operations. One tip: You'll discover more about this from the "outs" than you will from the "ins."

In many states, for instance, the job of lieutenant governor has very few official functions. Lieutenant governors sometimes officially have so little to do that they spend a lot of their time running for governor. When that happens, you often get the best tips on what is going wrong in the governor's administration by paying attention to the lieutenant governor and his or her staff.

PITFALLS

Jargon

All professions, journalism included, have their jargon. It's a shorthand way of explaining the world that is understood by the in-group and helps define it against the out-group. Covering the in-group on a beat exposes a reporter to their jargon and, before long, stories begin to be peppered with it.

Court stories tell of *writs of certiorari;* welfare stories are filled with *implemented viable feasibility criteria;* police stories begin to sound like detectives' reports full of *juvenile male perpetrators.*

Don't forget your readers and viewers. Avoid excessive use of jargon that will not be easily understood by your audience.

The Problem with Friendships

Develop comfortable, first-name relationships with the people on your beat without having those relationships turn into friendship. This is important because getting too chummy with a regular news source can interfere with doing your job.

Tips for Beat Reporters

Don't walk in and ask "What's new?" If your source knew the news, he or she would be an editor. Ask busy officials a specific question about what they are doing about some problem with which they are dealing.

Do read professional publications affecting your beat. Trends occurring elsewhere will sooner or later trickle into your town.

Do ask *why* on every story.

Do get out and talk to people; don't be a "telephone reporter." Reporting works best with personal contact.

Do leave your business card with news sources (and add your home phone number). Encourage them to give you a fast call when they know of a hot breaking story either on or off your beat.

Do remember that the best stories are those that affect the greatest number of people. A story about insurance men interests insurance men. A story about insurance can interest anyone who reads it.

Do be helpful to sources when you can do so without violating any ethical rule. If your source wants a short story in the paper about a Kiwanis dinner or his or her daughter's marriage, walk that extra mile. Such items may get you a page-one story some day.

Don't fear anger. The anger of most sources will be short-lived if you were fair and were doing your job in a professional manner.

Because you are dealing with these people day in and day out, it's easy to find yourself identifying with them instead of with the vague "public interest" taught about in textbooks. If that happens, you can easily begin writing for your sources instead of for your audience.

This is a problem that will never go away as long as reporters are assigned to regular beats. The same closeness and familiarity that helps to breed good news sources can cause conflicts of interests when you find yourself faced with a "negative" story about a "friend" on the beat.

There is no panacea. Some news media will bring in an outside reporter to handle an unpleasant story, to avoid destroying the beat reporter's relationships with regular sources. Other news organizations rotate beat reporters at regular intervals to ensure that no reporter gets too close to the people he or she is covering. Be aware that problems can arise. If you see that they have, ask to be transferred to another beat.

Public Relations Contacts

Public relations (PR) people have a growing role in government and commerce. In many ways, it would be more difficult to do your job without PR people. Public relations people can get out the news on bureaucratic developments with great efficiency, which enables reporters to avoid much wheel spinning. They help provide access to key news sources, and can furnish background information.

On the other hand, PR people also can be roadblocks, can gloss over situations, can hide problems, can omit important detail. When you are dealing with a PR official, remember who is working for whom. Although the title may be "press secretary" or "press assistant," the ultimate goal of a PR person is not to serve the press, but to serve his or her boss. Don't expect this person to subvert the boss's interests in order to serve yours.

What should you expect from a PR professional on a beat?

1. *Fairness.* They should treat you the same as they treat other news media people.

2. *Confidentiality.* If you've got a tip on an exclusive news story and work through a PR official to track down information or comment, you have a right to expect that person not to alert other reporters to what you're working on.

3. *Timeliness.* Government or business officials don't always understand deadlines. PR people are paid to understand them. When you make a request, the PR person needs to understand how quickly you need it answered. Notice of a routine event—such as a meeting or press conference—must be given far enough in advance to enable a reporter to plan coverage. Advance notice of a meeting is a legal requirement in many states.

4. *Honesty.* "No comment" is, in some circumstances, an acceptable—if unwelcome—response from a PR official operating under instructions from the boss. A lie is never acceptable and should earn your undying mistrust.

5. *Completeness.* Documentation should be made available to substantiate claims made in a press release.

DEALING WITH BUDGETS

A government budget is full of numbers, but unless you can see beyond the numbers to their impact on human lives, you won't be very good at writing budget stories.

"Appropriations in the budget can determine how long a pregnant woman waits to see a doctor in a well-baby clinic, how many children are in a grade school class, whether city workers will seek to defeat the mayor on the next election," said Melvin Mencher in his book *News Reporting and Writing.*

If reporters had been doing a better job of covering budgets, New York City might never have been on the brink of bankruptcy in the 1970s. "Because the esoteric nature of public finance tends to frighten off all but the most stalwart, city watchers trusted the government 'experts'. . . . New York's elected officials found it difficult to say 'no,' and the media did not watch the process carefully," said Professor Donna E. Shalala of Columbia University, who was appointed treasurer of Municipal Assistance Corporation, the fiscal agency for New York City.

Knowing what is in a budget and who is making the decisions about what's in and what's out will tell you where the power lies. In Hawaii, for instance, there is an elected state board of education that is supposed to set policy for the public schools and run them. However, the real key to understanding who has power over the schools, as is true with any other government agency, is to know who gets to spend how much money for what. And that decision is not made by the board of education. The budget for the public school system is sent to the state legislature not by the board of education but by the governor.

Once the budget gets to the legislature, it is the senators and representatives—not the board of education members—who decide how much money the schools will receive for operating expenses and for what the money will be spent. In the same fashion, when you want to know where the power lies within your school board, city council, or state legislature, find out who has control over the purse strings.

The budget will tell you the priorities of the people with the power. It is one thing to make a speech denouncing crime, or promising to beef up "the basics" in the public schools, or proposing to preserve open space in an area ripe for development. It is quite another to put your money where your mouth is and appropriate funds for more police and prosecutors and prisons, for hiring more teachers or buying more books or classroom computers, or for purchasing land for a park.

Dealing with a budget document can be overwhelming, especially if you are given it to read and digest on deadline. In such a situation, reporters are generally at the mercy of the budget drafters. The reporters must look at the summaries and take somebody's word about what is in the budget and what is important about it. But when you do have time to look at a government budget critically—or, after churning out the first-day story, once you can get back to the budget again—ask these questions:

Where is the money coming from? Are there any declines in local tax revenues? Who are tax changes most apt to hit? If the sales tax is increased, you ought to know that proportionately it will hit poorer people harder. Say so. Explain why. Give examples. How much more a year will a family of four in a typical income bracket pay? (The Internal Revenue Service's own Form 1040 tax tables for sales tax deductions are a good place to start.)

If the liquor tax is being raised, how much will it add to the cost of a six pack or a bottle of wine or Scotch? When you put it in these terms, it means a lot more to your audience than if you were to report that the new tax will raise $3.7 million in a fiscal year.

If changes in property tax rates are being proposed, either through raising assessments or changing the rates, find examples of how this will affect taxes on typical properties. Take a picture of two or three houses you choose as typical. Tell how much the owners now pay, and how much they will pay if the mayor's new tax schedule goes through. Illustrate this with graphics.

If the "new" money isn't being raised locally, where then? Are new state or federal fund grants built into a municipal budget? Are these apt to be permanent sources of income, or is Johnson City about to hire 25 people based on a federal grant only to find out that, two years down the road, the federal money will lapse and Johnson City must either fire the 25 or pick up the financial load using local property taxes?

What are the changes in this year's budget? Are new people to be hired? How many? For what? What are the new things the city/county/state plans to do that it isn't doing now? Who will this affect and how? Get down to the neighborhood level and figure it out.

How is the budget organized? Are the shares going to the big categories—education, welfare, public safety, defense—in about the same proportion as in the past or not? A pie chart can show you and your readers any dramatic changes that ought to be explained by the people who put the budget together.

Is there a "miscellaneous" category way down at the bottom that seems pretty fat? Is it being used to hide something that the budget drafter doesn't want you to find?

Is the budget balanced? Does the income equal the outgo? Is it really balanced, or is some unusual source of funds—say, a surplus from the year before—being drained to make this year come out even? Is the government borrowing more than normal? Is the borrowing for a reasonable purpose? (There's nothing wrong with a family taking out a mortgage that will be paid back over the useful life of their home. If the family is borrowing to pay the grocery bills, that's trouble! It's the same for a city or a state—borrowing to build a new school makes sense; borrowing to pay the teachers' salaries means financial trouble.)

How much room do legislators really have to use a budget to achieve political goals? Often, very little. The actual maneuvering room in a budget is limited by predetermined fixed costs such as paying off prior borrowing and paying salaries fixed by law or union contract. One estimate said only 10 percent of New York City's multibillion-dollar budget was discretionary because of such constraints.

How good a job is the government doing? This is probably the weakest spot in government budget drafting and in the reaction of reporters to it. Once a program gets going in the bureaucracy, seldom is it looked at seriously by top-level administrators or by the politicians who make budgetary decisions; it's taken as a "given" in the following year's budget.

Proposals for new programs generally get some kind of scrutiny by legislators, however cursory. But once those 25 extra police or building inspectors get hired, once the new neighborhood service center gets built, they usually become permanent items in the budget.

Journalists don't need to be bystanders in this process. You can look for answers. Sometimes an agency already will exist to do the job for which additional money has been budgeted. In Washington, the General Accounting Office is the best-known example of people whose function it is to review how well government performs. At the state level, often auditors or legislative reference bureaus churn out useful analyses of government agencies. Such government watchdogs are less common once you get to the local level, however. At any level of government, a penetrating look by an outside journalist can do a lot to uncover how well a particular part of the bureaucracy is doing its job.

WHAT TO KNOW ABOUT BEATS

Politics

"The successful political reporter must be totally detached about politics," says veteran journalist Jack Germond. "The political writer can't give much of a damn who wins an election. He must be confident the system will survive even if the worst poltroon he knows has just been elected mayor."

On the other hand, Germond advises, political reporters "must like and enjoy politicians as individuals . . . because the important stories of politics rarely come from speeches or television interviews or press conferences. Instead, they come from knowing people who know things and are willing to tell you about them."

Courts

Political science courses will tell you about the court structure and jurisprudence in America. Here we'll talk about the mechanics of covering the courthouse.

Just about all the papers filed in connection with court cases—and there can be tens of thousands of them in a complex civil case—are public records and accessible to reporters. You get at them through the court clerk. Often, you'll need to decipher a coding and filing system to track down a particular case, but once you've found it you normally can either get a copy of the paperwork or actually hold the file in your hands, review it, and take notes about the contents.

Remember that, by definition, there are at least two sides in every court case. In a criminal case, the filing of a charge or an indictment is just that—a charge or an indictment. The defense hasn't had a chance to put on its case yet. In a civil case, anybody can sue anybody over anything and ask for any outrageous amount of monetary damages. That doesn't mean the suit has merit or that the dollar damages requested bear any relationship to reality. A $200-million lawsuit is not by definition 200 times more important than a $1-million lawsuit. It may just mean that a more flamboyant attorney is handling the $200-million case, one who figures he or she can get more publicity with big numbers.

Don't fall for it. Remember that the defendant in a civil suit usually has several weeks to respond. If you've reported the initial suit, be fair and watch the clerk's office for the defendant's response. Report that, too. Don't feel the need to report on every scurrilous allegation just because it's contained in a suit.

Grand juries operate in secret. Many news media have made ethical decisions not to report on grand juries, feeling that to do so might prejudice the rights of potential defendants. At times there will be a prominent case and a grand jury session that cannot be ignored. But if it's secret, how can you cover it? Only by waiting outside the grand jury room (unless the prosecutor has quietly secreted the jury in some unusual place to avoid reporters doing just that), talking to witnesses, and watching for subpoenas to be filed on the public record. Then you need to make an ethical decision about what to publish. In this way grand juries can be covered, after a fashion, despite the secrecy.

The earlier caution about civil suits applies here as well. Grand juries are a one-sided proceeding in which the defense does not get its day in court. If you decide to write something about an ongoing grand jury, you can give the defense a fair hearing by requesting comment from any targets of the grand jury that you publicly identify.

Court hearings and trials themselves usually are open and can be covered by news media. (Common exceptions, however, are cases involving juveniles and family court matters such as divorce or child custody.) Increasingly, TV cameras and newspaper still cameras are being allowed into courtrooms.

There will be occasions, however, especially in pretrial proceedings, when an attorney will try to bar press and public. At times, the attorney succeeds, only to have appeals courts later overrule the decision. Be aware of the law in your jurisdiction about closing

court proceedings. Whenever you come up against a potential closing, alert your supervisors and, possibly, the attorney representing
your news organization, so a formal objection may be made. On
occasion, there will not be enough time to do even this, and you
may need to stand up in court and make an appeal for openness on
behalf of yourself and the public.

Some news media have drafted standard language on a wallet-
sized card so that a reporter covering a court case may rise, ask for
leave to speak, and read into the record some nice legalese citing
appropriate precedent and asking for a proceeding to be kept open.
Sometimes this works; often it doesn't—but it's worth a try as a last
resort.

Juries are off limits to a reporter while a trial is in progress
but are fair game once the verdicts are in. Often some of the most
revealing reporting about a trial comes from asking jurors how they
reacted to the evidence and how they went about reaching their
verdict. How many ballots? How were jurors' minds changed?
Which witnesses did they believe, and which did they not? The
functioning of a jury long has been a subject of interest to lawyers,
novelists, and filmmakers, and can be an engrossing topic for a
reporter, too.

Here are tips on trial coverage from William Ringle, who has
covered everything from municipal courts in Rome, New York, to
the U.S. Supreme Court:

1. Whenever possible, review the paperwork on file ahead of
time. As many explosive stories came from court papers filed before
the trials during the 1973–1974 Watergate cases as from the trials
themselves.

2. Before the trial begins, talk to each lawyer about his or her
"theory" of the case, so you'll have some idea of where each witness's testimony fits in and what each bit of evidence is intended
to prove. You'll also recognize genuinely unexpected evidence
when someone blurts it out.

3. Remember that you won't be able to hear what's going on
during most bench conferences involving only judge and attorneys,
but almost all are transcribed and later become part of the record.
(Ringle knew this and broke the story about a Watergate trial at
which it was revealed that President Nixon called the Canadian
prime minister an "asshole.")

Police and Crime News

Initial word that a crime has been committed normally comes to a reporter either from the police blotter, the police radio, or police officers themselves. How much information a reporter can get from individual police officers depends in large part on the reporter's ability to get to know sources. Access to the police blotter is largely a function of local law and custom. Some police departments offer free access; others offer none. Contents of the police radio are available to anyone with the proper receiving and scanning equipment.

Once a reporter has gathered the news of a crime or an arrest or both, however, a variety of ethical considerations come into play in constructing a story. In recent years, concerns about fair trial rights and privacy have wrought large changes in the way many news media write about crime and its participants and victims.

In the 1960s, for instance, the *Toledo Blade* adopted a code for crime news that, among other things, avoids mentioning "any prior criminal record of the accused" while proceedings are still ongoing. The Toledo paper and many others also step gingerly around reporting of any police claim that a confession has been made, and reporting of any evidence that a judge rules inadmissible—if, for instance, it was gathered as the result of an illegal search and seizure.

Many media still are thrashing about for the proper mix of disclosure and confidentiality. For instance, it may protect the rights of the accused to avoid reporting that police engaged in an illegal search and seizure in Case X, but if media consistently avoid reporting these incidents, how will the public ever find out that the local police do sloppy evidence-gathering work week in and week out? A confession may be extracted when police fail to advise a suspect of his or her right to an attorney, then later be thrown out by a judge on those grounds. How will the public ever learn of this failure by police unless the media report it? How much pressure will there be on police to improve their work if their failings never are reported?

Many media also are broadening their rules concerning the privacy of crime victims. For decades, most media have not published the names of the victims of sex crimes. Now, many media have extended that rule so that victims of robbery and other crimes are not identified by name or address. The idea is that some people might be dissuaded from reporting a crime because they don't want to see their names publicized or, in some instances, because their assailant might not know whom he or she has assailed unless the name shows up in the news.

For the most part, suspects are not named by news media until they are formally charged, which often doesn't occur for hours or days after the initial arrest. There are exceptions, however. If the mayor is arrested in a liquor store robbery, you can be sure most local media will immediately reconsider their no-names-until-charged rule. On the whole, news media prefer to wait until there is a formal charge, a step that usually requires a review by a prosecuting attorney. However, most arrests are made by a police officer, with the prosecutor having had no prior involvement. Many suspects are discharged after arrest and no charges are ever filed. After publicity has been given to the suspect, the damage is done to the reputation of a person who not only never has been convicted, but also never was even formally charged with a crime. For this reason, news media usually wait.

On these matters, a reporter is pretty much bound by the rules of his or her employer. Even where rules have been laid down, however, there will be individual instances that generate an argument for exceptions to be made. Police reporters often will be involved in debate with their editors about whether a particular case should be grounds for violating the general rule.

Business News

A constant challenge for the business beat reporter is deciding what is legitimate business news and what is puffery by advertisers looking for free space. Creed Black, publisher of the *Lexington Herald-Leader,* once put his policy this way: "If it's news, no amount of advertising will keep it out of the paper; if it isn't news, no amount of advertising will get it in."

The detailed implementation of such a philosophy will vary from town to town and newsroom to newsroom. In a small town, the opening of a three-employee business may very well qualify for publication; in a big city, probably not. In West Bilgeville, the 25th anniversary celebration of a local florist may warrant a short story or even a picture; in many places, it will not.

Many of the public relations-produced releases that come across the business reporter's desk deal with personnel changes—promotions, appointments, and retirements. Kit Smith, *Honolulu*

Advertiser financial editor, concedes that rewriting this stuff is "hardly fascinating journalism, but feedback is that these items are well read." Furthermore, occasionally such an item gives a lead to a good story. "Changes in senior executive posts may signal a policy split of some significance," Smith says. "One clue to a split? When the name of a departing executive isn't listed in a press release."

Labor News

Covering the labor beat requires familiarity with the federal laws that govern this segment of society (National Labor Relations Act, Taft-Hartley Act, or Landrum-Griffin Act). As with coverage of many public agencies, coverage of labor unions benefits from legally mandated openness in many areas. Unions are required to file a variety of information with the federal government dealing with salaries of key leaders, pension and insurance funds, and other financial affairs of the unions themselves.

The vocabulary of labor reporting over the years has tended to favor the management side to some extent. For instance, the employers make "offers," whereas union leaders make "demands." Work hard at leveling out the terminology so that it's fair to both sides.

Perspective and history are particularly important in describing any labor—management conflict. How do wages (and fringe benefits) in this industry or this company compare to those in others? Has the industry been strike prone in the past, or has it tended to take negotiations down to the wire and settle without a strike? Has the firm been losing work to nonunion companies that pay lower wages? Place contract terms in context—saying carpenters won $3 an hour more in wages tells little unless you know what they were earning before and the length of the contract.

POINT OF VIEW

Most reporters' beats are set up to coincide with bureaucratic structures—the White House, the state house, city hall, the police department—and that tends to breed in many reporters a point of view that parallels that of the bureaucrats. Resist this.

"In planning and executing news coverage, we usually start by asking: What did the president (governor, mayor, Congress, legislature, council, board, or court) do today?" said Robert S. Boyd, Washington bureau chief for Knight-Ridder Newspapers.

> But we should ask: What's important and interesting to readers that involves—or should involve—the government? For example, instead of assigning a reporter to tell what the EPA did today, we should tell that reporter to answer these questions: Is the environment cleaner or dirtier? What is the government doing about it? At what cost? Are there better ways of accomplishing the goal?

Too many reporters confuse a beat with its buildings or its bigwigs. As a result, covering local government often is viewed as dull business. Sometimes it is, yet a reporter will soon learn whether local government is functioning effectively, as a result of his or her examination of the responsiveness of the police and fire departments, condition of the streets, rate of apartment construction, price of water, and number of public-access channels on your cable television. This list could be very long. Reporters can look into crevices, and should.

The best kind of coverage of any bureaucracy occurs when reporters spend time with the people in the middle or at the bottom who actually do the work. At city hall, for example, the offices that directly touch the citizens are those dealing with parks, sewers, water, planning, traffic, and street repair. The people working in these offices love attention, but reporters often spend all day in the mayor's office or at council meetings, neither of which touch their audience as directly as do the lower levels of the city hall bureaucracy.

Covering city hall, says Chuck Haga, city editor of the *Grand Forks Herald*, involves more than just showing up at the stylish old building where "twice a month, the mayor and 14 city council members take over comfortable, wide-backed chairs in a room upstairs, where they enact a few ordinances, repeal some old ones and argue whether cats should be leashed." City hall is out there—where potholes and parking tickets are fixed, and where streetlights aren't always lit. Most of us do not pay much attention to these services except when they break down or when city/county taxes to support them are raised. But we do quickly notice when the trash is not picked up, the police do not respond quickly to our call, the streets have potholes, or neighborhood dogs make—well, distressing—use of our lawn.

The quality of our lives in the nation begins with the quality of our lives at home. One of your major jobs as a journalist is to monitor the quality of this life and, if the public wills, to help improve it.

Citizens have expectations about government that influence what local government can do. Political scientists have suggested that citizens have four types of expectations of government. They see governments at all levels as

Promoters of community growth
Suppliers of life's good things
Custodians and caretakers
Judges who decide among conflicting interests

Differences of opinion always arise. For example, a government that promotes growth of new housing may arouse the ire of citizens who feel the community already has enough housing, schools, police, or fire protection. Local government fits a social system. A change in one part normally causes adjustments throughout the system, as a slight shift in the rudder causes an airliner to slightly change direction. One part can move the whole thing, a little at first, a lot later. Public affairs reporters need to think long range.

REFERENCES

Berman, David R. *State and Local Politics*. 4th ed. Boston: Allyn and Bacon, 1984.

Brooks, Brian S. *News Reporting and Writing*. New York: St. Martin's Press, 1980.

Burns, James MacGregor, J. W. Peltason, and Thomas E. Cronin. *State and Local Politics: Government By the People*. 4th ed. Englewood Cliffs, NJ: Prentice-Hall, 1984.

Keller, Mike. *The Book: Or How to Succeed at the Honolulu Advertiser by Really Trying*. Honolulu, 1976 (Adapted from *Learning in the Newsroom*, American Newspaper Publishers Association Foundation, Reston, VA, 1973).

MacDougall, Curtis D. *Interpretative Reporting*. 8th ed. New York: Macmillan, 1982.

Mencher, Melvin. *News Reporting and Writing*. 2d ed. Dubuque, IA: William C. Brown, 1981.

CHAPTER 9
Mining Documents for Information

Remember that the foundation stone for effective investigative reporting is the dull, often boring, repetitious record-checking chores at a police station, a city hall, or a courthouse.

Clark Mollenhoff

People you interview can be forgetful, or just plain liars. Or they can change their stories afterward, leaving a trusting reporter swaying gently in the breeze.

When you directly observe "reality," you are really seeing only a part of it. The view from your vantage point—or the view of the incident or handful of incidents you happen to see—may mask important parts of the real world.

Gathering information by using documents solves some—but by no means all—of these problems. Documents can lie, too, if the person who prepared the document is a liar, or misinformed, or biased. But documents usually don't change their stories afterward. The author of the document may have seen only a part of reality, too, and thus be unable to paint a full and accurate account in writing. But in many public proceedings there is a systematic, thorough attempt to gather facts from several perspectives to "fill in the blanks" on whatever forms must be prepared and filed.

For these reasons, the use of documents is sometimes the best way to gather the information needed to paint a journalistic picture of reality. Because of our society's penchant for "putting it in writing," file cabinets—and, increasingly, computers—are often the best source of a thorough accounting of what has gone before. This

163

is especially true when you are dealing with government, which seems to require every form filled out and filed in triplicate.

Prosecutors can tell you they have a 95 percent conviction rate. But a check of court records may demonstrate that the cases that go to trial have only 58 percent convictions. Or the 95 percent figure may be built upon faulty reasoning—for instance, someone charged with murder, rape, robbery, and driving without a license may be counted as a "conviction" if he pleads guilty to the license charge. The law may instruct city tax assessors to list property at 60 percent of its market value. But property tax records may show that the mayor's compaign manager has his house assessed at 40 percent of what homes on that block were selling for last year. A legislator may deny having outside financial interests, but finding his name on the mortgage for a plot of land just condemned by the state for a new highway route argues persuasively that it just isn't so.

America is the home of the ubiquitous filing cabinet. If it happened and it's worth putting on the TV news or writing about in a newspaper, there is a fair chance that somewhere, in some office, somebody filled out a form about it. Those collected forms can be a gold mine for a reporter seeking to find out how the world really works, as opposed to how officialdom says it works.

EXPLORING DOCUMENTS

Documents can be explored by reporters in two major ways:

1. A search for a single document that produces the "smoking gun" of an investigation story. The Geraldine Ferraro story in the box on p. 166 is a good example.

2. A structured attempt to summarize what a whole set of documents says about the real world—for instance, the real world of drunk-driving arrests, of tax assessments, of government non-bid contracts awarded to political campaign contributors, of sentencing practices by criminal court judges. Chapter 10 demonstrates ways to approach this sort of systematic job using *content analysis*.

With either goal in mind, the reporter must start with some idea of what is there in the first place. Often, a story will seem impossible because the reporter too quickly despairs of being able to find the documentary evidence necessary to prove a hypothesis or to later provide protection from a libel suit. But numerous sources of documentary information easily can be explored by an industrious journalist.

Vital Statistics

Births, deaths, marriages, divorces, and name changes all have to be recorded. The record may be filed with a county clerk or health department (births or deaths), a family court (divorces), a secretary of state or courthouse (name changes). Somewhere, the government keeps track of the rites of passage that mark all our lives.

Generally, such events are public record at the time they occur. Many newspapers still carry agate-type summaries of all recent births, deaths, and marriage license applications, for instance. However, concern over *rights of privacy* in recent years has led some jurisdictions to deny access to such information at later times by journalists and others not directly involved. For instance, although you can obtain a copy of your own birth certificate or marriage license, in some places a reporter could not.

Don't assume you can't get such information, however. Try! And don't take the first "no" for an answer. When seeking vital statistics, as with any other arguably *public record,* operate on the premise that you have a right to it. You may be cut off at the pass by some mid-level civil servant afraid of erring on the side of openness, but pressure on a higher-up by you (or the news media lawyer) often can free the originally denied material.

For what would you want this sort of information?

A divorce file is perhaps the best example of a useful lode of facts in the vital statistics category. When a couple divorces, often there is a property dispute. To resolve the dispute, the judge needs full information on their assets: income earned, stocks owned, real estate in husband's or wife's name (or both), cash balances in the bank. Names and ages of children are often in the record, something that can be of use years later if you are trying to cross-check names of a public official's relatives for a story on nepotism. (Birth certificates are another good source for nepotism stories, because they tell the mother's maiden name and can help you track in-laws on her side of the family.) One major obstacle, as mentioned, may be rights of privacy. Some states keep most divorce proceedings hid-

Ferraro Owns Half of Firm, Records Show

James Asher,
Ray Holton,
and Gilbert M. Gaul,
Knight-Ridder Newspapers

ALBANY–A document on file in a state office here shows that Democratic vice presidential candidate Geraldine Ferraro, who has downplayed her involvement in the real-estate operations of her husband, owns one-half of the stock of P. Zaccaro Co. Inc., the family real estate firm founded by her husband's father.

She is also a vice president of the firm, according to the document, which is an application for a broker's license. The document is a sworn statement signed by both Ferraro and her husband, John A. Zaccaro, under penalty of perjury, and filed with the New York State Insurance Department on Aug. 5, 1983.

The firm that Ferraro owns jointly with her husband has managerial involvement in at least 14 properties owned by 14 different companies, partnerships and individuals. Those properties are in the Little Italy and Chinatown section of Manhattan.

The scope of the firm's operations was documented in a review of New York City property-tax bills that show that real estate tax bills for the affected properties are forwarded to P. Zaccaro Co. for payment—a common practice for firms that manage real estate.

The company is not Zaccaro's only real-estate enterprise. According to mortgage documents on file in the offices of the Borough of Manhattan and the public statements by an attorney who is a partner of Zaccaro, he has an interest in two other real-estate companies that own shares of five Manhattan properties. Ferraro is not listed in public records for those two companies. . . .

den behind a veil of secrecy in a family court where only the principals have access to the facts. Confidentiality is also a problem when a birth occurred out of wedlock. Statistics indicate that presently as many as one sixth of the births in the United States are out of wedlock, and some jurisdictions treat these birth certificates with more secrecy.

Police Records

Almost every reporter at one time or another has dealt with police records. The old, familiar *blotter,* which contains a record of everybody arrested and charged, in chronological order, is a primary source for police reporters across the land.

Blotters from months or years earlier can be a source of information, if they are available. (Often, however, the privacy hurdle gets in the way of access to them). It is important, however, to remember the limitations of an arrest record. People get arrested all the time without being charged. Often, people are charged only to have the prosecutor drop the charges before trial because the evidence just isn't there or is weak. Some people go to trial and are acquitted. Thus, finding an arrest record is only the first step in a long process.

Normally, you can get the name, age, and address of the person arrested, time and place of arrest, and legal citation of the charge involved, but the amount of access you get and the amount of detail on the blotter once you do get access vary from locale to locale. Furthermore, many officials tend not to regard access as a right. One Texas attorney general said police blotters in that state were made available to reporters "only as a matter of courtesy." On the other hand, a Wisconsin decision said denial of access was justified "only in the unusual or exceptional case."

Tax Information

Generally speaking, it is difficult or impossible to obtain state or federal income tax records. Once again this information is withheld on grounds of privacy. There are exceptions, however. The Internal Revenue Service does have procedures for making available certain tax information on nonprofit entities and other charitable groups. Your local IRS office can explain the procedures to you.

Property taxes are another matter. Just about everywhere, you can find in public records detailed information on every taxable parcel of real property: who owns it; who used to own it; the amount for which it is assessed; to whom the tax bill is sent. There are ways to keep some of this information concealed—such as by holding property in the name of corporations, partnerships, or blind trusts— but generally, property tax records are among the most valuable repositories of public information for the journalist.

Voting Lists

These are public record everywhere. Voting lists have names and addresses. Sometimes they show party affiliation, social security numbers, telephone numbers (even unlisted ones), birth dates, or even arcane bits of data like the voter's mother's maiden name (obtained at time of registration so that, if challenged at the polling place, the voter can be asked a question that will verify the identity of the person who is voting). If voting registers are available from past years, you can use them to trace a person's previous address— at least where they *said* they lived—at given times in the past. Or you can demonstrate that some civic-minded candidate for public office never even bothered to vote until he decided to run.

You also can compare voting lists with other public records to find inconsistencies. Let's say Sam Sleazy is registered to vote in the 19th District. Sam also owns a house in the 23rd District and the property tax records on that house show that Sam is getting a $10,000 homestead exemption on that house because he claims it's his personal residence. You have a story. Either Sam is voting illegally or he is claiming the exemption illegally.

Reverse Telephone Book

Most television stations and newspapers have such phone directories, which list phone numbers in numerical order and tell you who has each number. These books also organize phone number information by street and house number. Thus, if you want to identify the neighbors of someone who lives at 336 West Siwash Avenue, this crisscross telephone directory will tell you the phone numbers and names of the people at 334 and 338 (assuming the phone numbers are not unlisted).

Building Departments

You need a building permit to build something or to make modifications to a building above a certain dollar value. City inspectors are supposed to check construction in progress to make sure that electrical, plumbing, and other building codes are being followed. Inspectors also go through completed buildings to make sure changes haven't been made that take the building out of compliance with the codes. Building or fire inspectors also check for compliance with fire codes. A building found in violation is issued a notice of violation and may be fined or brought into court. Permit, inspection, and violation records normally are on file at your municipal building department.

City Directories

Private firms publish city directories for most mid-sized and large cities in the United States. These can be found in almost every newsroom. In addition to the basic information you would find in the phone book, they often give name of spouse, place of employment, officers of a corporation, and what kind of business it's in. Also, occasionally a phone number that is unlisted by the phone company will creep into the city directory because its information is compiled independently. Because people move every five years, on the average, one thing to watch out for is that some data in city directories is outdated. Double-check it.

Corporate Records

The laws vary from state to state, but every state has some procedure for formally organizing a corporation. Even with small, privately held local companies, normally you can track down information about its original owners and officers, capitalization, and stockholders. Original incorporation papers for a small company may be misleading. In most cases, an attorney will have done the incorporating and the attorney's name or the names of legal secretaries in the attorney's law office may show up in various official positions on the incorporation papers. The names may have little to do with who really owns the company, so make sure you don't put outdated information into a news story.

DOMESTIC PROFIT CORPORATION ● **STATE OF HAWAII** ●

MAKE REMITTANCE PAYABLE TO: DEPARTMENT OF COMMERCE AND CONSUMER AFFAIRS   ORIGINAL-RETURN BY MARCH 31
FILING FEE $10.00   BUSINESS REGISTRATION DIVISION   PENALTY FOR LATE FILING
                                                1010 Richards Street   YOUR CANCELLED CHECK IS YOUR RECEIPT
                                    Mailing Address: P.O. Box 40, Honolulu, HI. 96810

ANNUAL CORPORATION EXHIBIT   FOR THE YEAR ENDED DECEMBER 31, _____
                                                                              (YEAR)

CORPORATE NAME AND MAILING ADDRESS:

IF THE MAILING ADDRESS HAS CHANGED, LINE OUT OLD ADDRESS AND TYPE OR PRINT NEW ADDRESS BELOW.
(INCLUDE ZIP CODE):

(READ INSTRUCTIONS ON REVERSE SIDE)

Authorized Capital   Paid-in Capital (CANNOT EXCEED AUTHORIZED CAPITAL)

Class (Common, Etc.)	Shares	Par Share	Par Total	Class (Common, Etc.)	Shares	Amount
		$	$			$
		$	$			$
		$	$			$

(If no par share, read instruction)

NUMBER OF SHARES HELD IN TREASURY, IF ANY _____ (not shares outstanding held by shareholders)

(IF MORE THAN ONE CLASS, STATE SEPARATELY BY CLASS) _____

OFFICERS: LIST ALL OFFICERS. EVERY CORPORATION, INCLUDING PROFESSIONAL CORPORATIONS, MUST HAVE A MINIMUM OF TWO PERSONS AS OFFICERS.

OFFICE HELD   NAME IN FULL   RESIDENCE ADDRESS (Do not list business address.) (INCLUDE NUMBER & STREET, APT. NO., CITY, STATE & ZIP CODE)

PROFESSIONAL CORPORATIONS: SEE INSTRUCTIONS ON BACK OF THIS FORM.

DIRECTORS: (MAY STATE SAME AS ABOVE IF APPLICABLE. AT LEAST ONE MUST BE A HAWAII RESIDENT.)   RESIDENCE ADDRESS (DO NOT LIST BUSINESS ADDRESS.) (INCLUDE NO. & STREET, APT. NO., CITY, STATE & ZIP CODE)

1. DATE INCORPORATED: _____

2. SPECIFIC NATURE OF CORPORATE BUSINESS: _____
    (IF NOT SPECIFIC, EXHIBIT WILL BE REJECTED. IF INACTIVE DURING PERIOD, STATE INACTIVE.)

DECLARATION

I DECLARE UNDER THE PENALTIES SET FORTH IN SECTION 416-94, HAWAII REVISED STATUTES, THAT THIS EXHIBIT HAS BEEN EXAMINED BY ME, AND TO
THE BEST OF MY KNOWLEDGE AND BELIEF IS A TRUE, CORRECT AND COMPLETE EXHIBIT, MADE IN GOOD FAITH, FOR THE PERIOD STATED.

DATE _____   _____   _____
                           (Signature of authorized corporate officer)   (office held)
                           (If attorney-in-fact signs, attach power of attorney.)

FILE NO.   015-0915-10

FILE THIS ORIGINAL COPY. PHOTO COPY WILL NOT BE ACCEPTED.

Figure 9.1   Annual corporation report required by the state of Hawaii.

In some states, the annual statements that corporations are required to file do have updated lists of officers and stockholders, and even financial information on how much business the corporation did during the year and in what broad categories of commerce.

Unfortunately, in most places you have to know what you're looking for in corporate files before you can find it. You can't, for instance, go to a secretary of state's office and ask for a list of all corporations that list Harvey Wallbanger as an officer or stockholder. The system normally doesn't work that way—although, as more places get computerized, it might someday. If that happens, reporters will find their jobs easier.

Sometimes you must track through records in more than one state to get a true picture of the activities of a corporation. An out-of-state corporation may file only minimal records in your state capital, but may have a full record on file in the state where it is headquartered. Delaware is a particularly useful place to look for corporate records. Many firms incorporate there because Delaware has written its law specifically to make it easier and cheaper to do. It takes about an hour to charter a corporation in Delaware, and the process provides that state with 10 percent of its revenues.

Publicly traded corporations must comply with the rules of the Securities and Exchange Commission (SEC). Reports filed with the SEC deal with major stockholders and the increases and decreases in their holdings, and with buying and selling of stock by corporate officers, directors, and other "insiders." Changes such as these can give a reporter insight into what is going on inside a big firm.

Lawbooks

Most newspaper libraries keep up-to-date versions of local and state lawbooks. Law libraries have even bigger collections. Tips to remember when checking out a law:

> Laws are changed often—amended, updated, repealed. Be sure to review not only the bound copy of the lawbook, but also the insert pamphlets in each book that give you recent changes, or the annual "session laws" volumes detailing each act passed by a legislature or city council. If you don't, you may write a story about how somebody seems to be in violation of Section 301-F only to find out later that 301-F was overhauled by the last legislature and the violation no longer applies.
>
> Watch the nuances of language. *May* and *shall* may have only minor differences in everyday conversation, but they have differing meanings in a law.

Look for interpretations of the law. Attorneys general and judges hand down opinions all the time applying the general language of a law to specific situations—or even challenging a law for some constitutional reason. Many lawbooks will list the important opinions, but check with a lawyer familiar with a particular field to see if you have overlooked a legal opinion bearing on the case at hand.

The Courthouse

When a person is charged with a crime, the system starts building a paper trail on the case. Ultimately, the file may contain information on the crime itself, the testimony of witnesses, details of an indictment, recommendations by probation officers, sentencing, and any appeals. Probation reports can be especially useful. Whereas a trial itself will only entertain testimony about the particular crime charged, a probation officer's presentence report generally contains a lot of detail about the person's background that a judge can use in determining the proper sentence. Alas, in many jurisdictions this helpful and informative report remains confidential for privacy reasons.

Criminal law is not the only thing that brings people into court. Thousands of civil suits are filed daily when people can't settle disputes over such matters as property or money. Again, the filing of a civil suit starts an official file in some court clerk's office. The plaintiff lays out the case in simple terms. The defendant files an answering brief stating his or her side of the case. Both sides begin the *discovery* process of obtaining records and interviewing witnesses. Transcripts of the trial itself appear. Appeals briefs again summarize the facts in support of the case for each side. By the time a civil case works its way through all these steps, a lot of material about it has been entered into the record.

Except in extraordinary circumstances, all the material relating to a civil lawsuit is public record. Even better, the fact that something you report comes from a court record usually gives it *privilege.* Generally, in most states, if you make a fair and accurate report of the contents of a court file, you cannot successfully be sued afterward for libel. This is why reporters get excited when they come upon a particularly interesting and useful fact in a courthouse file.

Civil lawsuits over money frequently expose to public view a broad look at the participants' financial status—income statements, outstanding loans, or business connections. The contents of a lengthy civil suit are often the best place for you as a reporter to get a good grasp of the financial and business connections of anyone about whom you are curious.

Two special categories of civil court records are worth separate mention: *probate* records and *bankruptcy* records. When a person dies, the distribution of the estate goes through a legal process in court known as probate. As *Honolulu Advertiser* investigative reporter James Dooley observes, "It's a little crass to say, but when people die suddenly, often secrets that they have labored all their lives to keep secret get stuck in the probate files." Probate files are public record. They can be helpful even if you are investigating living persons. Often, their parents or other relatives have died and left them something in a will. Details on this property can be found in the courthouse's probate file on the deceased.

Going bankrupt is a little like dying in one regard—all your financial affairs get spread out in public view. When people file for bankruptcy (the bankruptcy laws are federal laws and the filings are in federal court), they generally must outline in detail their assets and liabilities. This information is available even about people and corporations who are just one step short of bankruptcy; the federal bankruptcy law has a provision (known as Section 11) that allows people to get under the wing of the bankruptcy court while they try to get their affairs in order and reorganize their overwhelming debts so they eventually can pay them. This, too, requires a public filing full of financial information.

Charities

Many states require charities to file at least some rudimentary financial information. From these records you can get names of officers and often full details on budgets, including how much of the donated funds are spent on administration and fund raising.

Two other useful sources of information about specific charities are the National Information Bureau in New York City, a 65-year-old group that compiles reports on nonprofit agencies, and the Philanthropic Advisory Service of the Council of Better Business

Using Computers

The filing cabinets of government and social agencies always have been key sources of the day's news. These traditional sources of information are now giving way to record-keeping systems that offer almost unlimited opportunities for you to increase the depth and scope of your reporting about the community. These new record-keeping systems use computers. Filing cabinets are being replaced by reels of magnetic tape, and record clerks are being replaced by computer programmers.

At all levels of government vast amounts of useful information about the community already are collected in the files of agencies and departments. The computer offers an efficient way of collating this information. The result should be increased in-depth reporting about the community—comprehensive, factual reports about the social and economic conditions that explain what is happening in declining neighborhoods, in the public schools of our changing cities, in the downtown and neighborhood business districts that compete with the shopping centers.

From the reporter's point of view, these new computerized files have two advantages over traditional sets of records: (1) rapid accessibility, and (2) the means to discover new information from the facts stored in the computer. (It is no problem at all for a computer to consolidate available information.)

Computers also enable us to obtain more precise descriptions of a set of information. For example, a rising juvenile crime rate might more adequately be described in terms of the crime trends among each age group. In the jargon of the pollster and survey researcher, this kind of information is obtained by cross-tabulations—a simple task for the computer, a tedious one for the clerk or reporter. The point is that the flexibility of the computerized file allows the reporter more creativity, more freedom in gathering news.

Obtaining cross-tabulations also illustrates the second advantage of computerized files: accessibility. Not only are computers incredibly quicker than human clerks or reporters leafing through manual records, computers as clerks are more accurate because they don't get tired.

Third, and most important, computers don't have the built-in biases of most humans. Any set of information about the community—whether in a computerized or traditional file—may contain biases arising from the manner in which it was gathered. Certain individuals may have been overlooked, certain events omitted. In compiling what is available, however, additional bias may be introduced in traditional files. A clerk may forget to check one file or one record book, or inadvertently skip a page. Problems also occur when records are temporarily removed from the file for routine use. Computers eliminate all these errors, except any bias in the way the information was gathered. Furthermore, clerks sometimes leave out marginal cases. Computers require precise definitions of the information desired and so eliminate this kind of bias also.

If the mass media are to utilize the potential of computerized information files, reporters and editors must come to view the computerized file itself—not just its keepers—as a news source. To exploit this new freedom for creative reporting, you must be trained to use these new sources. This means learning the rudiments of electronic data processing and data analysis. As long as you are content with computer printouts that are simply replicas of traditional files, then the ability to directly search computerized files will not be necessary. But for creative reporters who want to exploit the advantages of these technological advances, the ability to properly and directly employ the computer becomes a necessary skill.

Bureaus (CBBB), 1515 Wilson Blvd., Arlington, Virginia 22209, which has a set of standards for charitable solicitations. The CBBB frequently publishes lists of charities that fail to disclose pertinent information or that generate many "inquiries."

Tax-exempt organizations also must file special reports (called Form 990) with the IRS. Unlike most IRS information, these are public and copies can be obtained from IRS offices. The form, which must be filed if gross receipts exceed $25,000, lists a balance sheet, expenses, salaries of officers, and data from earlier years as well. Another useful form is IRS Form 1023, the one the charity fills out to persuade the IRS to give it tax-exempt status.

Licensing Records

State and local governments license and regulate all manner of professions from doctors and dentists and lawyers to masseurs and barbers and escort agency operators. David Anderson and Peter Benjaminson, in their book *Investigative Reporting* note that, in New York City, "a person must have a license to hold a block party, be an able seaman, embalm, exterminate, grade hay and straw, smoke on piers, establish a seaplane base, store rubber cement, make sausages, transplant hard shell clams, and open a deli."

Although you are not apt to run across many unlicensed sea-plane bases to expose during your journalistic career, by now it should be obvious that there are a lot of files, filled with licensing information. Keep them in mind as a source. Applicants often file personal background information to get licensed, and that material is often public record for the journalist to peruse. Unfortunately, many jurisdictions are beginning to lock these files from public view to preserve the licensees' privacy. At a minimum, however, you can normally determine if Person X is properly licensed by State Y to do business in Profession Z.

That in itself can be a story. You may find that the Amalgam-ated Towing Company got a city contract to haul away overparked cars even though the company lacks a city towing license in the first place, or that Dr. John Doe, who got his medical license yanked in North Dakota after pleading guilty to Medicare fraud, is happily practicing in your state even though the law prohibits convicted criminals from having medical privileges.

Regulatory Agencies

This century has seen the proliferation of a new kind of government agency—arms of the executive branch that function like courts or legislatures. Examples at the federal level include the Federal

Communications Commission (FCC), Federal Trade Commission (FTC), and National Labor Relations Board (NLRB). At the local and state level, zoning and land use boards and public utilities commissions function in this way. These government panels, which often have part-time members, are given wide authority to adopt regulations having force of law, to carry out licensing activities, to sit as judicial panels and settle disputes, and to set rate schedules for private companies or utilities.

Records of their meetings and hearings are generally open and often instructive. For instance, the best place to look for insight into a labor union or a labor dispute is often in the National Labor Relations Board records, which may contain filings by the union, by the employers with which it does business, and by the NLRB's own investigative staff. For a given labor–management dispute, the NLRB file can give you the same sort of information that courthouse files provide on a civil lawsuit.

Campaign Spending Records

The laws fluctuate widely, but the federal government and most states now have some requirement that candidates for public office file reports telling where they got their campaign funds (at least the larger contributions) and how they spent them. The filing of these reports makes news while a campaign is taking place, as political reporters write stories about who gave how much to whom and which candidate has the big war chest. The reports then sit in a file cabinet somewhere and often are overlooked when, years down the road, a reporter is trying to establish a history of the political ties of someone in the news.

Scouring campaign spending reports for meaningful information can be trying. The lists generally are not alphabetical or structured in any fashion calculated to make analysis easy. In most states, there is no need for the candidate to supply information about the business ties of each contributor. Thus, if you want to find out how much money came to Governor Phoghorn from Wallcrack Architectural Partners, Inc., you must look for the names of all the principals (and their spouses) and probably you still will not feel too certain that you have found everything. Nonetheless, the search often can be worthwhile. The task can be eased by using a computer to match up lists of, say, campaign contributors against government contractors.

Grantor–Grantee Index

Most land transactions and mortgages are filed in some public place. The *grantor–grantee index* for property in your area may be located in a land court, or a bureau of conveyances, or a register of deeds, or some other office with an obscure title. Whatever its name, this office can be well worth a visit when you are gathering information for a story. This is where you will find answers to questions such as, When did John Jones buy and sell any land or real property? What are his outstanding mortgages and from which bank and at what rate? Has any creditor placed a lien on his home that he must pay off before he sells it? What was the purchase price of a parcel of land? In many jurisdictions, you will find the latter information in the form of tax stamps that give you at least a rough idea. Because of the existence of two sets of property records, you can find out both who owns a particular piece of property (property tax records) and what property a particular person owns (grantor–grantee index).

Although property records are fairly complete, thorough, and up to date, they may not be perfect. In recent years, with bank mortgage rates soaring, more and more people have resorted to private financing for property transactions. These transactions may or may not be publicly filed. One common method is for the seller to *take back* a mortgage, accepting a down payment and agreeing to formally transfer the property some years down the road after the buyer has come up with the rest of the money. In some areas this is called an *agreement of sale,* in other places a *contract for deed.* Practices vary from state to state. Often the existence of such a sales agreement will show up on property tax records because the buyer assumes responsibility for tax payments right away, even though the deed has not formally changed hands.

Plain Old Files

Every government office keeps some sort of files about what it does. What's in them? Expense account information for civil servants or members of boards and commissions who travel at public expense; information on who has guns registered and who is allowed to carry a concealed weapon; results of health inspections of restaurants and inspections for water pollution, air pollution, sewage outflow. (For a more thorough look at hundreds of types of documents, how to get them and use them, pick up *The Reporter's Handbook: An Investigator's Guide to Documents and Techniques,* edited by John Ullmann and Steve Honeyman for Investigative Reporters and Editors, Inc.)

Depending on how useful your state's "sunshine law" is (see Chapter 11 for a discussion of these laws), you can get at some, most, or all of what you want with just a simple request for access to the particular file drawer or folder that contains what you need.

A final caution about public records: All such information is put on file by people, each of whom can sometimes make mistakes or act wrongly. Double-check findings with other sources. Some public records are privileged, meaning that you are not apt to be successfully sued *if* you write about them fairly and accurately. However, just the fact that this information is privileged does not absolve the journalist from double-checking and trying to determine whether it is accurate. No piece of information is true just because it's in writing.

The Reporter as Detective of Documents

There are two basic kinds of investigative reporters—documents people and source people. Documents people are the ones who spend all their time in the basement of the courthouse, the Bureau of Conveyances and places like that. And source people try to find somebody who has done all that research and get him to tell them the results. Sometimes, combining the approaches works quite well.

If you do the documentary research yourself, you'll familiarize yourself with the subject. Your depth of understanding will increase; you're not going to have it if you get it from somebody else. It will also stand you in very good stead if somebody sues you for libel because you can then produce pieces of paper—tangible evidence—to prove what you said in the story. This is a much better position to be in than if you simply went on the word of an unidentified source.

If you printed a story quoting an unidentified source and someone sues you for libel and asks, "Where did you get that information? Prove this is true," and you can only say you got it "from an unidentified source—I can't tell you who it is"—you're in deep trouble in that libel action. But if you have the documents and evidence, you're a lot better off.

I have a standard kind of research pattern—with variations—that I run through to begin any investigation. If I'm trying to find out about a particular person, there are a number of things which I will always try to do. The first thing to do is go into the library at your newspaper—the so-called morgue—and pull clippings on that particular individual or corporate entity.

Second, go to the local courthouse to look up the individual's name in the indexes in the clerk's office, (a) looking for both the individual's name and any corporate entities that the individual is involved in and (b) pulling out lawsuits and just taking a look at them to familiarize myself with the person's legal history or litigation history.

Third, if you know what corporations the individual is involved in, go to the proper state government office and pull out the corporate papers on those companies. Another source of information about companies is the annual reports. They tell you the current officers and directors. Depending on the size of the company, the annual reports also tell you who the accountant is or the person who does the books for the company, which is sometimes useful to know.

Fourth, make a stop by the Bureau of Conveyances to find out if the individual has been involved in real estate transactions. Often the Bureau of Conveyances has other things that are filed there as a legal record: (a) mortgages; (b) tax liens; (c) if he has ever assigned his power of attorney to anybody, that will be there. There are a number of different things in there besides real estate purchases.

Fifth, probate court handles cases arising whenever a person dies without a will or there's a problem with the deceased's estate or there is a legal dissolution of the estate. The probate court is a wonderful source of information. You find things in there that you just can't find anyplace else. There's no longer a way to hide the fact that you have investments you may not want publicly known. If you die accidentally and haven't had time to set up your affairs as you'd have liked to, these secrets are going to show up in the probate court file.

A sixth source of good information is property tax records. You look up property by the tax map key, which is just a number. The title history sheet traces each transaction on that property for the past two decades or so. There are also maps of the property.

I like to approach a story on which I'm working by originally doing as much documentary research as I can. You learn a lot by studying the materials. You go through all these documents, which are sometimes hard to figure out. You learn about the subject. You arm yourself in advance so that when you go to interview the people who are actually involved, they are impressed that you have taken the time and the trouble to find out about the details before you talk to them. And they sometimes will be a little bit more willing to talk to you about the matter, simply because they realize that you'd done some work on it already. But it also gives you the ability to cut through all the crap because you have already done some work and you have a working understanding of the subject you're interested in.

James Dooley, Investigative Reporter, *Honolulu Advertiser*

REFERENCES

Anderson, David, and Peter Benjaminson. *Investigative Reporting.* Bloomington, IN: Indiana University Press, 1976.

Ullman, John, and Steve Honeyman, eds. *The Reporter's Handbook: An Investigator's Guide to Documents and Techniques.* New York: St. Martin's Press, 1983.

CHAPTER 10

Unobtrusive Community Portraits

Sometimes people can't tell you what you want to know. If you ask several judges, for example, to tell you whether or not they are biased for or against any particular group of people—for example, women or blacks—most certainly the unanimous answer will be no. All of us believe that we are doing our jobs fairly, yet that may not be true.

If people cannot tell you, then perhaps the trail of documents that most of us leave behind us will provide fingerprints of our actions. If so, you may be able to use *content analysis*—a social science research technique for the *systematic* study of documents— to find out things about officials of which they may not be aware, or only dimly aware. One document may provide only a glimpse. Several may provide answers.

Public records exist by the tons—as do private records, although they may be less accessible. Records can overwhelm you, unless you have a systematic approach to them, but if you can unravel entire sets of documents they may tell you much more than an individual record. If you are skilled, you can make them add up to far more than the sum of the individual parts.

Documents will let you make supportable inferences about job performance, for example. Looking at how a particular judge handled several hundred cases allows you to draw reasonable inferences about whether or not the judge is fair to, say, teenagers charged with drug offenses. Does Judge Browne "throw the book" at them? Does Judge Greene "let them off easy"? Lawyers freely admit (privately) that they shop for judges for certain types of clients

183

and certain types of offenses. How accurate are their assumptions? Content analysis can tell you.

Social scientist Bernard Berelson defined content analysis as a research technique for the objective, systematic, and quantitative description of the manifest content of documents. A key term in this definition is *objective*, a term familiar to journalists. This word, to Berelson, implies *reliability* and *replicability,* which mean being able to define a task so explicitly that anyone else can follow the directions and obtain the same results. For example, Sears Roebuck provides directions simple enough so that different people can follow them to assemble toy wagons that look alike.

To "assemble" a content analysis, you need to establish clear rules regarding what you are looking for, rules so clear that others could follow them without difficulty. That is easier said than done because what seems crystal clear to you often is difficult to explain to others. But, as we shall see, making this effort is essential in content analysis.

USING CONTENT ANALYSIS

Skillful use of documents offers unique ways to evaluate community organizations. In 1983 the *Richmond Times-Dispatch* assigned a special team the task of answering a simple question: Is justice dispensed fairly in Virginia? Two reporters, Mike Grimm and Ray McAllister, assisted by the research department of Media General, which owns the newspapers, obtained information about all the robbery cases (there were 171) decided in courts in 28 state localities during the final three months of 1982.

Grimm and McAllister studied robbery because, they reported, "unlike some other serious crimes (such as murder), it does not often have elements that are difficult to quantify (such as passion), and because unlike others (such as drug crimes), it occurs with relative frequency across the state." For every case they recorded information about 94 items (variables), such as race and age of defendant, length of sentence, whether or not a weapon was used during the robbery, existence of a prior criminal record, and so forth. The reporters used a coding form to record the information and a computer to do the analysis.

Some findings that surprised many outside and inside the court system were these:

> Conviction for robbery in different parts of the state can bring different sentences.
>
> Blacks can expect longer sentences than whites.
>
> A jury trial, if you are convicted, is likely to result in a longer sentence than a trial before a judge alone.
>
> Having a prior criminal record does not have much effect on sentence length.
>
> Robbing someone in a business is likely to get you heavier sentence than robbing someone on the street.
>
> Using a gun will get you a longer sentence than not using one.
>
> Your court-appointed lawyer is about as good as a private lawyer.
>
> A married person who is convicted is likely to get a shorter sentence than one who is single, separated, or divorced.

These findings could not emerge from a single case or even from a few cases. It is necessary to look at a group of them before the picture begins to develop. One surprised Virginia judge looked at the differences the study found in treatment of blacks and whites and concluded: "I can't say that every single judge [treats the races evenly]. But as a group, I cannot believe they consciously treat [them] differently. . . . It must be," he continued, "an unconscious decision." Content analysis of documents is one way to unlock the results of unconscious decisions.

As another example, the state of Hawaii had a tough drunk-driving law—on paper, at least. It called for fines up to $1000, jail of up to a year upon conviction, and a mandatory license suspension if a suspected drunk driver refused to take a breath or blood test. Nevertheless, plenty of people were dying on the state's highways each year in accidents that police linked to alcohol.

The *Honolulu Advertiser* and reporter Robert Hollis decided to take a look at the real world of drunken-driving prosecution, as opposed to the theoretical world of the lawbook. The newspaper, with the help of a University of Hawaii professor, developed a coding sheet summarizing the main facts about each drunk-driving arrest and prosecution. The newspaper systematically went through police and court documents related to 432 cases—every drunk-driving arrest in two separate months chosen at random. A newsroom clerk and several University of Hawaii students helped collect the data. The university's computer did the analysis. This study enabled the *Advertiser* to report as follows:

> None of the 53 persons arrested who had refused to take a breath or blood test lost a driver's license, as the law required.
>
> The average fine was $108, well below the $1000 maximum.
>
> Licenses were suspended for less than 10 percent of those convicted.
>
> Nearly three fourths of the arrests were made within two miles of the main Honolulu police station. On rural roads, including principal commuter routes outside the city, only rarely did police stop suspected drunk drivers—generally, only after an accident had occurred.

Figure 10.1   Reporter and photo editor consult (*The Honolulu Advertiser*).

The newspaper's reports facilitated passage of a new state drunk-driving law in 1982. A year later, Hollis and the *Advertiser* examined another set of cases, all of which had been processed under the new law, and found not only that the new law made little difference, but that, in some ways, it worked even more leniently than the old one. Within 10 days, the legislature had passed an even tighter law.

Others have used content analysis to determine the most dangerous street intersections, or the areas in which women should avoid walking alone, or which type toys are most likely to be dangerous (using police accident records). Content analysis also has been used to spot trends in public opinion, by using letters mailed to the editor (not just those published, unless a newspaper has the rare policy of publishing everything mailed to it.) Here are some examples of how content analysis has been used.

The *Indianapolis News* checked a month's worth of municipal court records for four courtrooms and found that the average amount of the fines varied from $24.32 for the "softest" judge involved to $36.52 for the "toughest."

The *Philadelphia Inquirer* examined records for 1034 persons indicted for murder, rape, assault, and robbery and used a computer to help draw a striking picture of the city's criminal justice system (see Figure 10.2).

The *Cleveland Plain Dealer* bought a court's data tape and studied sentencing, bail, probation, and other facets of the justice system there. A computer enabled them to work with data from more than 27,000 cases.

The *Dubuque Telegraph Herald* used a year's worth of traffic accident records—2378 of them. They found that drivers involved in injury-producing accidents were charged with fewer violations than those causing just property or vehicle damage.

A *Minneapolis Tribune* reporter used U.S. Census data to produce a story on commuters.

The *Lexington Herald-Leader* sampled 330 property tax assessment appeals and found that the average appeal brought a $5700 reduction in assessment.

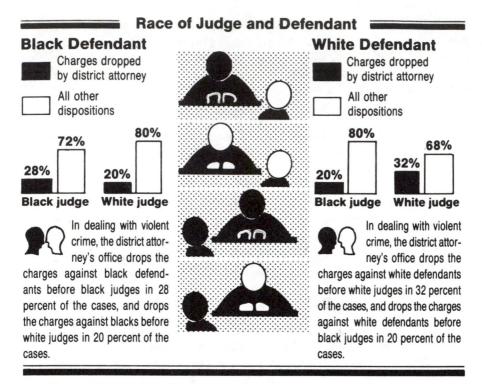

Race of Judge and Defendant

Black Defendant

■ Charges dropped by district attorney

☐ All other dispositions

72%   80%

28%   20%

Black judge   White judge

In dealing with violent crime, the district attorney's office drops the charges against black defendants before black judges in 28 percent of the cases, and drops the charges against blacks before white judges in 20 percent of the cases.

White Defendant

■ Charges dropped by district attorney

☐ All other dispositions

80%   68%

20%   32%

Black judge   White judge

In dealing with violent crime, the district attorney's office drops the charges against white defendants before white judges in 32 percent of the cases, and drops the charges against white defendants before black judges in 20 percent of the cases.

Figure 10.2   Race of judge and defendant (Reprinted by permission of *The Philadelphia Inquirer*, 1973).

CONTENT ANALYSIS TECHNIQUES

If you have never conducted a content analysis, you will find it seems more difficult than it really is. But you can break down the task into distinct steps.

Locate Appropriate Documents

In the *Richmond Times-Dispatch* example, the reporters used court records. Many kinds of records have been used by others, everything from personal letters to classified ads in newspapers.

Sample the Records

Generally speaking, you do not need to examine every record, especially if they are very numerous and you are trying to discover some general trends. Because the Richmond reporters were inter-

"Random Lottery" in Courts—Why Sentences Vary So Much

Mike Keller,
Staff writer,
Honolulu Advertiser

Circuit Judge Robert Won Bae Chang has little use for robbers. Of the 21 convicted robbers who faced him for 1973 offenses, he sent all but one to prison or jail.

Circuit Judge Masato Doi took the opposite tack. He placed most robbers on probation, and sent only one of nine to prison. He did order one of the probationers to spend six months in jail, however.

But Doi came down hard on other types of violent offenders. He didn't think much of rapists, for instance, especially if they also robbed their victims. He sent three of five rapists and three of four rapist-robbers to prison.

What makes their sentencing practices so curious is that both judges were relatively stern compared with their colleagues on the bench, yet they varied radically from one another in deciding what types of offender belonged in prison.

Overall, Chang sent a little more than half the defendants who faced him for violent offenses to prison. Doi's overall average was 40 percent.

But of these totals, Chang sentenced 62 percent of the defendants originally arrested for robbery to at least five years in prison. Doi, on the other hand, by sending one robber to prison, had an 11-percent-to-prison total for robbers.

The breakdowns lead to one obvious conclusion, perhaps best summed up by Norval Morris, dean of the University of Chicago Law School. He stated in a recent nationally syndicated article about "sentencing disparities. Put curtly, like cases are not treated alike, so sentencing is a random lottery."

ested in determining whether the judicial system treated varying types of defendants differently, they limited their study to the records dealing with robberies in selected judicial districts for part of one year.

They could handle the 171 cases with 94 pieces of information coded from each case, especially by using a computer to assist with the analysis. But if there had been 1710 robbery cases or 17,100 cases, they no doubt would have sampled. They could have determined the total number and then randomly selected a reasonable number to study, say 200 or 300. Or, they could have randomly picked a starting number, say 9, and selected every 10th case (or some other number) after that: the 19th, 29th, 39th cases and so forth.

Many wrongly view sampling as a lazy man's cop-out—they say to themselves, "I have to look at all of these records"—or as potentially leading to wrong results because all records were not examined. Both of these common notions are unsound. First, human activities tend to be quite consistent across time and, as we discussed in Chapter 7, if you have seen a carefully selected part of the whole, then, in a sense, you have seen it all (at least within a known margin of error).

Determine Exactly What You Are Seeking

List the information that the records can supply. In the Richmond example, reporters were readily able to determine from available public records the name of the ruling judge, the race and age of the defendant, the length of any sentence, and a variety of other types of information.

Before you start, check that the information you want is noted on the record, or can be obtained from other sources. If the information is not available and you cannot readily obtain it from another source, do not build your investigation around it.

It is wise to draw tables in which you plan to display your investigation results. For example, in the table on p. 191 the entry in each box will be the number of cases falling in that category.

Drafting such tables ahead of time helps you determine if you have made plans to obtain all needed information. This avoids the sometimes unfortunate discovery at the conclusion of an investigation that you forgot to write down the race of the defendant,

Length of Sentence for Robberies, by Race

	Sentence Length			
Race of defendants	Light	Moderate	Heavy	Totals
White				
Black				
Other				
Totals				

thereby preventing you from being able to analyze your information by this variable.

In the example cited here you also need to define exactly what is meant by a "light," "moderate," and "heavy" prison sentence, as the reporters did in the Richmond study (see Figure 10.3). Your definitions should be reasonable *and* be explained to your audience. Not everyone will agree with your definitions, but at least make your terms clear. In Richmond, for example, the reporters decided that a prison sentence of three years or less would be judged *light*; four to eight years, *moderate*, and nine years or more, *heavy*. If you spent eight years in prison, would you regard it as a "moderate" sentence? Such terms are relative. That is why you must explain your terms to your audience.

Develop a Coding Sheet

A coding sheet is nothing more than a form specially devised to help you systematically record information from the documents you examine. For example, if you were coding trends in the type of letters people are writing to your broadcast station or newspaper, you probably would develop a coding sheet with spaces to record the date of the letter, any government agency mentioned, the general topic(s), and background information about the letter writer. You could add many more variables—for instance, the number of misspelled words! A simple coding sheet for letters to the editor is illustrated in the box below.

This idea can be greatly expanded, but you must keep it simple enough that others can follow your lead. You will need to be able to define what you mean by *mayor/mayor's office, city council, local courts, taxes,* and *police protection.*

Coding Sheet

Date of letter to editor _____

 Local government agency mentioned
  Focus is on Mayor/Mayor's office ____
  On the City Council ____
  Police Department ____
  On local courts ____
  No mention of specific agency ____
  [Etc.]

 Letter is about
  Taxes ____
  Police Protection ____
  [Etc.]

Letter Writer: Male ____   Female ____
  Can't determine from name or unsigned letter ____

Apparent section of town (from return address)
 Expensive ____
 Middle class ____
 Poor ____
 Out of town ____
 Can't determine ____

Examples help, so it is a good idea to provide them. The same is true for determining that certain addresses belong to "expensive," "middle-class," or "poor" areas. Tax records, combined with local knowledge and common sense, will aid you in doing this. This is important because you will need to defend all these judgment calls.

Make a Test Run

After you select your sample and develop your coding sheet, make a test run. Use your coding sheet to see if it works conveniently; you may find you need to rearrange it. For example, you will quickly notice that one of the first pieces of information you see (using our letters-to-the-editor investigation as an example) is the date of the letter (on the letter or envelope). It is easy to record (code) that first. Any specific public agency mentioned (if any) is probably next easiest. The topic is next. Several topics may be mentioned. How many will you note? (Investigators often note only the first topic mentioned, on the assumption this probably is more important in the mind of the letter writer than topics mentioned later. Most of us first mention what bothers us most.)

Background information on the letter writer normally is provided at the bottom of the letter (if it is not an anonymous letter), making that easiest to record last. Your coding sheet should mirror the easiest way to record the needed information, which normally is coded from easiest to hardest judgments. Use the test run to make adjustments.

Also notice the amount of time it takes to locate a document, record the needed information, and move to the next document—one complete cycle. Multiply the amount of time needed for one document by the number of documents you plan to investigate. You should keep in mind that experience will enable you to save some time as you go along, although not always very much.

Can you examine all the documents you originally planned to use? You may need to cut back your sample if it takes a long time to code one document. On the other hand, you may find it easier than you thought (not likely) and thus be able to add more documents. Either way, remember you have to draw a new random sample.

Investigators using content analysis for the first time often seriously underestimate the amount of time required to employ the technique. Careful preplanning, and a test run (or two), will help you keep the time allocated in line with the importance of the project. Any investigation is only worth so much time. Just as you should draw the *smallest* (not the largest) sample consistent with the level of findings you desire, you should spend only as much time as needed to answer the questions your investigation asks— not a minute more.

Gather Facts Systematically

When your coding sheet is adjusted for ease of use, begin to gather your facts. You will find this easier to do as you gain experience. Be careful, however, that you do not unconsciously change established rules as you go along. This can happen without your realizing it. For example, if several letter writers complain about the mayor's office and, separately in the letter, about the functioning of the police department, how would you code these complaints? Be careful that you do not code them one way (e.g., "mayor's office") during the early part of the investigation, and differently (e.g., "police department") later in the investigation. (That is why some investigators only code the first-mentioned problem.) Your mind will play subtle tricks on you, but you can check for this and, in fact, you must.

Conduct a Reliability Check

After you (or your helpers) have coded a certain number of documents, have someone else code them to see if they apply your coding rules the same way you do. You need to have reasonable agreement. One formula to compare your agreement is the following:

$$\frac{\text{Number of items coded the same way by person A and by person B}}{\text{Total number of items coded}}$$

The percentage of agreement should be reasonably high for easy judgments and will naturally fall lower for hard judgments. There is no "right" level. Most investigations strive for 80 percent agreement or better. You need to determine which level you will accept. If your coder agreement is too low, you need to examine your coding sheet and its explanations. Is it too hard to follow? Have you done a sufficient job in learning it or in training other coders? Most books on content analysis include detailed discussions of reliability. Without a reasonable level of agreement, you have no claim to objectivity, and without objectivity, you are not doing content analysis.

Finish Gathering Data

Once you are reasonably certain that others would code your data the same way as you, proceed to finish gathering all the information. If at any point you become uncertain about whether the coding continues to be consistent, stop and conduct another reliability check.

Analyze Your Information

Normally you can use computers, which are fast and precise, to analyze the information. Nearly all newspapers now have computers on which you can use excess time, or you can use computer facilities at a nearby college or university. Some microcomputers have statistical packages that can handle many of your jobs, although at slow speed.

Visualize the Best Way to Communicate to Your Audience

Quantitative studies often lend themselves to graphs and charts. If you can help the audience visualize differences, you can help them remember the most important points about your research. For example, the Richmond study that compared conviction rates for black versus white robbery defendants displayed its findings as shown in Figure 10.3.

The same study found that jury decisions of guilt more likely result in longer sentences than judges' decisions of guilt. The differences found by reporters between jury and judge trials are shown in Figure 10.4.

GENERATING NEWS

You will find it laborious to use content analysis, but it is rewarding. Using ordinary documents, you will find unique ways to examine the life of your community. Content analysis can help you ask ques-

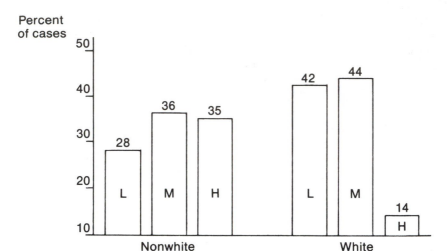

Light sentence (L): 0 to 3 years
Medium sentence (M): 4 to 8 years
Heavy sentence (H): 9 years and over

Figure 10.3   Sentence length by race in Virginia (from "Unequal Justice," reprinted from the *Richmond Times-Dispatch* series, published October 16–21, 1983, page 8).

tions of officials that are more original and probing—just as the Richmond reporters could ask focused questions about judicial performance after they completed their investigations.

With content analysis you can generate news of interest and importance to your community. For example, let's take a quick look at some documents that the police department in your town regularly uses. We will use the standard form (see pp. 198–99) used by one police department (forms differ with different departments) to record details of a robbery investigation.

If you wanted to study the robbery records of your community for a year (using sampling if you are examining a large community or looking over the accumulated documents of several years) you could, among other things, discover:

> Where robberies are most likely to occur in your community (block 2)
> What time of day (block 4) and day of week (block 5) robberies occur

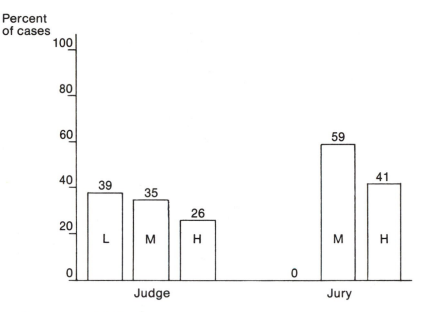

Light sentence (L): 0 to 3 years
Medium sentence (M): 4 to 8 years
Heavy sentence (H): 9 years and over

Figure 10.4 Sentence length by jury vs. judge trial (from "Unequal Justice," reprinted from the *Richmond Times-Dispatch* series, published October 16–21, 1983, page 14).

The "type" of person (race, age, sex) most likely to be a victim (block 10)

The "type" of business (if any) most likely to be involved (block 13)

Robber "characteristics" (block 27) (Later you can compare this with arrest warrants to see which "type" of robber the police are most successful in arresting.)

The general circumstances of robbery in your town (block 32)

You can obtain other types of information as well. Perhaps you are interested in checking the performance of an individual arresting officer—how successful has he been in arresting those charged with robbery, for example? What can you do with this information? You can check to see if the police provide extra protection to those areas most likely to be robbed, and if they are sensitive

POLICE DEPARTMENT

Robbery

1. Case No. 13817674

2. Address of Occurrence	3. Zone	4. Occurred	5. Day	6. Disp.	7. Arr.	8. In Ser.	9. Date
1634 Holden Ave.	8	8:40 p.m.	Tuesday	On Stakeout		10:05 am	

10. Victim's Name	Age	Sex	Race	Res. Address	Res. Phone	Bus. Address	Bus. Phone
Thomas A. Molay	57	M	W	1203 Texas Ave	671-8437	1634 Holden Ave.	671-4744

11. Owner	12. Victim's Occupation	13. Type of Premises	14. Weapon Used—Serial No.
Thomas A. Molay	Liquor store owner	Liquor store	2 handguns 14387162 SB8231442

15. Method Used to Commit Crime	16. General Type of Property Taken	17. Value
Strongarm robbery	Cash	$312

18. Weather Clear

19. Trade mark or unusual event   One suspect entered the store when it appeared to be empty, except for the owner, showed a gun and demanded the money.

20. Vehicle Used by Offenders	Model	Make	Year	Body Style	21. Color	22. License	State	Year	23. Ident. Marks
	Mustang	Ford	'74	Sedan	White	D812-175	Yes	Cur.	Badly rusted

24. Storage Receipt
84-3822

25. What Did Offenders Say "Give me all the money you've got in the register, all of it, and do it fast. This gun is loaded, and I'll shoot."

26. No. of Offenders	27. Subject	Sex	Race	Age	Res. Address	Incarcerated	Occupation
Two	Calvin Louis Jones	M	W	27	Louisville, Kentucky	No	Unknown

28. Disguises	29. How Offender Approached - Flight	30. Hospital (14)	31. Condition
Bandana over face	Car driven by accomplice	Memorial	Very grave

32. Remarks: We were on a routine stakeout, hiding in a back room in the liquor store when the suspect entered. When he displayed his weapon and grabbed the money we entered the area, identified ourselves and ordered the suspect to drop his weapon. The suspect turned toward us, seemingly pointing his gun at us, and we both opened fire. Tucker fired one shot from a shotgun and Nicks three shots from his service revolver. The shotgun blast struck the suspect in his groin area and one shot from the revolver struck him in the stomach and another in his right arm. The second suspect, who made no attempt to flee, was apprehended outside in their car. He has been identified as Norman F. Smith, also of Louisville. Jones is in the hospital's intensive care unit. Smith is being held in the county jail.

33. Reporting Officers Signatures

	Badge No.	34. District
a) Roger Nicks	482	3
b) Lee Tucker	789	3

199

to the time and day of highest risk. What if police more heavily patrol upper-class white housing areas, reducing the risk in those areas, while leaving a skeleton crew in lower-class areas? The product of your own investigation can lead to additional important stories. In other words, by using content analysis of local public documents you can generate unique and important news about your own community. What kind of stories could you develop from the arrest records for murder?

UNOBTRUSIVE PULSE TAKING

You do not have to limit your search to public documents. What could you do with published business records such as annual reports? With annual reports of such quasi-public agencies as the Red Cross, Boy Scouts, or Heart Fund you can identify trends to guide your questions. The method is *unobtrusive* because you do not necessarily need to tell officials what you are seeking. The word may get around, of course, but if this happens, you will be ready with some interesting questions. Either way—ideally, both ways—you have a story.

REFERENCES

Berelson, Bernard. *Content Analysis in Communication Research.* Glencoe, IL: Free Press, 1952.

Holsti, Ole R. *Content Analysis for the Social Sciences and Humanities.* Reading, MA: Addison-Wesley Publishing, 1969.

Krippendorf, Klaus. *Content Analysis: An Introduction to Its Methodology.* Beverly Hills, CA: Sage, 1980.

Webb, Eugene J., Donald T. Campbell, Richard D. Schwartz, and Lee Sechrest. *Unobtrusive Measures: Nonreactive Research in the Social Sciences.* Chicago: Rand McNally, 1966.

CHAPTER 11
Freedom of Information Laws

> It is hereby declared to be the policy of the United States that the public is entitled to the fullest practicable information regarding the decision-making process of the Federal Government.
>
> *Government in the Sunshine Act,*
> Public Law 94-409, 1976

Sounds nice, doesn't it?

The federal government and most states in recent years have passed "sunshine laws" such as the act quoted above guaranteeing public access to government records and meetings. These laws presume that information is public unless it falls into a category exempted by the law. Detailed procedures exist for requesting access to government records and for appealing when some bureaucrat says, "No, you can't have these."

These laws often have worked to the advantage of press and public. For instance, the Freedom of Information (FOI) Service Center in Washington says the federal Freedom of Information Act has been used by journalists and others to obtain documentary information "on stories such as the Rosenberg spy trials, FBI harassment of civil rights leaders, automobile design defects, consumer product testing, international smuggling operations, environmental impact studies, the salaries of public employees, school district compliance with antidiscrimination laws, sanitary conditions in food processing plants, and CIA spying on domestic political groups."

However, the laws are only as good as the legislators who wrote them, the bureaucrats who administer them, and the judges who have the final authority over whether Reporter X gets to look at File Y—and of course they aren't much help to reporters who don't know about and use the laws. Unfortunately, these laws— particularly, the many "exceptions" to open access—have at times proved to be obstacles to reporters instead of aids.

That said, however, it is still important for you to know about the "sunshine law" in your state and the federal FOI act. This chapter discusses the theory behind sunshine laws and the ways in which they are written. The federal FOI act applies only to federal government agencies; different states have different statutes covering the same issues. This chapter does not pretend to be a comprehensive discussion of the 50 state laws, but attempts to show you what to look for in making use of these laws, federal or state, in gathering information.

PUBLIC RECORD LAWS

Some public records laws really do insure public availability of most government records, whereas others are little more than a compendium of ways for bureaucrats to deny access to files. Here are some key points you should know about making use of the public records law in your area. First, what exactly is a "public record"? In California, for example, a public record "includes any writing containing information relating to the conduct of the public's business prepared, owned, used, or retained by any state or local agency regardless of physical form or characteristics." In these days of increasing computerization, the words "regardless of physical form or characteristics" can be important in assuring access to files on electronic tape or disks.

State laws, as well as the federal government through its Freedom of Information Act, make exceptions to the definition of public records. North Dakota law, for instance, says, "Except as otherwise specifically provided by law, all records of public or governmental bodies . . . shall be public records." Be aware of the "except as otherwise provided" language. Sometimes it provides gaping loopholes in which bureaucrats can stow the records you want to examine.

The exceptions in the federal FOI act are fairly typical of what you find in a state "sunshine law." According to this act, the federal government is required to let you see all of its records except the following:

1. Classified defense and foreign policy information.

2. Internal personnel rules and practices of an agency.

3. Data exempted by another law. (This has been dubbed the "catch-all" exemption by the FOI Service Center, which reports that federal agencies at one time or another have cited nearly 100 other laws as justification for withholding documents. The "catch-all" covers such predictable areas as income tax forms, Central Intelligence Agency and Census Bureau records. The "catch-all" also has made it difficult to obtain information from the Federal Trade Commission, farm loan and parity programs, and some postal service information.)

4. Trade secrets.

5. Internal memos or communications—the so-called executive privilege exemption that applies to internal working papers, preliminary drafts, and letters between bureaucrats. The FOI Service Center says this exemption, which also includes communications between bureaucrats and the government lawyers serving them, is widely used by the government to deny public access to records.

6. Personnel, medical, or other files that would "constitute a clearly unwarranted invasion of privacy."

7. Current law-enforcement investigation files.

8. Records relating to bank regulation.

9. Information about geology and geography of oil and other wells.

Clearly, many of the exceptions are based on legitimate goals—such as privacy, or national security—that should be balanced against the public's right to know. On the other hand, if you were a bureaucrat intent on denying a reporter access to a particular file that ought to be public or that falls in a gray area, it wouldn't take much imagination to find a category you could stuff it into, forcing the reporter to file an appeal, take you to court or just give up. In the end, then, the success of a particular request for information under the FOI act can depend on the commitment to openness by the agency or the particular employee who fields the request.

Different federal administrations have shown different attitudes about FOI matters, and the attitudes at the top clearly can influence decisions far down the line. Jimmy Carter's Justice Department said even if a document fell within one of the FOI act's exemptions, an agency should make it public unless release would be "demonstrably harmful" to the government. When Ronald Reagan took office, his attorney general rescinded that policy, sending a signal to agencies to hew closely to the language of the exemptions.

State laws allow many of the same exceptions as the federal FOI act. Hawaii's law exempts "records which invade the right of privacy of an individual." Louisiana exempts "books, records, writings, accounts, letters, letter books, photographs or copies thereof, ordinarily kept in the custody or control of the governor." That's a broad notion of "executive privilege," which could be used to cover a multitude of sins.

New Hampshire exempts "records pertaining to internal personnel practices, confidential, commercial or financial information, personnel, medical, welfare, and other files whose disclosure would constitute invasion of privacy."

How much are government employees being paid? Maryland's law specifically includes "the salaries of all state, county, and city employees" as a public record. Other jurisdictions won't give out salary information, citing privacy considerations.

This concept—invasion of privacy—is becoming an increasing hurdle for reporters trying to evaluate government. The U.S. Congress in its Privacy Act of 1974 said, "The Congress finds that . . . the right of privacy is a personal and fundamental right protected by the Constitution of the United States." The same concept is being used to shape state laws as well.

The concept of a "right of privacy" is an attractive one. Journalists daily grapple with the ethical questions that crop up when the public's right to know collides with the individual's right to be left alone. As with most other such issues, balancing tests must be applied. To be sure, there are occasions in which publication of the contents of records would invade someone's privacy. On the other hand, governments deal with people every day; it would be difficult for news media and voters to evaluate how well government is doing its job if the evidence of those dealings were automatically sealed up just because the papers that document those dealings happen to have somebody's name on them.

On the practical level, this growing cognizance of the concept of privacy can change the frame of mind of the civil servants in charge of records. When Congress passed the Freedom of Information Act in 1966 and tightened it up in 1974, federal employees were put on notice that openness was the theoretical ideal. Exemptions were made allowing certain records to be kept confidential, but the law was titled Freedom of Information, giving some idea of its overall thrust, and the 1974 version of the FOI act encouraged bureaucrats not to go overboard with secrecy. It ordered the Civil Service Commission to discipline any federal employee who "arbitrarily or capriciously" withheld records that ought to have been released. (The threat remains largely theoretical. As of 1983, the FOI Service Center in Washington reported, "only one case is known to have been referred for disciplinary action and in that case the government official was not punished.")

The 1974 Privacy Act, however, states that government workers can be disciplined for being too free with information. A federal worker who discloses records with "individually identifiable information" in violation of the law "shall be guilty of a misdemeanor and fined not more than $5,000." The message: When in doubt, don't release it.

SUCCESS STORIES

Here are some of the cases newspapers have fought to get access to records that they thought were public, but bureaucrats said were not.

> The *Charleston* (West Virginia) *Gazette* used the federal Freedom of Information Act to get information on state banks making insider loans to officers or bank directors.
> The *Miami Herald* also used this law to get a list of companies that had not repaid Small Business Administration loans.
> A North Dakota judge allowed the *Grand Forks Herald* to inspect the personnel files of a former police chief.

The Supreme Court of Pennsylvania came to the aid of a newspaper seeking certain welfare records in order to expose
welfare abuse. (Most of the time, however, journalists
have been frustrated by privacy standards when seeking
information about welfare.)

A judge ordered the University of Wisconsin to give the *Mad-
ison Capital Times* access to records detailing outside employment of faculty.

The *Des Moines Register and Tribune* forced the FBI to turn
over hundreds of pages of documents dealing with investigations of Iowa colleges during the 1960s and even convinced a federal judge that the government should pay
$4700 in legal fees for pressing a lawsuit on the matter.

The *Washington Post* tried to use the FOI act to find out from
the U.S. State Department whether two prominent figures
managing the Iranian government's side of the U.S. hos-
tage crisis were in fact American citizens with valid U.S.
passports. The *Post* won in lower courts, but ultimately
lost when the Supreme Court ruled in 1982 that Exemption 6 to the FOI act (the one dealing with "invasion of
privacy") covered "great quantities of files" other than
personnel and medical records. Included in the "great
quantities" were the State Department files on the Ira-
nians in question. The *Los Angeles Times* said the high
court had taken the "privacy" exemption and "broadened
it beyond recognition."

Occasionally, journalists win a limited victory. They get some
of the records, but not all. Or they get "edited" versions. A *Honolulu
Advertiser* reporter once used the Freedom of Information Act to
obtain a packet of records relating to a federal probe of medical
reimbursements to nursing homes. After lengthy delays and negotiations, he got the file—with all the names of the people involved blacked out. Included in the packet of files was a Xerox copy
of his own letter asking for the records—with his own name duti-
fully expunged by someone who had been told to cross out every
name.

Some critics accuse news media of being too shy about using
public records laws to pry loose government information. Rep. William Moorhead, D-Pa., who helped draft and pass the Freedom of
Information Act through Congress, says his experience has been

Grading the High Schools

Andrea Meditch
TEXAS MONTHLY

You can give all the SAT tests, achievement tests, and basic skills tests you want—and all are given in Texas in profusion—and you still won't know how well high schools prepare their students to survive that first year in college. The only way to find out is to actually measure how well graduates from particular high schools do during their freshman year.

As it happens, it is precisely what the University of Texas has been doing, quietly, for the last six years. Since 1978 UT has been compiling an average grade for each of the 1465 accredited high schools in the state based on the grades of the freshmen they send to UT. What UT has not done is rank the high schools to see how well— or poorly—they do compared with each other. But we did it, and the results are listed below.

UT released the information only after a Texas Open Records Act request. An administration official said the university was reluctant to part with it because "we don't want a school to open a newspaper or magazine and read that they're the worst high school in the state." Fair enough. A few caveats are in order. First, only those high schools that sent five or more students to UT are included in the list. Second, the results reflect only the grades of 1983–84 freshmen. Last, and most important, obviously not all Texas high school students attend UT. Some of the top high schools, for instance, place many of their best students elsewhere, while the best students at more modest schools might well end up at UT.

With that in mind, these rankings can still give you a pretty fair idea of how well Texas high schools are preparing their students for college, or at least for UT. In the lists that follow, each school has a grade-point average, which is figured by averaging the GPAs of the UT freshmen from that school. (A GPA, you may remember from your own college days, can be anywhere between 0 and 4, with 4 being an A, 3 being a B, and so on.) If a high school ended up with, say, a 2.8, that means its graduates averaged about a B- at UT. The 1983–84 UT freshman class of 5873 had a GPA of 2.47, or about a C+.

The list points to some fascinating—and unexpected—conclusions.

Don't buy the myth that small-town kids can't make it at UT. Small-town high schools make up a third of the top-twenty list, including number one: A & M Consolidated in College Station.

As a region, West Texas sends the best-prepared students to UT. There are five West Texas schools in the top twenty, none in the bottom twenty. Central Texas freshmen fared the worst: there were four Central Texas schools in the bottom group and, unless you consider La Grange part of that region, none in the top.

Another surprise: despite obstacles like poverty and a large Spanish-speaking population, freshmen from the Rio Grande Valley did well. Two schools placed in the top twenty; none were in the bottom group. And Valley freshmen from schools that fell between the two lists generally outperformed the UT average. . . .

Reprinted with permission from the September issue of TEXAS MONTHLY. Copyright 1984 by TEXAS MONTHLY.

that "the reporters, editors and broadcasters whose job it is to inform the American people have made little use of the FOI Act."

And Stanford University professor Elie Abel, formerly chairman of the New York Citizens' Committee on Public Access, said, "Journalists by and large don't use documents. They're lazy. They wait for a spokesman to say it. Younger reporters are a little more likely to use the [freedom of information] mechanisms. The old pros call up a source and ask. It's a more congenial way of doing things."

PUBLIC MEETING LAWS

In addition to dealing with documents, many sunshine laws also provide for open meetings so journalists and members of the public can attend. Generally, all public meeting laws make similar points:

1. Most meetings of public agencies or bodies must be open to the public.

2. Meetings may be closed for specific exemptions. The federal Government in the Sunshine Act, for instance, allows meetings to be closed for discussions of national defense or foreign policy matters, internal personnel rules and practices, trade secrets, matters involving invasion of personal privacy, criminal accusations against or formal censure of any person, law enforcement investigations, bank regulation or civil lawsuits or subpoenas. In other words, many of the grounds for denying access to public records are also legitimate grounds for closing an otherwise "public" meeting, and equally difficult to monitor. The Nevada law, like many others, allowed closed meetings for personnel matters. Said one Reno editor: "They held personnel meetings that had nothing to do with personnel."

3. Meetings may be closed only by following certain procedures. The federal law, for instance, requires a recorded public vote in which a majority of the entire membership of an agency votes for closure. Some state laws require a two-thirds vote or more than a simple majority.

4. Meetings must be announced in advance in a specified manner. Federal meetings, for instance, normally must be announced at least a week in advance, with information about time, place, and subject matter published in the Federal Register. There are provisions, however, for short-notice meetings by majority vote.

5. Decisions to close a meeting may be appealed. Federal courts may order that the transcript, minutes, or tapes of a closed

meeting be made public if the meeting was improperly held in secret. In some states, a court may also invalidate an action taken by a public body violating the state public meeting law.

Within those broad parameters, however, there are dozens of different details in the various statutes and even more court interpretations on exactly what the statutes mean in practice. For instance, what constitutes a *meeting*? Typically, it is defined by the number of officials attending. In Arizona, a meeting is "the gathering of a quorum of members of a public body to propose to take legal action." It must be a quorum; it must involve action. These provisions are common. However, Colorado law governs "all meetings of two or more members of any . . . policy-making or rule-making body of any state agency." There is no need for a quorum in Colorado—just two members, whenever they take a formal action or whenever "any public business is discussed."

Sometimes meetings exempt from sunshine laws are the most important ones. New York Governor Mario Cuomo, the speaker of the state Assembly, and the majority leader of the Senate met behind closed doors in 1982 to cut a deal compromising their major differences over the state budget. It's hard to envision a single more important meeting in all of New York state government that year, yet the press and public were not present. Reporters were reduced to skulking in the hallways, waiting for a smile, gesture, or nod of the head when somebody came out to go to the restroom.

Must the attendees of a meeting all be present in the same room for a "meeting" to fall under the public meeting law? In Oklahoma, yes. A public meeting "means the conducting of business of a public body by a majority of its members being personally together." In Iowa, no. There, a public meeting means "a gathering in person or by electronic means." A conference telephone call may fall under Iowa's public meeting statute. But the Virginia Supreme Court ruled in 1983 that the state's Freedom of Information Act does not bar officials from holding unannounced "meetings" through telephone conference calls.

What if all the members of a state utilities commission are invited to the same cocktail party? Is that a public meeting if they wind up in a corner discussing the electric company's pending rate request? It depends.

In Ohio, they may be in the clear if it was an unplanned, chance contact. There, a public meeting is any prearranged discussion of public business. In other states, it depends on just how sneaky they all were. The Connecticut law says such a "chance meeting or social meeting" is not a public meeting if the board members "neither planned nor intended" to discuss official business. In Idaho, they would be in the clear; in that state, a public meeting means only "the convening of a governing body of a public agency to make a decision or to deliberate toward a decision."

For the most part, the state laws that refer to "chance gatherings" or "social gatherings" say they are not covered by the public meeting law unless they were set up specifically to circumvent the law itself.

What kinds of bodies are covered by public meeting laws? Again, it depends on where you are. Most state laws cover quasi-judicial bodies (such as utilities commissions), governing bodies of political subdivisions (such as city councils), boards of education, and boards of regents. Generally, the courts are exempted, as are grand juries and trial juries. Often, a state legislature will exempt itself from its own state's law on open meetings. Some state laws include advisory commissions; others include only panels with authority to make decisions. In California, the meetings of "the official student body organization" at any state college or community college are governed by the state public meeting law.

Some examples of using public meeting laws to bring sunshine into otherwise dark corners:

A Wisconsin judge ordered the Milwaukee City Council to hold an open meeting on renegotiating a contract with a recycling plant.

A Tennessee judge said the Chattanooga school board violated the state public meeting law by holding a secret meeting to negotiate teacher contracts. In many states, however, labor negotiations are outside the purview of public meeting laws, in part because the entire memberships of public bodies usually do not participate in the actual negotiating.

Never underestimate the ingenuity of a public official bound and determined to do things in secret. Consider the Rome, New York, zoning board of appeals, which came to grips in an unusual way with a new state open meetings law requiring zoning boards to conduct their business in public.

At a July 1983 session, the board members met in public but communicated with each other by whispers. They couldn't be understood by the public or the reporters in attendance. The board's presiding officer told a reporter for the *Rome Daily Sentinel*, "We don't have to speak into the microphone. We [only] have to stay in the same room as you." After some bad publicity and a ruling from a state agency that inaudible deliberations violated the New York open meetings law, the board relented.

OPENNESS AND THE COURTS

It used to be assumed that whatever the rules for school boards or zoning panels or utilities commissions, at least the courts were a paragon of openness. In recent years, however, with increasing debate over free press–fair trial disputes, numerous requests have been made to close proceedings in criminal cases.

The Supreme Court generally has come down on the side of open trials, but has suggested there are valid reasons for closing pretrial hearings. One example is a hearing to decide whether certain evidence obtained by police will be admissible in a trial to come later. Defense attorneys argue that even if they succeed in getting the evidence suppressed, it does little good if the matter receives such wide community publicity that the potential pool of jurors hears about the incriminating evidence anyway.

Journalists and media attorneys argue that there are ways other than closing courts to assure a free trial. Close questioning of prospective jurors and changes of venue to assure impartial jurors are two that immediately come to mind.

In practice, however, journalists often are confronted with a fait accompli. They show up to cover a hearing and find it closed. Or they sit helplessly by in the audience while an attorney moves to close a hearing and a judge quickly assents.

In an effort to assure news media their day in court before such actions are taken, the Gannett Corporation in 1981 distributed wallet-sized cards to its reporters. The cards contain a speech that a reporter can read if ever confronted by an about-to-be-closed trial or hearing. Here's what you can say if you ever find yourself in such a situation:

> Your honor, I am _____ , a reporter for _____ , and I would like to object on behalf of my employer and the public to this proposed closing. Our attorney is prepared to make a number of arguments against closings such as this one, and we respectfully

ask the Court for a hearing on those issues. I believe our attorney can be here relatively quickly for the Court's convenience and he will be able to demonstrate that closure in this case will violate the First Amendment, and possibly violate state statutory and constitutional provisions as well. I cannot make the arguments myself, but our attorney can point out several issues for your consideration. If it pleases the Court, we request the opportunity to be heard through counsel.

HOW TO USE PUBLIC RECORD LAWS

Once you have a nodding acquaintance with both the federal records laws and those in your own state, you are in a position to attempt to use them to your advantage. Here are the steps to follow:

1. Try to avoid confrontations. Contact people by telephone or in person. Make informal requests for records from a press officer or head of an agency office. If you can keep on the good side of the records custodian and avoid confrontation, it will make finding things in the files easier. After all, the bureaucrat knows what's in there and how the files are organized. You don't—yet. If things don't go smoothly right away, the FOI Service Center suggests that you make a point of telling any officials with whom you speak that you intend (if you do) to file a formal request for the records under the FOI act or your state's open records law.

The federal FOI act requires, in fact, that you "reasonably describe" the records you seek. The law also requires each federal agency to make available public information about the jobs it does and the information available in its files. State laws sometimes have the same sort of requirement to help the record seeker. In New York, for instance, each agency must maintain a "subject matter list" describing the categories of records it keeps, whether or not the records are available. But the easiest way to locate the right file is by enlisting the help of a cooperative civil servant who can help you "reasonably describe" what you need and tell you where to ask for it.

2. Be specific in your request. Asking a civil servant to get you "all the Health Department records on water pollution inspections for the last five years" is one way to make sure you won't

miss something, but may backfire. Bureaucrats are human beings, too; if your request appears to promise the bureaucrat a lot of work, he or she may look for a way to avoid filling it. The easiest way out is for the bureaucrat to decide that, no, you can't have those records because they fall under exemption 3(b)(III) of the public records act.

On the other hand, there will be times when you must ask for a large body of records because you don't know exactly what you are looking for. Or you may want to examine an agency's performance over a long period of time in order to systematically evaluate it. If, however, you can focus on a particular file folder that you know is there, you may have a better shot at getting it on the first attempt.

3. If informal negotiations don't work, put the formal operation of the law to work. In the boxes on pages 215–216 and 217 are sample letters to use. One, from the FOI Service Center, is the form for requesting records through the Federal Freedom of Information Act. The second is an example of how to appeal denial of a records request under the New York state law.

Watch the deadlines. The federal government is required by the FOI law to act on a records request within 10 working days and to decide an appeal of a denial of access within 20 working days. State laws differ. The New York law requires an initial decision within 5 business days and says any appeals should be processed within 7 work days. In most cases, denials of access must be in writing, stating the reasons.

Although the deadlines are in the law in black and white, they simply don't work in many cases. The FOI Service Center reported in 1983 that the FBI had a 6–12-month backlog of FOI requests to process and that long delays also were probable when dealing with the State Department, Justice Department, and CIA.

4. Don't give up easily. If the first bureaucrat you contact balks, pursue your chase up the ladder. It may just be a case of a mid-level civil servant afraid of breaking new ground. Historian Daniel Boorstin once quoted a maxim of the French civil service: "Never do anything for the first time." For the most part, a civil servant will not get into trouble with his or her boss by refusing a reporter access to a particular file. It is often easier for the bureaucrat to say no as a matter of routine, bucking you upstairs to someone with real authority.

Sample FOI Request Letter

Name of Public Body
Address

To the FOI Officer:

This request is made under the federal Freedom of Information Act, 5 U.S.C. 552.

Please send me copies of (*Here, clearly describe what you want. Include identifying material, such as names, places, and the period of time about which you are inquiring. If you wish, attach news clips, reports, and other documents describing the subject of your research.*)

As you know, the FOI Act provides that if portions of a document are exempt from release, the remainder must be segregated and disclosed. Therefore, I will expect you to send me all nonexempt portions of the records which I have requested, and ask that you justify any deletions by reference to specific exemptions of the FOI Act. I reserve the right to appeal your decision to withhold any materials.

I promise to pay reasonable search and duplication fees in connection with this request. However, if you estimate that the total fees will exceed $, please notify me so that I may authorize expenditure of a greater amount.

(*Optional*) I am prepared to pay reasonable search and duplication fees in connection with this request. However, the FOI Act provides for waiver or reduction of fees if disclosure could be considered as "primarily benefiting the general public." I am a journalist (*researcher, or scholar*) employed by (*name of news organization, book publishers, etc.*), and intend to use the information I am requesting as the basis for a planned article (*broadcast, or book*). (*Add arguments here in support of fee waiver.*) Therefore, I ask that you waive all search and duplication fees. If you deny this request, however, and the fees will exceed $, please notify me of the charges before you fill my request so that I may decide whether to pay the fees or appeal your denial of my request for a waiver.

As I am making this request in the capacity of a journalist (*author, or scholar*) and this information is of timely value, I will appreciate your communicating with me by telephone, rather than by mail, if you have any questions regarding this request. Thank you for your assistance, and I will look forward to receiving your reply within 10 business days, as required by law.

Very truly yours,

(Signature)

Expect to have this sort of trouble often. Many public officials can envision only trouble when a reporter starts asking for records. Given the way most sunshine laws are structured, it is seldom difficult for a government official to find a loophole to avoid giving you the records you want. Thus, the bureaucrat's instinctive reaction may be to stonewall and look for a legal way to keep you away from the office files. You'll see how true this is after you have made a few sorties into government files during your journalistic career.

5. Follow the formal appeal process. Often, this will take you upstairs to some elected official or political appointee who may decide there is more woe in fighting off the press than there is in releasing the records.

6. In a pinch, get a lawyer. Ultimately, it will be necessary for a media lawyer to get involved if you file suit to obtain records. Even before that stage, however, a lawyer often can be persuasive with bureaucrats or government attorneys just as a sign that you are serious. The drawback is that when a lawyer is involved the effort starts costing you money. Lawyers don't browbeat government agencies for free.

At times, a civil servant may find that delay is the most prudent course to follow. If you are on a fishing expedition and don't really know what you'll find, and if your lawyer tells you the law is on the government's side, you may decide to give up the chase once it starts to get expensive.

Sample Appeal Letter

Name of Agency Official
Appeals Officer
Name of Agency
Address of Agency
City, NY, zip code

Re: Freedom of Information
Law Appeal

Dear _____ :

I hereby appeal the denial of access regarding my request, which was made on _____(date) and sent to _____(records access officer, name and address of agency).

The records that were denied include: _____ _____(enumerate the records that were denied).

As required by the Freedom of Information Law, the head or governing body of an agency, or whomever is designated to determine appeals, is required to respond within seven business days of the receipt of an appeal. If the records are denied on appeal, please explain the reasons for the denial fully in writing as required by law.

In addition, please be advised that the Freedom of Information Law directs that all appeals and the determinations that follow be sent to the Committee on Public Access to Records, Department of State, 162 Washington Avenue, Albany, New York 12231.

Sincerely,

Signature
Name
Address
City, State, zip code

When dealing with either the federal FOI act or the equivalent law in your state, however, there is one source of free legal help for both you as a journalist and for your media lawyer: the FOI Service Center in Washington, a joint project of the Reporters Committee for Freedom of the Press and the Society of Professional Journalists, Sigma Delta Chi. This center maintains a 24-hour First Amendment/FOI Hotline in Washington (202-466-6313). Either you or your lawyer can call the hotline to get advice on using open-records and open-meeting laws, or getting into closed courtrooms. The FOI Service Center also has current publications on these topics that your newsroom should have on file. If it doesn't, write the FOI Service Center, 800 18th Street NW, Washington, DC 20006. Currently, about 10 states have hotlines similar to the Federal FOI Hotline. Often these are financed by media organizations that put an attorney or law firm on retainer. The Minnesota Newspaper Association hotline, for example, gets 60 calls a month and signed up more than 110 clients in its first six months.

7. Write about your problems, when you can do so without blowing the cover off something you are investigating and without alerting competing media. This can help make the case that secrecy is costing the government more than any possibility of bad publicity resulting from your getting the records.

8. Try to avoid paying fees for any information obtained under FOI laws. The federal FOI act allows the government to charge you fees for searching out the documents you asked for and for making copies of them. The copying fees are generally about 10 cents a page, about what you would pay anywhere else. But, of course, if you need several hundred or thousand pages, the cost can run pretty high. As an alternative, if the documents are filed in an office near you, review them there and don't have them all copied. What can really run the costs up is the search fees, which an agency can charge for locating the documents you requested. Search fees vary widely among federal departments. Find out in advance what they will be.

The federal FOI law requires that documents be given free or at a reduced cost if furnishing the information would "primarily benefit the general public." It can always be argued that publicizing the work of government agencies is in the interest of the general public, although the argument is not always successful.

State laws vary on the questions of fees. In New York, for instance, search fees generally are not allowed and duplication fees cannot exceed 25 cents per page. Try to settle the matter of fees up front—ideally, by getting them waived in advance. At a minimum, establish a ballpark figure for how much the fees will be, then find out if your boss will pay for them.

REFERENCES

Pember, Don R. *Mass Media Law*. 3d ed. Dubuque, IA: Wm. C. Brown, 1984.

Rush, Tonda F., ed. *How to Use the Federal FOI Act*. 3d ed. Washington, D.C.: FOI Service Center.

Weinberg, Steve. *Trade Secrets of Washington Journalists*. Washington, D.C.: Acropolis Books, 1981.

CHAPTER 12
Social Indicators

Communities increasingly demand that their local newspapers and broadcasting stations push journalism beyond surface reporting of the day's news events. Caught up in the major changes of our society, communities seek answers to a broad variety of questions. One general strategy used by media to guide these explorations of life in our communities and where they are headed is called *social indicators*. Social indicators are "statistics, statistical series, and all other forms of evidence that enable us to assess where we stand and are going with respect to our values and goals, and to evaluate specific programs and determine their impact." Although this statement may sound like the policy statement of a Pulitzer-prize-winning news outlet, it actually comes from social scientist Raymond Bauer's benchmark book, *Social Indicators*.

Whether applied by social scientists or by journalists, the social indicators strategy yields a comprehensive, systematic view of the community. Social indicators tell both the good news and the bad news.

Traditional news beats, or more contemporary news beats organized around social functions, can yield most of the social indicators that journalists need. But there must be a new point of view on the part of the observers stationed on the news beats. This new approach aims at a broader, more systematic look at the data compiled by public agencies. It looks beyond the single obtruding event to see the mosaic, to see how all the pieces fit together.

Social indicators reporting is not a radically new approach to reporting. What is different is that it is more systematic and comprehensive. In other words, social indicators add the *scientific method* to the reporter's repertoire. The fundamental values of social indicators reporting are those of traditional journalism. What is introduced is a new *strategy* for implementing the traditional goals and values, and a new strategy introduces new *tactics*. That is what this book is about: the new tactics of reporting and the techniques of behavioral science observation that can be applied in journalism.

One key element of the scientific method, the *hypothesis*, is especially important for social indicators reporting. A hypothesis is a point of view, a vantage point, a focus on some specific set of elements in a situation; it is not a stubbornly retained bias or opinion. Hypotheses are frequently rejected and constantly modified as our experience in the real world of fact dictates.

Why employ a hypothesis? Actually, all observers and journalists use hypotheses to guide their reporting. Sometimes they call them *story lines*. What differs from observer to observer is the explicitness of their hypotheses. How well do they specify what he or she is seeking? An explicit hypothesis is a navigational aid through the buzzing, blooming confusion of the real world.

When you set out on your news beat to work the gold mine of statistics (social indicators), you will quickly appreciate the value of explicit hypotheses. Reading page after page of statistics with nothing in mind except that they are somehow newsworthy is an exhaustive and, usually, unproductive task. Sets of statistics, budgets, and similar lists of facts too often are approached in terms of an event orientation. "Give me 2000 words on the new city budget," says the city editor. "See what you can get from this Agriculture Department bulletin," says the news director. The end result is often something like a casual rewrite of the world almanac. The story may make a good filler, but it is not good news copy. Don't rush in to write up all the social indicators at hand—set hypotheses, ask useful questions, use social indicators to tell a story. Statistics are interesting news copy only when they are translated into human terms.

Newsday succeeded in converting the statistics from over a half million reported crimes and thousands of arrest records, plus the newspaper's own polling results, into a comprehensive series on crime in suburbia. Here's a sample of the results:

> Community-by-community statistics suggested wide differences in crime rates, dependent on factors such as income, family stability, and the amount of rental housing. Among other things, the

study found that while Long Island as a whole is relatively crime free, there are pockets where poverty and overcrowding translate into levels of crime approaching those in urban areas. Several such crime cores were pinpointed. While such cores are old stories in America's inner cities, they are relatively new in the suburbs.

In Bay Shore, for instance, where an 11-square-block area accounts for nearly half the community's total crime, Laurie Papell, a YMCA social worker, explained: "What we're talking about . . . are the basic problems in American society—poverty, unemployment, child neglect." In the community's crime core, a man named Gator nursed a beer in a small bar and delivered his own summation. "People are desperate, they do crazy things. . . ."

Burglary is Long Island's most pervasive crime, striking about 24,000 times in 1982. Despite a recent decline, it is also the crime that most worries Long Islanders. Sixty-three percent of those polled by *Newsday* expressed fears about their homes being burglarized. For victims, the chances of recovering their possessions are very slim. Stolen property is usually sold rapidly, often within days or even hours—sometimes to local businessmen who act as fences.

Fears that New York City criminals are operating on Long Island are overblown. Long Islanders commit the overwhelming number of crimes on Long Island. But while the impact of city criminals is felt most along the Nassau–Queens border, the fear spreads much farther. In Suffolk, one out of five residents believes that a majority of burglaries and robberies are committed by city criminals.

Few criminals get caught. On Long Island, *Newsday* found that 90% of the murders are solved, but only about 30% of all robberies and 25% of burglaries are solved. Norman Carlson, director of the federal prison system, says: "The average criminal is gambling on the odds . . . and right now they feel the odds are in their favor."

Of those who do get caught, most live near the crime scene and are teenagers. For instance, 60% of the burglars arrested in 1982 were between 13 and 20. But there is increasing belief by police that these young people they are arresting are not committing the majority of crimes, particularly burglaries and robberies. A cadre of career criminals—men in their late teens and twenties, often driven by drugs—may actually be responsible. Suffolk Police Capt. Richard Dormer estimates, for example, that 200 career criminals may be responsible for 80% of the burglaries in the county's five western towns.

Social indicators are not limited to the statistics available from surveys and from the sources on your beat. The Bureau of the Census, plus other federal and state agencies, routinely compile vast amounts of data on local communities. For example, there is considerably more in the census records for your coverage area than the headcount from the 1980 national census. In fact, the statistic on how many people live in each geographic area is both the most frequently reported and the least interesting part of the vast data collected by the Bureau of the Census. Every 10 years when the national census is conducted, most newspapers and TV newscasts use a story reporting the new population count for their area, with, of course, a comparison to 10 years ago. Although this tells everyone something about their community, region, or state, and how it is changing, a considerably more detailed portrait of change can be produced from census data.

USING CENSUS RECORDS

Glance at the 1980 Census questionnaire reproduced on pp. 226–230 and note the vast detail available about the people in your audience. All the initial questions are about demographic characteristics—age, sex, race, or ethnic background, years of schooling, marital status, and occupation. The categories of these demographic characteristics can be combined in many different ways to describe segments of your community and how they are changing. If your newspaper or broadcasting station has a marketing research person, he or she spends a considerable amount of time looking at these demographic segments to see how fast they are growing or shrinking. Ask to see some of this material.

However, you don't have to get into the complexities of population segments defined by two, three, or a half dozen demographic characteristics in order to use census data for both strategic planning and specific news stories. The data on one characteristic alone can provide a wealth of information.

Take *age*, for example. The shrinking size of the young age cohorts in our national population—children between the ages of 8 and 12, for example—has resulted in the closing of many elementary schools in recent years. Compared to the post-World War II baby boom generation, which required many new schools, our public school systems now are dealing with a significantly smaller population of children. Census data on age will answer many questions about the people in your audience: Does your coverage area

The 1980 Census Questionnaire

The first seven population questions and housing questions H1–H12 are asked of every household (see Figure 12.1). The rest of the questions are asked on a one-in-six random sample basis, except in localities of less than 5000 population, where a one-in-two sample is taken.

The first question appears on the cover of both the short form (used with 100 percent of the population) and long form (used with the sample population). It asks, "What is the name of each person who was living here on Tuesday, April 1, 1980, or who was staying or visiting here and had no other home?" Personal data from this question are not published by the Census Bureau.

fit the national pattern, or does it display a different trend? How large is the population of children under age six? Are school enrollments going to increase or decrease? What are some of the other implications of the changing sizes of various age groups in your community or state?

The data on *sex* offer an equally rich source of information. Most geographic areas of the United States have considerably more females than males in their population now. Sociologists are beginning to study the implications of this for marriage and divorce patterns and many other aspects of our social life. Journalists should engage in similar research. There are major social implications here, and most likely they involve the majority population group in your area.

Combining the data on sex and occupation, the census also tells us that a majority of women now are working outside the home—or, building up the portrait another way, it tells us that the "traditional" American family of a husband and wife, plus two or three children under age 18, is now a minority. In 1983 only 16 percent of all households fit that description. If the definition of a "traditional" household is further restricted to a family composed of a breadwinner husband and housewife, plus two or three chil-

How to fill out your Census Form

See the filled-out example in the yellow instruction guide This guide will help with any problems you may have.

If you need more help, call the Census Office The telephone number of the local office is shown at the bottom of the address box on the front cover

Use a black pencil to answer the questions. Black pencil is better to use than ballpoint or other pens

Fill circles "O" completely, like this. ●

When you write in an answer, print or write clearly

Make sure that answers are provided for everyone here.

See page 4 of the guide if a roomer or someone else in the household does not want to give you all the information for the form.

Answer the questions on pages 1 through 5, and then starting with pages 6 and 7, fill a pair of pages for each person in the household.

Check your answers. Then write your name, the date, and telephone number on the back page.

Mail back this form on Tuesday, April 1, or as soon afterward as you can. Use the enclosed envelope; no stamp is needed.

Please start by answering Question 1 below.

Question 1

List in Question 1

• Family members living here. including babies still in the hospital

• Relatives living here

• Lodgers or boarders living here

• Other persons living here

• College students who stay here while attending college. even if their parents live elsewhere

• Persons who usually live here but are temporarily away (including children in boarding school below the college level)

• Persons with a home elsewhere but who stay here most of the week while working

Do Not List in Question 1

• Any person away from here in the Armed Forces.

• Any college student who stays somewhere else while attending college.

• Any person who usually stays somewhere else most of the week while working there.

• Any person away from here in an institution such as a home for the aged or mental hospital.

• Any person staying or visiting here who has a usual home elsewhere.

1. What is the name of each person who was living here on Tuesday, April 1, 1980, or who was staying or visiting here and had no other home?

Note

If everyone here is staying only temporarily and has a usual home elsewhere, please mark this box ☐.

Then please
• answer the questions on pages 2 through 5 only. and
• enter the address of your usual home on the back page.

Please continue ⤴

Figure 12.1   The 1980 census questionnaire.

dren under age 18, then we may have defined an endangered sociological species.

There is virtually no end to the strategic plans or numbers of reporters' questions that could be drawn from the personal information compiled by the Census Bureau, but it compiles much more than the information on people. Since 1940 our decennial national census also has included a census of housing that asks questions

Page 2

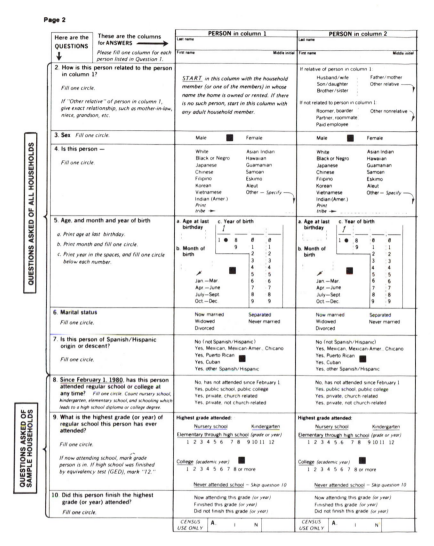

Figure 12.1 (continued)

equal in detail to those asked about personal characteristics. For each household the census obtains the occupant's estimate of the value of the property, whether the current occupants own or rent their residence, the amount of rent paid if they do rent, the total number of rooms, and a variety of other information. On a sample basis the census also ascertains the age of the house or building,

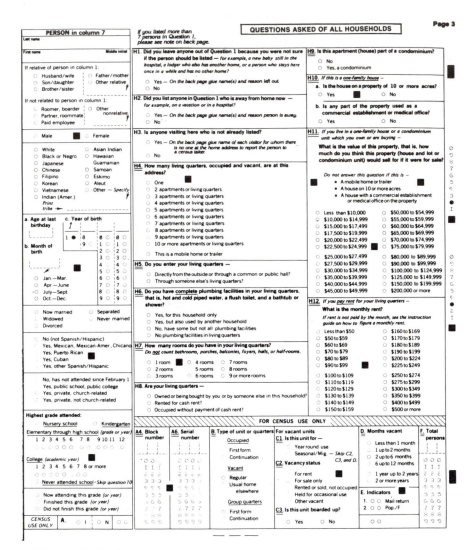

Figure 12.1 (continued)

estimated costs of utilities for the household, presence of a telephone, air conditioning, and automobiles, and a host of other indicators on the family's pattern and quality of daily life. These data can be the basis for a very thorough portrait of daily living conditions in your community.

The sample questionnaire also contains population questions 11 to 33, shown here on pages 6 and 7. These questions appear on pairs of facing pages of the sample form (i.e., 6 and 7, 8 and 9, etc.) for each person in the household. Note that questions 17 to 33 do not apply to persons under 15 years of age.

QUESTIONS ASKED OF SAMPLE HOUSEHOLDS   Page 7

c. When going to work last week, did this person usually —

Drive alone — *Skip to 28*   Drive others only
Share driving   Ride as passenger only

d. How many people, including this person, usually rode to work in the car, truck, or van last week?

2   4   6
3 ■   5   7 or more ■
After answering 24d, skip to 28.

25. Was this person temporarily absent or on layoff from a job or business last week?

Yes, on layoff
Yes, on vacation, temporary illness, labor dispute, etc.
No

26a. Has this person been looking for work during the last 4 weeks?
Yes   No — *Skip to 27*

b. Could this person have taken a job last week?

No, already has a job ■
No, temporarily ill
No, other reasons *(in school, etc.)*
Yes, could have taken a job ■

27. When did this person last work, even for a few days?

1980   1978   1970 to 1974 ⎫
1979   1975 to 1977   1969 or earlier ⎬ *Skip to 31d*
Never worked ⎭

28–30. Current or most recent job activity

Describe clearly this person's chief job activity or business last week. If this person had more than one job, describe the one at which this person worked the most hours. If this person had no job or business last week, give information for last job or business since 1975.

28. Industry

a. For whom did this person work? *If now on active duty in the Armed Forces, print "AF" and skip to question 31.*

(Name of company, business, organization, or other employer)

b. What kind of business or industry was this?
Describe the activity at location where employed.

(For example: Hospital, newspaper publishing, mail order house, ■ auto engine manufacturing, breakfast cereal manufacturing)

c. Is this mainly — *(Fill one circle)*

Manufacturing ■   Retail trade
Wholesale trade   Other — *(agriculture, construction, service, government, etc.)*

29. Occupation

a. What kind of work was this person doing?

(For example: Registered nurse, personnel manager, supervisor of order department, gasoline engine assembler, grinder operator)

b. What were this person's most important activities or duties?

(For example: Patient care, directing hiring policies, supervising order clerks, assembling engines, operating grinding mill)

30. Was this person — *(Fill one circle)*

Employee of private company, business, or individual, for wages, salary, or commissions ■

Federal government employee
State government employee
Local government employee *(city, county, etc.)*

Self-employed in own business, professional practice, or farm —
Own business not incorporated
Own business incorporated

Working without pay in family business or farm

31a. Last year (1979), did this person work, even for a few days, at a paid job or in a business or farm?

Yes ■   No — *Skip to 31d*

b. How many weeks did this person work in 1979?
Count paid vacation, paid sick leave, and military service.

Weeks

c. During the weeks worked in 1979, how many hours did this person usually work each week?

Hours

d. Of the weeks not worked in 1979 (if any), how many weeks was this person looking for work or on layoff from a job?

Weeks

32. Income in 1979 —

Fill circles and print dollar amounts.
If net income was a loss, write "Loss" above the dollar amount.
If exact amount is not known, give best estimate. For income received jointly by household members, see instruction guide.

During 1979 did this person receive any income from the following sources?

If "Yes" to any of the sources below — How much did this person receive for the entire year?

a. Wages, salary, commissions, bonuses, or tips from all jobs . . . *Report amount before deductions for taxes, bonds, dues, or other items.*

Yes ➤ $ .00
No   *(Annual amount – Dollars)*

b. Own nonfarm business, partnership, or professional practice . . . *Report net income after business expenses.*

Yes ➤ $ .00
No   *(Annual amount – Dollars)*

c. Own farm . . .
Report net income after operating expenses. Include earnings as a tenant farmer or sharecropper.

Yes ➤ $ .00
No   *(Annual amount – Dollars)*

d. Interest, dividends, royalties, or net rental income . . .
Report even small amounts credited to an account.

Yes ➤ $ .00
No   *(Annual amount – Dollars)*

e. Social Security or Railroad Retirement . . .

Yes ➤ $ .00
No   *(Annual amount – Dollars)*

f. Supplemental Security (SSI), Aid to Families with Dependent Children (AFDC), or other public assistance or public welfare payments . . .

Yes ➤ $ .00
No   *(Annual amount – Dollars)*

g. Unemployment compensation, veterans' payments, pensions, alimony or child support, or any other sources of income received regularly . . .
Exclude lump-sum payments such as money from an inheritance or the sale of a home.

Yes ➤ $ .00
No   *(Annual amount – Dollars)*

33. What was this person's total income in 1979?

Add entries in questions 32a through g; subtract any losses.
$ .00
(Annual amount – Dollars)
If total amount was a loss, write "Loss" above amount.   OR   None

Figure 12.1   (continued)

UPDATING THE CENSUS

By this time the thought probably has crossed your mind that although 1980 Census data may be a useful basis for strategic planning, it lacks the timeliness that journalists deem necessary in a news story. Don't despair. The basic data of the Census is compiled

QUESTIONS ASKED OF SAMPLE HOUSEHOLDS

Name of
Person 1
on page 2:

_____
Last name   First name   Middle initial

11. In what State or foreign country was this person born?
Print the State where this person's mother was living when this person was born. Do not give the location of the hospital unless the mother's home and the hospital were in the same State.

_____
Name of State or foreign country; or Puerto Rico, Guam, etc.

12. If this person was born in a foreign country –
a. Is this person a naturalized citizen of the United States?
- ○ Yes, a naturalized citizen
- ○ No, not a citizen
- ■ Born abroad of American parents ■

b. When did this person come to the United States to stay?
- ○ 1975 to 1980   ○ 1965 to 1969   ○ 1950 to 1959
- ○ 1970 to 1974   ○ 1960 to 1964   ○ Before 1950

13a. Does this person speak a language other than English at home?
- ○ Yes   ○ No, only speaks English – Skip to 14

b. What is this language?

_____
(For example – Chinese, Italian, Spanish, etc.)

c. How well does this person speak English?
- ○ Very well   ○ Not well
- ○ Well   ○ Not at all ■

14. What is this person's ancestry? If uncertain about how to report ancestry, see instruction guide.

_____

(For example: Afro-Amer., English, French, German, Honduran, Hungarian, Irish, Italian, Jamaican, Korean, Lebanese, Mexican, Nigerian, Polish, Ukrainian, Venezuelan, etc.)

15a. Did this person live in this house five years ago (April 1, 1975)?
If in college or Armed Forces in April 1975, report place of residence there.
- Born April 1975 or later – Turn to next page for next person
- ○ Yes, this house – Skip to 16
- ○ No, different house

b. Where did this person live five years ago (April 1, 1975)?
- **(1) State, foreign country, Puerto Rico, Guam, etc.:** _____
- **(2) County:** _____
- **(3) City, town, village, etc.:** _____
- **(4) Inside the incorporated (legal) limits of that city, town, village, etc.?**
  - ○ Yes   ○ No, in unincorporated area

16. When was this person born?
- Born before April 1965 –
  Please go on with questions 17-33
- ■ Born April 1965 or later –
  Turn to next page for next person

17. In April 1975 (five years ago) was this person –
a. On active duty in the Armed Forces?
- ○ Yes   ○ No

b. Attending college?
- ○ Yes   ○ No

c. Working at a job or business?
- ○ Yes, full time   ○ No
- ○ Yes, part time

18a. Is this person a veteran of active-duty military service in the Armed Forces of the United States?
If service was in National Guard or Reserves only, see instruction guide.
- ○ Yes   ○ No – Skip to 19

b. Was active-duty military service during –
Fill a circle for each period in which this person served.
- ○ May 1975 or later
- ○ Vietnam era (August 1964–April 1975)
- ○ February 1955–July 1964
- ○ Korean conflict (June 1950–January 1955)
- ○ World War II (September 1940–July 1947)
- ■ World War I (April 1917–November 1918)
- ○ Any other time

19. Does this person have a physical, mental, or other health condition which has lasted for 6 or more months and which . . . .
- **a. Limits** the kind or amount of work this person can do at a job? . . . . .   Yes No
- **b. Prevents** this person from working at a job?
- **c. Limits or prevents** this person from using public transportation? . . . .

20. If this person is a female –   None 1 2 3 4 5 6
How many babies has she ever had, not counting stillbirths?
Do not count her stepchildren   7 8 9 10 11 12 or more
or children she has adopted.

21. If this person has ever been married –
a. Has this person been married more than once?
- ○ Once   ○ More than once

b. Month and year of marriage?   **Month and year of first marriage?**

_____   _____
(Month)   (Year)   (Month)   (Year)

c. If married more than once – Did the first marriage end because of the death of the husband (or wife)?
- ○ Yes   ○ No

22a. Did this person work at any time last week?

| ○ Yes – Fill this circle if this person worked full time or part time. (Count part-time work such as delivering papers, or helping without pay in a family business or farm. Also count active duty in the Armed Forces.) | ■ No – Fill this circle if this person did not work, or did only own housework, school work, or volunteer work. |

Skip to 25

b. How many hours did this person work last week (at all jobs)?
Subtract any time off; add overtime or extra hours worked.

_____ Hours ■

23. At what location did this person work last week?
If this person worked at more than one location, print where he or she worked most last week.
If one location cannot be specified, see instruction guide.

a. Address (Number and street)
_____
If street address is not known, enter the building name, shopping center, or other physical location description.

b. Name of city, town, village, borough, etc.
_____

c. Is the place of work inside the incorporated (legal) limits of that city, town, village, borough, etc.?
- ○ Yes   ○ No, in unincorporated area

d. County _____

e. State _____ **f. ZIP Code** _____

24a. Last week, how long did it usually take this person to get from home to work (one way)?

_____ Minutes

b. How did this person usually get to work last week?
If this person used more than one method, give the one usually used for most of the distance.
- ○ Car   ○ Taxicab
- ■ Truck   ○ Motorcycle
- ○ Van   ○ Bicycle
- ○ Bus or streetcar   ○ Walked only
- ○ Railroad   ○ Worked at home
- ○ Subway or elevated   ○ Other – Specify

If car, truck, or van in 24b, go to 24c.
Otherwise, skip to 28.

Figure 12.1 (continued)

only once every 10 years, but these statistics constantly are being updated. Every month the Census Bureau's trained staff of interviewers conducts about 60,000 interviews across the nation. From your knowledge of sampling error gained in Chapter 7, consider how precise these updated estimates are—even when broken down by states. It is these interviews that generate the monthly unemployment statistics as well as considerable other new data on our population. Thus, the decennial census of each decade provides the benchmark data, and the current population surveys keep our information up to date.

GOVERNMENT AND BUSINESS

Beyond the mountains of data on people and their homes, the Bureau of the Census also compiles extensive data on local government and businesses. The traditional concerns of journalism in these areas can be richly augmented with these census reports.

Again, just as is the case for census information on people and housing, numerous opportunities exist for comparing these data on your local community with the same kinds of data from other geographic locations or from earlier points in time. Identical procedures are used by the Bureau of the Census to collect its data from all locations and to prepare state and national totals or averages. This means that data about your community can be placed in context and compared with communities nearby or in other states, your entire state, or the nation. Most importantly, trends over time can be examined both for your community and for any of these comparison groups.

Remember that numbers, such as those from census reports, lend precision to your reporting, but that numbers in isolation do not have a lot of meaning. You really need to compare any number with at least one other number in order to transform data into information.

Because much of the data on government and business is compiled every 5 years, rather than at 10-year intervals as is the Census of Population and Housing, a wealth of recent data is available at nearby public and college libraries, or you can order reports directly from the Bureau of the Census. The costs are nominal—virtually free compared to the costs of most books these days.

CENSUS OF GOVERNMENTS

If you seek out the most recent *Census of Governments*, it will be easy to spot this two-foot plus thick set of books on the library shelf. Here is extensive information on everything from local county government and every school district enrolling 5000 or more pupils to

As Redevelopment Moved In, Many Residents Moved Out

Betty Roccograndi
Staff Writer
Wilkes-Barre Times Leader

KINGSTON—The quiet, residential streets along the river in Kingston have been rebuilt since the 1972 Agnes Flood.

But because of the flood and younger people leaving the area for better jobs, the area lost population during the decade and the average age of its residents increased.

Federal census statistics show the area lost 19 percent of its population during the decade, while the county population rose slightly.

They also show the area grew more transient. According to the 1970 census, 73 percent of the people had lived in the same house five years or more—close to the county average. By 1980, that figure had fallen to 57 percent, while the county rate stayed about the same.

The quiet residential district is lined with a mixture of single-family homes, duplexes and apartment buildings.

To the north of Pierce Street is a newly-developed area on Third Avenue, which includes the Shop Rite supermarket and other stores, the Kingston Recreation Center and the Roller King Skating Center.

The flood probably played more of a part in changing the area than anything else did, according to Kingston Mayor Charles Bankes.

Although many people defied another flood and stayed to remodel their homes, some did move to other areas, such as Mountaintop and Oakwood Park.

"They wanted out under any condition," said Kingston real estate broker William Rolland Sr., former chairman of the Flood Victims Action Committee of Wyoming Valley. "If it rained, they were gunshy," he said.

Another noticeable difference was the total number of households.

Here, the census showed a decrease of 104 households, from 830 to 726. But Irvin Patterson, executive director of the Luzerne County Redevelopment Authority, said the construction four years ago of Kingston Manor, an approximately 100-unit apartment building for senior citizens, would have since raised the number of households for the area.

The area also differs from the county in the age of the population. Here, the median age increased from 40.3 to 43.1. County-wide, the median age decreased from 36.2 to 35.9.

The median household income also rose, but not as much as it did throughout the county. Here, it increased from $8,273 to $11,812, or by about 43 percent. But county-wide it jumped from $6,928 to $13,990, or by about 102 percent.

The median value of homes increased as well, from $16,800 in 1970 to $40,300 in 1980. Through the county, median home value rose from $10,700 to $30,800.

Overall, the area has seen some vast improvements, from newly-constructed and remodeled homes on the south side of Pierce Street to the new commercial area on the north side.

And according to William Kratz, relocation director of the Luzerne County Redevelopment Authority, there's still potential for further development in the area's commercial district.

---

government-operated liquor stores. Four major aspects of government are covered:

Organization of government within each state
Taxable property values
Public employment
Government finance

This last category is an especially valuable lode of information for in-depth reporting because these reports neatly summarize a wealth of data on the revenues and expenditures of local government. Furthermore, the comparative figures for placing these financial statistics in perspective are always available.

Among the financial data provided about each school district, for example, are the sources of its revenue: the amount of federal aid, both that provided directly and that provided indirectly through some intermediary agency, such as the state government; direct state aid; revenue obtained from school taxes, usually taxes on local property; and any other sources of revenue available to the school district. Also reported is the enrollment in each district, which facilitates comparisons with other school districts. Data on revenue and expenditures can be divided by the enrollment and reported per pupil or per 100 pupils.

The money spent by the schools is summarized in three principal categories: salaries and wages, construction, and interest on debt. For any indebtedness of a school district, information is provided on the total amount of debt, plus new debts added and old debts paid off during the previous fiscal year. During a time when the voters in many districts continue to complain about property taxes while enrollments are declining due to major demographic shifts in our population, this summary data from the *Census of Governments* is a valuable news source.

To take another example, the *Census of Governments* contains more than two dozen entries for every county government in the United States. Among the information provided are the amounts of revenue obtained from various sources; spending on such activities as police, transportation, public welfare, parks, and government administration; and the amount of debt owed by the county. Again, these neat summaries and the ability to compare counties with each other and across time make this portion of the *Census of Governments* a key news source.

CENSUS OF RETAIL TRADE

For data on the private sector there is the *Census of Retail Trade*. Like the *Census of Governments*, these reports are prepared every five years, in the years of each decade that end in 2 and in 7. Organized by state, these volumes report a wealth of data for every city of any size. For 10 major categories of retail stores and shops, there is information on the number of stores, their total sales, their payroll, and their number of employees.

Comparisons of these data, across time and across communities, provide an excellent economic barometer for your community. Any creative journalist can spend hours browsing through these reports and converting this dry statistical data into a living, readable economic portrait of the community.

Once you have grasped the continuing potential for these kinds of news stories, your professional exploration through the library shelves can continue to yield discovery after discovery. For example, annual reports on the geographic distribution of federal funds contain detailed grist for the continuing debate between the Sunbelt and the Frostbelt on the distribution of federal largesse. These reports also provide raw material for the continuing story on the impact and importance of federal money for a wide variety of local activities.

Examination of the 1980 data for Longview, Texas, a modest city of approximately 50,000 in the northeast corner of the state, shows that Longview and its residents received $55,576,000 from 18 federal agencies that year. Topping the list was $17,530,000 from the Department of Health and Human Services, mostly in Social Security payments. Longview also received $10,991,000 from the Department of Defense. This hefty sum included nearly $5 million in contracts to Longview businesses and about $5.6 million in military retirement pay to Longview residents.

The examples and sources cited here represent only a casual use of census records as news sources. Many other stories can be found in these sources and in many other federal and state sources as well.

Once you begin to pose questions and hypotheses about life in your community and to seek indicators of these conditions, numerous unobtrusive measures will come to mind. By *unobtrusive measures* we mean techniques where the very act of observation does not distort or bias the behavior under observation. By this definition, interviewing is an obtrusive technique, and content analysis is an unobtrusive technique.

Even observing something as ordinary, nonstatistical, and unobtrusive as trash and garbage can test a variety of hypotheses.

> Numerous reporters have tested the efficacy of "dry" laws by counting the liquor bottles and beer cans found in the trash of allegedly "dry" areas.

The effectiveness of state laws requiring deposits on beer and soft drink containers has been tested by observing the amount of litter along roadways and in public parks.

For years the *New Orleans Times-Picayune* measured the "party spirit" of the annual Mardi Gras by asking the city sanitation department how many tons of bottles, cans, and other debris were retrieved from the streets and gutters after Mardi Gras Day.

Toronto Star reporter David Miller's qualitative assessment of what is left out for the garbageman verified the severity of economic conditions during the summer of 1984:

> *Times are tough for pollikers.*
>
> *Pollikers? They're the folk that travel Metro at night or early morning in old cars or trucks, checking out the garbage for appliances, furniture, returnable bottles (especially beer), metal, you name it.*
>
> *Before the recession hit, garbage officials say, a polliker, a term invented by the garbagemen, could make $50 a night salvaging the junk we dump on our lawns for 7 a.m. pickup.*
>
> *But now, with high unemployment, the dollar sinking and the inflation rate rising, people aren't throwing out things with the same vigor.*

Testing your hunches about trends or conditions in the community is not constrained by available statistics or what you can get a quote on from some official. Use your imagination and you will think of dozens of unobtrusive social indicators that are useful and revealing. To further stimulate your thinking, Eugene Webb and his colleagues at the Medill School of Journalism have published an entire book on this approach to observation: *Unobtrusive Measures: Nonreactive Research in the Social Sciences.*

The news is more than today's events. It includes systematic reports of today's situations, which are likely to produce the obtruding events of tomorrow. Creativity and imagination are the principal elements of social indicators reporting and its use of the scientific method—they have always been the hallmarks of good journalism.

REFERENCES

Anderson, Elijah. *A Place on the Corner.* Chicago: University of Chicago Press, 1978.

Bauer, Raymond A., ed. *Social Indicators.* Cambridge, MA: M.I.T. Press, 1966.

Festinger, Leon, Henry Riecken, and Stanley Schachter. *When Prophecy Fails.* Minneapolis: University of Minnesota Press, 1956.

Liebow, Elliot. *Tally's Corner: A Study of Negro Streetcorner Men.* Boston: Little, Brown, 1967.

Webb, Eugene J., Donald T. Campbell, Richard D. Schwartz, and Lee Sechrest. *Unobtrusive Measures: Nonreactive Research in the Social Sciences.* Chicago: Rand McNally, 1966.

Whyte, William F. *Street Corner Society.* Chicago: University of Chicago Press, 1955.

Part IV
DIRECT OBSERVATION

CHAPTER 13

Participant Observation

The reporter's name was Neville St. Clair. He worked for an evening newspaper in London, and his editors wanted a series of stories about begging in the city.

"It was only by trying begging as an amateur that I could get the facts upon which to base my articles," he recounted. He had done some acting before going into journalism, so it wasn't hard for St. Clair to make himself up as a pitiable character with a scar on his face and a red wig.

St. Clair discovered (this was in the days before the Newspaper Guild) he was such a good beggar that he was making more on the streets than in the city room. He took a leave from his paper, and ultimately quit his reporting job to become a full-time panhandler. His suburban wife and kids never knew. In the end, however, he was unmasked by a clever detective named Sherlock Holmes.

The story is Sir Arthur Conan Doyle's *The Man with the Twisted Lip*. It's one of the earliest accounts—albeit a fictional one—of a journalist using a popular social science tool, *participant observation*, in search of a story, and, perhaps, freelance opportunities too. Other examples, all nonfictional:

Nellie Bly of the *New York World* faked insanity to look at an asylum from the inside in the 1880s. That ploy has been repeated over the decades.

Philadelphia Inquirer reporter Eric Harrison spent two weeks undercover in a housing project, then went back as a re-

241

porter for nearly three months, finding "an isolated world in which a different set of rules applies . . . lawlessness is the norm, sanitation is a hopeless struggle, and something as simple as taking out the trash becomes a fearful task."

Mike Keller of the *Honolulu Advertiser* spent five nights in Hawaii State Prison with "32 murderers, 17 rapists, and 114 other convicted felons" and wrote an eight-part series on problems behind bars. His conclusion: "It's an intriguing place to visit. But I sure as hell wouldn't want to live there. . . . Animals at Honolulu zoo are housed better."

Wall Street Journal reporter Beth Nissen worked three weeks on an electronics factory assembly line in 1978 to look into charges of unfair labor practices.

Mike Goodman of the *Los Angeles Times* posed as an employee in a detention home for juveniles. After his story about abuses appeared, many top-level supervisors were out of jobs.

SEEING EVERYDAY LIFE

Social scientists Howard Becker and Blanche Geer describe participant observation as "that method in which the observer participates in the daily life of the people under study, either openly in the role of researcher or covertly in some disguised role, observing things that happen, listening to what is said, and questioning people, over some length of time."

Participant observation enables you to work in situations where the overt presence of a journalist could change people's behavior. Participant observation can be as simple as a newspaper's restaurant critic making reservations under a false name to conceal his or her identity from restaurateurs—because if it's known by the owner, the maitre d', the waiter, and the chef that *The Daily Bugle* restaurant critic is in the house, the meal and service will be far from typical. The journalist's goal is to describe normal times, not an artificial reality constructed for the benefit of a reporter.

But working without a "cover" does not mean you can't successfully use participant observation. Elliot Liebow, a white man,

Our 'Bar' Uncovers Payoffs, Tax Gyps

Pamela Zekman
Zay N. Smith
Chicago Sun-Times

It looked like any neighborhood tavern in Chicago. The beer was cold, the bratwursts hot.

But the Mirage, 731 N. Wells St., was never quite what it seemed.

It was a tavern operated by the *Sun-Times* and the Better Government Assn.

The bartenders were reporters and investigators. The repairmen were photographers headed for a hidden loft.

All were investigating years of complaints from small businesses about the day-to-day corruption they have to endure in Chicago, the city that works if you know how to work it.

The *Sun-Times* will tell the Mirage's story—with names, dates and amounts—in the days to come.

This newspaper will detail:

Payoffs of $10 to $100 grabbed by city inspectors who ignore health and safety hazards when the price is right.

Shakedowns by state liquor inspectors who demand whatever is in a tavern's cash register for their silence about liquor violations.

Tax fraud by accountants who consort with taverns to cheat on state and federal taxes in a practice so widespread it may be costing Illinois $16 million in sales tax alone.

Misconduct and negligence by public employees who loaf on the job, use city equipment for private gain and routinely demand cash under the table for what should be public services.

Illegal kickbacks, tax skimming, and offers of political fixes from jukebox and pinball machine operators—including one from policemen who alone may be failing to report a half-million dollars a year in taxable income.

wrote his sociological classic *Tally's Corner* based on his experiences in a black area of Washington, D.C. He later wrote of his work:

> On several different counts I was an outsider, but I also was a participant in the full sense of the word. The people I was observing knew that I was observing them, yet they allowed me to participate in their activities and take part in their lives to a degree that continues to surprise me.

Author George Plimpton has made a career of participant observation, trying his hand at being a pro football quarterback and a professional golfer, among other things, and then writing books about the experience. For him, he admits, it's a "gimmick"—but a useful one for information gathering.

Plimpton enjoys the understanding of professionals he writes about "because I've tried to do what they've done. They talk to me slightly differently from the way they talk to reporters. So the point of the gimmick is to open the door to a kind of relationship with the subject which is a little different from the one they'd have with an ordinary interviewer."

Plimpton is known to his subjects, and the technique still works. Mike Keller's subjects also knew who he was, during his five-day stay in Hawaii's prison, but he wrote that the inmates "were eager to talk, even though I had not expected it. I thought they would be resentful of me as an outsider who didn't rightfully belong." One inmate slipped him drugs, even though he was known to be a reporter, to show how easy it was to obtain and conceal drugs behind bars.

Participant observation frees the journalist from relying solely on "official" versions of the truth. It's one thing for a nursing home supervisor to tell you that bedridden patients are bathed every second day. It's quite another to see for yourself as an orderly that once a week is the rule.

Sociologist Elijah Anderson spent a good deal of his time over a three-year period with the habitués of "Jelly's" bar and liquor store in a black area on the south side of Chicago. "I socialized with the people—drinking with them, talking and listening to them, and trying to come to terms with their social world," Anderson explained.

He wrote about the different social strata he found: The "regulars," the "wineheads" (on whom everyone looked down), the young "hoodlums." From his research he produced a 216-page book, but much of the anecdotal material used to illustrate his sociological conclusions would have made riveting reading or viewing if recast into a newspaper or television series on life in the Chicago ghetto.

The participant observer technique can add the richness of human interaction and emotion to news. It can capture the flesh and blood of a situation.

HUMAN OBSERVATION

Novel approaches or perspectives, such as participant observation, often let you see things in a new light. Frequently this happens when you study a foreign language. For the first time you gain a real appreciation of the structure of English, a language we mostly learned piecemeal as children. An analogy with reporting methods holds. Most of us learned piecemeal the traditional methods of journalistic observation. We learned them by doing simple interviews, rewriting press releases, and scanning a variety of reports and records. Participant observation has the same relationship to traditional reporting methods as the study of a foreign language has to English. Some attention to participant observation provides useful sensitization to the observation methods of journalism.

Participant observation uses the human as an observation instrument. This is true of the other methods of observation discussed in this book, but the point is sometimes obscured by such intermediate tools as questionnaires, coding sheets, and public records. And even the most alert, sensitive, and professional journalists bring a certain amount of intellectual baggage and previous experience to any observation task. The themes, ideas, and concepts we use to organize our observations impose an order on reality that it does not inherently possess.

Although two naive observers will not come up with the same set of facts, two journalists will, because, consciously or unconsciously, they apply the news values of professional journalism to their observations. This too can structure—a tactful way of saying *distort*—the observations.

To grasp the variety of possibilities raised by the strategy of participant observation, consider this method of reporting as a bridge between the very distinct roles assigned to reporter and source by traditional journalistic practices. Traditional journalism is based on some kind of link—commonly an interview or press release—between a participant (the source) and the observer (the journalist). The technique of participant observation fuses these two roles, but not in a single, fixed way.

In describing any particular application of participant observation, either of the two words in the phrase *participant observation* can be emphasized. This is even clearer if we reverse the phrase and call the reporter's role *observer participant.*

In some instances, the degree of participation is actually quite small, in part because the observer does not want to actively influence the process under observation. In such a situation, the reporter is an *observer* participant and the technique of observation is participant *observation.*

In other instances, the reporter is fully a participant in the activities under observation. The reporter's identity may be known to all the others around, as in George Plimpton's books; known only to a few members of the group, as in William Whyte's *Street Corner Society*, or not known to any members of the group at all, as in *When Prophecy Fails*, by Leon Festinger et al. In these instances the reporter is an observer *participant* and the technique is *participant* observation.

At least two considerations govern what role the reporter plays. The first is the efficiency of collecting material for a news story or series of stories. This includes both the ease with which the reporting situation can be set up and the probable effects of observation on the behaviors and events under observation. Second, ethics must be a major consideration also. When reporting involves less open observation and more clandestine participation, is it ethical? Could the information be collected in other, more open ways?

SOME GUIDELINES FOR PARTICIPANT OBSERVATION

Participant observation is not right for every situation. It poses major logistical problems for the television reporter in particular. Some key characteristics of participant observation are as follows:

Make it up as you go along. Typically, you don't enter a situation seeking to prove or disprove a particular hypothesis. You discover the rules of the game as you watch it and participate in it.

Give yourself enough time to understand things. Recognize that you will not gain instant acceptance in any group. When Elijah Anderson began studying "Jelly's," he started by just hanging around the bar regularly, an outsider.

> It was a place where I would be relatively unobtrusive, yet somewhat sociable. It was here that the process of getting to know Jelly's began, where increasingly I gained some license to exist and talk openly with people.

Make complete notes on what you observe as soon as possible after observing it. Walking around with a note pad will not work most of the time, and simply cannot be done if you're working under cover. Nonetheless, at the end of each day, make a record of what you saw, heard, and felt. Go overboard in notetaking. When you begin a project, you can't know what will be significant or illustrative. An anecdote that seems trivial at first may prove to be central to what you eventually deduce about a situation. Your notes should encompass the physical setting of the place, the identities of the people you observed, the purpose for which they gather, the actual behavior you saw.

Don't take sides. In any participant observer setting, but particularly in cases where you are watching a situation in conflict (union vs. management, factions in a psychiatric ward, inmates vs. guards in prison, "regulars" vs. "wineheads" in a neighborhood bar), you cannot effectively observe the whole scene if you tie yourself to one camp. Position yourself socially so that you can communicate with all factions.

You need to do this right from the start, or you may permanently forfeit any chance to obtain rapport with some subgroups. This is a danger inherent in getting permission for a project from the higher-ups in an organization. If the rank-and-file see you being endorsed by the leaders, they may suspect that your allegiance is elsewhere. They will never act naturally in your presence, and your reporting will suffer.

Pay attention to how other people around you view the world. You are there to see how reality is perceived by others, not to impose your theories of reality upon them.

When you are finished you do not have numbers to analyze and discuss. This is unlike many of the techniques discussed in this book—surveys and document research, for instance. You have a series of qualitative impressions instead.

It costs time and money. Sociologists can spend months or years on a project. That kind of commitment is not typical for news projects of this type, but it may sometimes be necessary to spend a week or two, even a month or more, on one project. An investment of this type is not taken lightly by editors and news directors.

The logistical problems of living with or at least living among your subjects are many. You need considerable planning if you are to succeed. As important as devising a careful plan is, there also may be ethical reasons which prevent you from gathering information through deception. Indeed, some news media have rules prohibiting or tightly circumscribing any use of deception by journalists. Some of the arguments pro and con on this issue are described in more detail in the article by David Shaw of the *Los Angeles Times* reprinted in the box at the end of this chapter. Decide in advance whether it is crucial to conceal your identity for the project to succeed. In many cases, it will be necessary. People in embarrassing, illegal, or emotionally trying situations may not act naturally if they know a journalist is around taking notes that will turn up in the newspaper or on television some day.

For other studies, however, revealing your identity with some vague statement of the purpose of your presence may work. Some experts in the field believe that people find it impossible to be on guard constantly for long periods. After a while, people often "let their hair down," forget what you're there for, and begin acting naturally. One advantage of not concealing your identity is that it gives you a plausible reason for asking people questions.

THINGS THAT CAN GO WRONG

Beware of becoming such an active, wholehearted participant that you change the nature of what you want to report. Social psychologists Leon Festinger, H. W. Riecken Jr., and Stanley Schachter had to walk an exceedingly fine line on this point when they joined a millenium religious group predicting the end of the world. This was not a situation where social scientists or reporters could sit around, notebooks in hand, asking questions about the beliefs and motivations of the faithful. They had to appear to be true believers, yet without such fervor that the very nature of the millenium movement would be changed by three college professor members. Reactions caused by the very act of observation are a major problem for many modes of reporting. The presence of a TV camera, in particular, can change events. People act differently on camera.

Also maintain an awareness that even as a participant observer, your view of the situation at hand is a limited, sometimes highly selective, view of reality. Even a participant observer cannot be everywhere and with everyone constantly. The observer's role also limits what can be observed. If you are closely aligned with the leaders of a group, you have the leaders' perspectives on the members and vice versa—you can't have it both ways. Although the traditional journalistic practice of interviewing all sides in a controversy is an attempt to have it both ways, it does not always succeed. Interviewing and participant observation can complement each other.

This question of the social distance between the observer and the observed has been discussed many times, including the explicit question of the distance between the reporter and his or her sources. It is not as easy in practice as it is in theory to maintain a distance that is sufficiently close to allow you to understand your subject but at the same time to avoid total identification and co-optation. Part of the task of the participant observer is to enter the world of the source's experience. But if we enter it too deeply and identify with his or her situation, then we have lost the neutral perspective of the professional journalist.

"The Ethics of Deception by Reporters"*

David Shaw
Los Angeles Times

Do the special rights granted to the press under the First Amendment also impose upon the press special responsibilities that preclude deception and misrepresentation?

Or is the public benefit to be derived from the disclosure of certain conditions sometimes so great—and the obstacles to such disclosure sometimes so difficult—that reporters are justified in pretending to be what they are not?

In short, does the worthwhile end sometimes justify the deceptive means?

As recently as five years ago, says Thomas Winship, editor of the *Boston Globe*, "we got an excellent story by having a reporter pose as a guard at a youth detention center and report on the maltreatment he saw. We wouldn't do that now."

"We in the press are arguing for an open, honest society, demanding certain behavior from our public officials," says William Hornby, editor of the *Denver Post*. "We ought to be just as open and just as frank and straightforward in getting information as we claim other people ought to be in giving it to us."

But some editors see such proclamations as both unrealistic and self-righteous. Says Michael J. O'Neill, former editor of the *New York Daily News*, "there are some situations where it's the only way to get the story."

That is the decision *Chicago Sun-Times* editors made when they assigned a team of reporters to operate the Mirage Bar incognito for four months in 1977 to expose graft and corruption in the city.

* The following is an excerpt from an article published in the *Los Angeles Times* on September 20, 1979. Since that time virtually everyone named in this story is either retired or has changed jobs.

The results: City inspectors volunteered to overlook health and safety violations at the bar in exchange for money. Jukebox and pinball operators offered kickbacks. Accountants offered counsel on the fine art of tax fraud. Contractors served as bagmen for payoffs to public officials.

The *Sun-Times* ran stories on its discoveries for four weeks.

In earlier years enterprising efforts like that of the *Sun-Times* had often won Pulitzers—right in Chicago. The *Chicago Tribune* won in 1971, for example, when one of its reporters worked as an ambulance driver to expose collusion between the police and private ambulance companies.

But the *Sun-Times* did not win—largely because several editors on the Pulitzer advisory board objected to their journalistic methods.

"In a day in which we are spending thousands of man-hours uncovering deception, we simply cannot deceive," says Benjamin C. Bradlee, executive editor of the *Washington Post* and a member of the Pulitzer advisory board.

However, insists James Hoge, at the time editor of the *Sun-Times*, "We couldn't have gotten that information and presented it as effectively any other way. We had reported for a number of years on bribery in Chicago . . . with no effect."

Even Hoge agrees, though, that the kind of journalism practiced on the Mirage Bar story "should be used only with extreme caution and selectivity and only when certain standards are applied."

Most editors seem to agree, in principle, on those "standards":

> The story involved should be of significant public benefit.
> Past experience, common sense and hard work should first demonstrate that there is no other

way to get the story, that conventional reportorial techniques just will not yield the necessary information. . . .

Executive Editor Gene Roberts of the *Philadelphia Inquirer* can remember using a variety of misleading tactics when he covered civil rights in the South for the *New York Times* in the late 1950s and 1960s.

"Reporters were systematically excluded from the first desegregated schools," he says. So Roberts, who has a Southern accent and could look quite young back then, always kept a sweater and a school notebook handy. On occasion he would throw his coat and tie under a nearby bush and stroll onto a high school campus, wearing a sweater, carrying a notebook and looking, for all anyone knew, like a typical white student.

Lois Timnick, human behavior writer for the *Los Angeles Times*, used a phony name and posed as a graduate student in psychology so she could work for two weeks at Metropolitan State Hospital and expose conditions for mental patients there.

Although Ms. Timnick signed her phony name to an "oath of confidentiality," promising "not to divulge any information or records concerning any client/patient without proper authorization," she did look at—and write about—patients' confidential medical records.

Did that violate her oath?

"No, I don't think so," she says now. "When I wrote about the patients . . . I changed their names and some of the details about them so other people couldn't recognize them."

But Ms. Timnick took the job precisely because it would give her access to confidential medical records—something she felt was essential to her story, but something many editors see as an invasion of the patients' privacy, despite her subsequent precautions in writing the story. (Even Ms. Timnick admits she would not want a reporter looking at her own medical reports, whether he wrote about them or not.)

Although Ms. Timnick says she does not think she could have gotten as good a story by conventional interviews with patients, doctors and other hospital employees, Eugene Patterson, president and editor of the *St. Petersburg Times*, says "She'd have a hard time convincing me of that." Twenty years ago, Patterson says, a reporter who worked for him in Atlanta won a Pulitzer Prize for exposing conditions in a mental hospital, "and he did it with routine, above-board, reporting—without posing as anyone he wasn't."

A reporter for another paper says that when she assumed another identity to do an investigative story, all the questions of professional ethics did not bother her as much as those involving her own personal ethics.

"When I did my story," she says, "I had to make friends with the people I was working with. . . . I shopped with them and babysat for them . . . trying to get them to talk to me. I'd never made a friendship before that was blatantly [a] fraud.

"That bothered me personally a great deal."

But she did it anyway. And her editors supported her.

REFERENCES

Anderson, Elijah. *A Place on the Corner*. Chicago: University of Chicago Press, 1978.

Becker, Howard S., and Blanche Geer. "Participant Observation: The Analysis of Qualitative Field Data." In Richard N. Adams and Jack J. Preiss, eds., *Human Organization Research*. Homewood, IL: Dorsey Press, 1960.

Festinger, Leon, Henry Riecken, and Stanley Schachter. *When Prophecy Fails*. Minneapolis: University of Minnesota Press, 1956.

Whyte, William F. *Street Corner Society*. Chicago: University of Chicago Press, 1955.

CHAPTER 14

Field Experiments

If you are a newsstand dealer here is some advice for you: Pile a stack of old magazines under the ones you want to sell and buyers will be more likely to pick them off the top. At least Bernard Green, founder and president of Eastern Newsstands, says so. He should know.

"Magazines sell best from a pile or full-cover display. The higher the pile, the fresher it looks," he says. "It's like groceries." One of Green's newsstands is in New York City's Pan Am Building and has more than 2000 magazines on display, organized into 18 sections.

With more than 100,000 people passing through the building daily, Green says he learned selling tactics by trying different techniques. He *experimented*, although Green perhaps would not use that word. He did what you as a public affairs reporter can sometimes do: try something to see how it works.

But you must plan carefully and keep ethical and legal considerations in mind. When you experiment, you go beyond observing events—you create them. Field experiments that are done well can tell you how things really work in the community. Let's look at some examples.

NEWSPAPER FIELD EXPERIMENTS

Shortly after Mecklenburg County passed a tougher law to control auto exhaust emissions, a local newspaper, the *Charlotte News*, decided to see how well inspection stations enforced the law.

The *News* selected four stations in different parts of town—from among the approximately 110 stations empowered to inspect cars—and had a 1977 model car inspected. The car had a number of defects besides high emissions of carbon monoxide, including worn brakes and no rearview mirror, the latter enough by itself to cause the car to fail a safety inspection.

However, only one mechanic said the car failed on the basis of exhaust emissions. The law allowed up to 5 percent carbon monoxide; the mechanic told the reporter/driver the car registered 7 percent, but even he marked only 5 percent in the inspection form's "idle engine" block and advised the driver to make certain repairs to reduce carbon monoxide emissions. Other station's readings were 4.3 percent, 2.8 percent, and .05 percent, representing acceptable emission levels, but widely variant station readings. Who was right?

Other inconsistencies emerged in safety judgments about tires, brakes, and the missing rearview mirror, about which the reporter/driver casually had said to all four stations, "As you'll see, my mirror is missing. I'm going to fix that myself." Three of the stations still disapproved the rearview mirror, but one did mark it "approved."

The day this story appeared in the *News*, another story in the paper quoted the county administrator of the auto emissions program: "I am going to get my men on it today." He promised more monitoring of inspection stations, better record keeping, and surer penalties for shoddy inspections. The investigation produced information that the official was able to use to improve law enforcement. Information from such field experiments where reporters become involved in the action is often just as useful for officials as it is informative for readers.

Journalism students under the direction of University of North Carolina professor Philip Meyer decided to see if bartenders really did check student identifications to see if customers were at least 18 years old, the legal age to buy beer in North Carolina at the time. Fifteen students visited 114 bars in Chapel Hill and the surrounding area.

In 78 percent of the visits to Chapel Hill bars and 94 percent of the visits to nearby out-of-town bars, this group of 18-year-old students bought beer without anyone asking for an ID. That was Saturday. On Monday, it was even easier in Chapel Hill, although a little more difficult nearby; 93 percent of the visits in Chapel Hill and 89 percent of the visits nearby resulted in no one asking for an ID.

The class also learned that you easily can order a fake ID from out-of-state companies by using an incorrect address and picture. Students used a picture of Meyer's daughter—taken when she was only 11 years old—along with an incorrect home address in one effort to find out how easy it is to order an ID. The ID arrived in the mail; apparently no one had checked the incorrect information. The class had learned that anyone could have an ID ready to produce at the door of a bar—*if* he or she somehow fell into the small group asked to prove age.

Published stories of these investigations made it harder, for a while at least, for youths to buy beer in Chapel Hill. North Carolina since has passed tougher laws to hold bartenders legally responsible if they sell beer to underage youths.

University of Windsor students mailed 528 letters in a test of the Canadian Post's efficiency and found that 85 percent of those with correct postal codes arrived within 24 hours of mailing within the same city and 48 hours between cities. When students mailed some letters with no postal code or with incorrect codes, 76 percent of them still reached their destinations at about the same time. But Windsor students also discovered that 78 letters, 15 percent of those mailed in the experiment, never arrived. "It's astonishing. I can't understand it," a Windsor Post official said. "I have no explanation."

The various investigations summarized here range from serious to lighthearted, but all tried to establish controls to measure *only* certain things or to make careful comparisons. In all the investigations, reporters actively gathered information or actually caused the action.

WHAT CAUSES WHAT?

Of all the questions you can ask yourself as a reporter, the most challenging is this: What is the cause of something else? Historians have discovered it is easier to determine the who, what, when, where, and how of events than the why. Lawyers find the same thing; so do doctors. There are many potential causes of any single

Figure 14.1   (*The Honolulu Advertiser*).

event. You must know exactly what you are looking for—for example, the efficiency of car inspections, or the determination of barkeepers to uphold the law.

Let's say star quarterback Bob Adams learns the Saturday morning of the final championship game that his girlfriend has left him (what timing!) for someone else. Adams also has just recovered from a mild case of the flu, and he has a mildly strained right ankle from the game last week. During the game he completed 16 of 36 passes, but his team lost 35–7. During the season he had never failed to complete fewer than 75 percent of his passes in any game, and he always threw at least 35 passes. What caused his poor championship game performance? Was it personal problems with his girlfriend? His ankle? His lingering flu? The performance of his pass receivers? The excellent defense of the other team? Poor coaching? Perhaps it was the weather; everyone uses that. The list could be very long.

In Adams's case you will never know for sure. Of course, you will ask him, the coach, and others about the game. Such can be the familiar journalistic challenge of finding causes. At other times, however, you can frame your assumptions or hunches into clear-cut questions, devise a field experiment, and see what results from a single, or at least controlled, cause. The cause often will be you or the situation you create by conducting your experiment.

If you conduct a field experiment you will need clear goals. Often you will be seeking the answer to a single question, other times to several questions. In each of our examples, reporters attempted to answer one or more major questions:

> Do auto inspection stations conduct proper and consistent safety inspections? (2 questions)
> Do bartenders check age before selling beer?
> How speedily does the Canadian Post deliver letters?

These questions seem simple, but you cannot be sure of the answers until you try to think of other factors that might influence the outcome, and then *control* for those factors.

SCIENTIFIC APPROACH TO EXPERIMENTS

Although you may not think deeply about causes when you devise a field test of a hunch, scientists try hard to design experiments to rule out everything except the "real" cause or causes of a phenomenon.

For the scientist, if the differences that are found can be easily explained by reasons other than the one hypothesized, the investigation has not been tightly enough designed. Generally, a scientist tries to establish the following conditions before he or she says one thing *causes* another thing to happen:

> First, cause and effect are always both present.
> Second, the cause always comes first in time and always causes some change in something else all by itself, without any help.

You know that dropping a hammer always causes it to fall to earth at nearly (not quite) the exact same speed each time. You know that a hot match nearly always burns your arm. But you also know that such clear causes seldom occur in everyday human behavior.

Excessive drinking does not always cause a hangover. Excessive speed does not always cause an accident. Reading too long does not always cause eyestrain. Yet there is a higher probability for these results if you drink and drive, speed, or read for many hours without a break. You will need a well-designed field experiment in order to determine *the* cause of an event.

Let's see how a scientist might test the apparently simple hypothesis that reading a newspaper for a long time will cause eyestrain. It certainly sounds simple: A lot of reading causes eyestrain. You hear statements like that all the time—in fact, you live by many of them—but you might find them hard to "prove."

Let's try. Our social scientist carefully designs his or her experiment ahead of time. The essence of a good experiment, whether conducted by a scientist or a journalist, is *the systematic gathering of information under controlled conditions*. Sketching a rough table into which you plan to place your findings often can help you design a field experiment. Let's take the reading-leads-to-eyestrain example. A social scientist might set up a table like the following:

Number of Persons Reporting Eyestrain

	Degree of eyestrain			
After reading	Severe	Mild	None	Total
6 Hours				
4 Hours				
2 Hours				
No reading at all				
Total				

The social scientist first would find some reading material of reasonable difficulty. Because reading ability and skill vary, he or she would have all people in the experiment read the same material, and at the same time, as time of day might make a difference. The experimenter would try to ensure that all readers have approximately the same interest in the material—otherwise some might be so interested that they would "forget" to get eyestrain. Likewise, he or she would need to be sure that some people do not have prior experience with the material—for example, if the passages selected were from the *New York Times*, some might already be familiar with the newspaper and thereby have an advantage. The social scientist needs to consider other factors as well: How about making sure that rapid and slow readers are distributed randomly into the different conditions? Also, some people are far more interested in reading than others. How can the research be designed to ensure that people in fact are reading when they should be, rather than looking out the window? And how can people be kept reading for six hours? How many breaks should be allowed and when should they occur? How will eyestrain be measured anyway; will the researcher simply ask the subjects if they have it? Are there ethical issues to consider in "making" people read for two to six hours?

The social scientist should have a control group of similar reading experience and demographic background that is also tested at the end of two, four, and six hours. But what will this group be doing at the time of the experiment?

The researcher would try to control or hold constant every factor except *amount of reading time*, in order to explain how lengthy reading might cause eyestrain. The point is this: Investigating the relationship between reading and eyestrain is not as easy as it appears, if you want to find out if reading *alone* is the cause of eyestrain.

You will always find it a challenge when you become the detective in search of a cause. Human behavior is complicated, and there often are many ways you can explain behavior. Even with experiments, you should be careful in planning and cautious in explanation.

JOURNALISTIC APPROACH TO EXPERIMENTS

You usually will not have as much time as social scientists to test hypotheses, and you may not be as interested as they are in finding a single cause for a particular development. However, you must be as thoughtful about controls on your observation as is our social scientist. You need to ask yourself many of the same types of questions.

For example, have you designed your field experiment so you are able to discover the influence of a single or few variable(s), while holding everything else constant? Have you selected your subjects at random, or is there something so special about them you cannot generalize to other people in your community? Is time of day important to your experiment? In Chapel Hill several years ago, a social scientist and his class compared how quickly students could catch a free ride when they "thumbed" or "hitched" a ride first dressed as a "hippie" and then as a "straight." The same students dressed two different ways. They measured the time that elasped from the time the student began thumbing to the time a car driver stopped to offer a ride (and was told this was an experiment!).

But what kind of people drive down a particular street at 8 A.M. versus 9 A.M. versus 10 A.M., or on Monday versus Wednesday versus Friday? Consider your own community. You would need to control for these kinds of variations by conducting the experiment at the same time over several days. Another aspect of this investigation you would need to control is to be sure all people involved agree on the meaning of "hippie" versus "straight."

A FLORIDA EXAMPLE

Despite these limitations, often you may discover interesting facets of your community. Two journalism students at the University of Central Florida in Orlando used a field experiment to see if people would help an obviously drunk person get into his car (where he would endanger any driver or pedestrian who came near him).

One student doused himself with gin, including rinsing his mouth with it, and asked passersby to help him get into his parked car. He was cold sober, of course, but acted so drunk that he could not even unlock his car door. One student played the same role each time while his friend waited down the street to explain the experiment afterward. Then the two students switched roles. The "drunk" student told each passerby he was unable to unlock his car door and asked for help. He tried to act the same way each time.

Did anyone help? Each student asked 50 people for help—a total of 100. Of these, 44 offered help. Interviewed afterward, these pedestrian helpers gave various reasons for helping. One man said he "had been in the same position." Others reported accepting the drunk student's claim that he was "okay to drive home." Another said, "If he wants to break his head, that's his business."

It did not make much difference if the students were dressed in business suits or in dirty, torn tee shirts. They included this extra variable in their experiment apparently on the assumption that people might more readily help a "respectable-looking" person.

These ingenious Florida students, Lee Lerner and Mike Griffin, may not have thought of their efforts as much more than testing a hunch about how much help people would offer to a drunk, but their data can be arranged in a simple "scholarly" table for comparisons. Griffin dressed in a business suit when he pretended to be drunk. Lerner worked in a dirty, torn tee shirt. As mentioned, each asked 50 passersby for help. (How were the passersby selected? Randomly?) These are the results:

Number of Passersby Who Helped the Drunk Driver

	Yes	No	Totals
Griffin (suit)	21	29	50
Lerner (tee shirt)	23	27	50
Totals	44	56	100

The way in which they added manner of dress, the extra dimension in their field experiment, is clear. (Should Griffin also have tried the tee shirt version? Should Lerner also have tried the business suit version?) Mode of dress did not make much difference in the results: Nearly one of every two people passing was willing to help this staggering hazard hit the road—and whatever else came across his path.

You might ask a number of questions if you decided to try the same experiment in your community:

> Was the car parked near the university? Perhaps people were more willing to help students, especially other students. Did young people help more than older people? (One 68-year-old retiree tried to find someone to help drive the

young man home, a sensible approach. "He's too young to get smeared into a pole," the man explained.) At any rate you would have to be cautious about generalizing to the population of the entire community without much more knowledge about the sample.

At what time of day did the field investigation take place? Would you get the same results at night?

Was there a difference in physical appearance between the two students? Were they equally "attractive" or "unattractive," aside from their manner of dress? Did they say exactly the same thing each time?

Did both Griffin and Lerner act equally "helpless"?

You can think of other control considerations if you decide to do something similar in your community. It is evident that Griffin and Lerner tried to set up their experiment so that each passerby would confront the identical dilemma: Should I help this (well-dressed or tee-shirted) very drunk young man? They field tested their hunch—they called it an idea "just off the top of our heads"—more carefully than most of us would do.

The results surprised them, and perhaps should surprise us, in this period of rising public concern over drunk driving. They had expected that perhaps 9 or 10 people of the 100 asked might help. Instead, nearly one half did. Like most good field experiments, their investigation produced more questions than answers. One wonders: How widespread is our natural inclination to help each other—widespread enough to create a community danger on our streets?

Such a field investigation demonstrates how reporters can raise public policy questions. Such an investigation also suggests doing a bigger, more tightly controlled follow-up experiment that blends results of a field investigation with traditional interview stories with police, health officials, or others connected with reducing the number of drunk drivers on our highways. And, as the Florida students demonstrated, such studies do not always need to be expensive or even time consuming. But you do have to plan carefully.

ETHICS

Important ethical considerations arise in conducting field experiments. Lerner and Griffin probably informed police ahead of time about their experiment. Someone often will report such activity and

To the Airport: Getting There the Fastest

Anne-Marie Schiro
The New York Times

Summertime is travel time. Every day thousands of people head for the roads, the rails or the skies. People in a hurry to reach their destinations take a plane, naturally. But the trip to the airport is sometimes as long as the flight itself.

Difficulty in finding a taxi, heavy traffic or bad weather can be nerve-racking. Limousines can be costly. So when the Metropolitan Transportation Authority introduced the JFK Express—better known as the Train to the Plane—it was welcomed. An average of 3100 riders use it every day, more in summer.

From the inception of the service in September 1978 until June 1980 it was considered experimental. Then it was put on a permanent basis. When there was talk last week of discontinuing it, many travelers were dismayed. Then the M.T.A. decided to keep it running. But is it really the best way to get to Kennedy International Airport?

The *New York Times* sent five people at rush hours on a Friday—each using a different method of transportation—to race the Train to the Plane, and to compare cost, comfort and convenience. All left from Times Square at 4 P.M. The experiment was repeated at 9 A.M. on a weekday.

One rider took the JFK Express from 42d Street and the Avenue of the Americas, another hailed a cab, the third went to the East Side Airlines Terminal, 38th Street and First Avenue, to catch a Carey bus. The fourth person went to the New York Statler Hotel at 33d Street and Seventh Avenue to test the hotel limousine service. The fifth person took the F train to the Union Turnpike stop in Kew Gardens, then boarded the Q-10 bus to the airport. The final destination for everyone was the Trans World Airlines domestic terminal.

The fastest time was one hour and five minutes, by the hotel limousine—actually a van. (That time included a five-minute subway ride to the hotel.) But the traveler was less than enchanted with the comfort. The van seated nine persons—three across—and with two tall men seated next to her, leg room was short. Also, the van was not air-conditioned. Smoking was not permitted.

But the driver loaded and unloaded baggage and was helpful about getting each person to the exact destination. Cost: $9, plus 75 cents for the subway. Reservations are required and tickets must be purchased one day in advance. Service from other hotels varies in price, departure time and other ways.

A Wednesday morning trip took exactly the same time, but was more comfortable because there were fewer passengers.

The second-fastest time was made by the taxi, which took one hour and 20 minutes. The driver chose the Triborough Bridge to avoid rush hour at the Midtown Tunnel but found heavy traffic going through the Central Park transverse at 65th Street, on First Avenue between 91st and 101st Streets, on the approach to the airport and at the airport itself. The cost: $23 plus $1 toll plus 50 cents for each bag, plus tip.

When the ride was repeated on Tuesday morning, the driver chose the Midtown Tunnel. Despite heavy traffic approaching the toll booths, the entire trip took 50 minutes. Cost: $23.40 plus $1 toll plus 50 cents for each bag. The passenger didn't tip this driver because he was surly, she said.

A close third was the JFK Express: one hour and 23 minutes from Times Square, including waiting time at the 42d Street and Avenue of the Americas station (the service runs every 20 minutes). Once the train was boarded, it was an hour and 10 minutes to the T.W.A. terminal.

The Train to the Plane is actually a train and a bus. Transferring from one to the other at Howard Beach adds an element of inconvenience, as does having to lug your own suitcases. But this can still be a pleasant journey.

Large arrows on the subway platform point to the exact place to wait for the train. Conductors and security guards were pleasant and helpful. The trains were air-conditioned, with no smoking allowed, and everyone had a seat. Luggage was placed in front of doors not in use, so the aisles were clear.

Buses from Howard Beach to the various airport terminals were also air-conditioned, but baggage cluttered the aisles and some people had to stand. You might also have to wait for a bus, but this did not happen on our trial runs.

On Monday morning at 9, the entire trip took an hour and 16 minutes. . . .

the police will come roaring up. Obviously, you should not do anything dangerous that will distract passing traffic in the streets. What if someone driving past looks at the "drunk" student and inadvertently runs into a pedestrian? How did people feel when they were informed about the experiment afterwards? You always should inform people about an experiment; if you do not, and they later read your story, they surely would feel used.

Social scientists confront the same ethical issues. Most universities have rules that must be followed in conducting experiments to ensure that human subjects are not unfairly or unsafely treated and are fully informed after the experiment. The use of hidden cameras in particular raises ethical questions, and you must always be prepared to justify the means you use on moral as well as on legal grounds.

Ends never justify unfair or unsafe means. Of all the methods you use as a reporter, field experiments clearly are the most intrusive. You are manipulating events to determine the outcome. You literally make news. The first priority is to be careful. You should ask yourself these questions

Is the experiment unsafe to those participating?
Have all officials at your company been informed, and do they approve?

Are there legal problems?

Have police or other public officials been notified?

Have you created any unanticipated or unnecessary public danger?

Will people be angry at your news organization after it participates in the field experiment?

Consider these questions carefully as you design your investigation. If you plan and execute it carefully, you may be on the edge of a fascinating test of some hunch about behavior or beliefs in your community. You may surprise yourself—and your community.

REFERENCES

Babbie, Earl. *The Practice of Social Research*. 3d ed. Belmont, CA: Wadsworth Publishing, 1983.

Campbell, Donald T., and Julian C. Stanley. *Experimental and Quasi-experimental Designs for Research*. Chicago: Rand McNally College Pub., 1966.

Cook, Thomas D., and Donald T. Campbell. *Quasi-experimentation: Designs and Analysis Issues for Field Settings*. Chicago: Rand McNally College Pub., 1979.

Stempel, Guido H. III, and Bruce H. Westley, eds. *Research Methods in Mass Communication*. Englewood Cliffs, NJ: Prentice-Hall, 1981.

CHAPTER 15

How Some Students Used Their Observational Skills: Report on Cocaine

WILLIAM CLOUD

Professor Cloud, with the help of three other University of North Carolina journalism professors, organized students in an effort to learn the scope of cocaine use in Orange County, where the university is located. Results were startling.

Professor Cloud assembled and reorganized this material—originally published in the April-May, 1985, issue of The Journalist, *the UNC School of Journalism publication—for presentation here. The project was originally directed by Philip Meyer, William Rand Kenan Jr. professor and a former director of research for the Knight-Ridder newspaper group. Professor Meyer is known as the father of precision journalism; he recently authored* The Newspaper Survival Book, *a guide to interpreting research. Professor Cloud for years worked as a reporter and editor for* Newsday. *Other professors from UNC contributed to this project: Professor Rich Beckman, who teaches photography, has many professional photo credits; Professor Jane Brown, who teaches research methods, has published many scholarly articles and most recently coauthored a book about the effects of television viewing on children. All the professors involved have worked as newspaper consultants.*

The students, many of them named in the following material, played leadership roles in planning, executing, and writing the

Reprinted from the April-May, 1985 edition of the *UNC Journalist*. Reprinted by permission of the School of Journalism, University of North Carolina.

series. They show what can be done in a short time (the project took about three months, from its idea to its execution) if you plan carefully and carry out skillfully, that is, if you combine good tactics with broad strategy.

PROJECT BACKGROUND

Our students conducted a county-wide survey and discovered that about one of every six persons had tried cocaine. Furthermore, they found that drug use was progressive for many—that is, often people graduated from alcohol through marijuana to cocaine and in some cases heroin.

That discovery might have appeared dramatic in itself, given the conservative nature of our (relatively) southern rural culture, *or* hardly surprising, given today's widely reported use of drugs. How could we—and how should we—interpret and present the survey findings? Figures alone often have little meaning for readers. Figures must be explained in human terms if readers are really to know about wasted lives and worried officials. After all, cocaine is a social problem, not a statistical one.

Taking the results of a poll of county residents and providing that human element was the challenge facing advanced reporting students in the School of Journalism at the University of North Carolina at Chapel Hill. Student efforts to meet that challenge led to a compelling special section in UNC's publication, *The Journalist.* Combining survey data with in-depth interview data produced a series that generated much local comment. Survey data alone would have missed the human story; interview data alone would have minimized the social significance of the story in terms of the number of people using cocaine.

As the project progressed, the series involved students in nearly every aspect of print journalism. The same methods could as easily be used by broadcast journalists. The project began with students from both an advanced reporting class taught by Professor Philip Meyer, and a media research class taught by Professor Jane Brown.

In February, the students conducted a telephone public opinion poll among Orange County residents (see pages 307–313). They analyzed their findings and then moved ahead on reporting their stories. The project included more than the poll findings. Students interviewed families and friends of the 17 people in North Carolina who died from cocaine overdoses in 1984. These individual profiles often proved poignant, and they put all-too-human flesh on the statistics. Students also interviewed police, lawyers, and officials from pertinent public agencies; these interviews produced separate stories.

By March students in Professor William Cloud's advanced editing program had begun to design the section that would appear just over a month later. Photography students, under the direction of Professor Richard Beckman, began work on their part of the project: They constructed a map of North Carolina locating where the cocaine victims died and a photo illustration to highlight the front cover of the special *Journalist* section in which the series would appear. (These two illustrations are not reproduced here.) A graduate student prepared charts to highlight key survey findings (reproduced on pp. 276–277).

Graphically, results were dramatic: Bold black headlines contrasting against areas of white space reflected the serious nature of the subject and drew readers into the section. Just as dramatic and compelling were the stories written by student reporters. This chapter presents some of the material from this student effort. It shows what students, with faculty editorial guidance and encouragement, can do.

The reporter who wrote the main story had to present the poll results, provide an overview of the drug problem, and at the same time keep the readers interested. He did this by frequently using quotes from a variety of sources, including law officers and drug users. At one point, the reporter compared poll findings with an unscientific poll conducted by *Ladies Home Journal*. Obviously, one has to be careful—as the reporter tried to be—with such comparisons.

PROBLEM is bigger than we think

By Bob McCarson

Nearly one of every six Orange County residents has tried cocaine at some time, a survey conducted by UNC-CH journalism students has revealed.

That comes to about 9,000 adults, more than enough to fill all the permanent seats in Carmichael Auditorium.

Among students at the University of North Carlina at Chapel Hill, the rate is even higher—21 percent, or more than 4,000 students of the 20,500 enrolled.

The use of cocaine persists and grows despite its grim reputation as a killer. Last year, 17 North Carolinians died from its use. Cocaine claimed 11 lives in North Carolina in 1983. In 1982, the total was two.

Nearly half of Orange County adults know at least one person who has used cocaine at some time. The number who admit current cocaine use is much smaller—2 percent of Orange County adults in the survey say they used cocaine in the past month.

To find who uses cocaine and why, students at the School of Journalism investigated each of those 17 North Carolina deaths blamed on cocaine in 1984 and polled 535 Orange County adults.

Four of five adults here believe there is less cocaine use locally than in the rest of the country. But self-reported cocaine use among Orange County adults is already as high as the national level of about 15 percent, last measured in 1982 by the National Institute on Drug Abuse.

Frederic W. Schroeder, dean of students at UNC-CH, was surprised at the percentage of students who have used cocaine. "I think it's two or three times more than I would have guessed it to be," he says.

Law enforcement officials say they aren't surprised by the Orange County figure in the survey. But one police chief, A. Sid Herje of Carrboro, says he is surprised the rate isn't closer to 20 percent.

"It's a problem we're seeing more and more of around here, because right now there's a glut on the market," he said. "The price of cocaine has really dropped, so more and more people have access to it."

The survey also shows that Orange County and Chapel Hill, the town that has always prided itself on its image as the quiet little village, are not in a vacuum.

The National Institute on Drug Abuse estimates that every day, 5,000 people smoke, snort or inject cocaine for the first time.

In Boulder, Colo., a college town not too different from Chapel Hill, a 1984 survey similar to the UNC-CH poll showed cocaine use among Boulder County adults to be 21 percent—well above the national level found in 1982.

Orange County residents have their own idea of what kinds of people use cocaine—professional athletes, UNC-CH students and professionals such as doctors and lawyers.

But Steven A. Bernholz, a Chapel Hill lawyer whose specialty is defending people facing drug charges, says cocaine knows no sexual or social biases. The survey tends to support his view.

"There are lawyers, business people, physicians, housewives, professional women, graduate students, students," Bernholz says. "No one is immune by virtue of their position or stature."

None of the 17 whose deaths were investigated fit the stereotyped idea that cocaine is "the trip of the hip," the drug for America's affluent, upwardly mobile sector.

The median age of the victims was 27. The youngest was 19 and the oldest

48. All but two were white—one was black, one a Lumbee Indian. Seven were women. They had varying backgrounds—waitress, power-plant technician, home builder, housewife, con artist.

Some had been drug users since junior high. Others picked up the habit as adults. At least two may have found the drug on the job.

Some people in Orange County blame students for a high level of local illegal drug use. But the survey shows that in the county's main college age group, 18 to 24, non-students are more likely to have used cocaine than students.

"That one really surprises me," Herje says. "I would like to think that means that the students are getting smarter, but I can't say that for sure."

Among older students, those 25 and up, the rate of cocaine use rises sharply. In the 25–44 age group, students are more likely to use it than non-students.

The survey shows the rate of cocaine use to be highest among young white males who are college-educated. One in five of all males reports use of the drug. Among females the rate is about 12 percent. That's 33 percent higher than a national level found last year in an unscientific survey by Ladies Home Journal.

Jimmy Campbell, a 37-year-old Chapel Hill man in prison for selling cocaine, says cocaine lures women.

"Coke traps women more easily than men," he says. "Lots of guys bought coke from me in order to lead to sex with women waiting for them."

Cocaine use in Orange County is not evenly distributed. An analysis shows it is more pervasive in the urban areas of southern Orange County. The rate is five times higher in Chapel Hill and Carrboro than in Hillsborough, the rural county seat that more resembles the traditional North Carolina town.

Bernholz says urban southern and rural northern Orange are becoming less polarized. More and more, he's seeing "a lot of what I would call rednecks" arrested on cocaine-related charges.

"That indicates to me a diminishment of the differences in attitudes about drugs in the county as opposed to Chapel Hill," he says. "There's probably more cocaine in Orange County and Chapel Hill in particular than in communities of North Carolina of a similar size."

Orange County lies in the path of huge shipments of the illegal drug from Colombia. The contraband is dropped by airplane or boat on North Carolina's sparsely populated Coastal Plain. Dealers then move it westward through the major population centers.

Analysis of the 17 N.C. deaths that resulted from cocaine in 1984 shows a concentration in the cities along the industrial crescent from Raleigh to Greensboro to the state's largest city, Charlotte. Along that stretch of Interstate 85 lie some of North Carolina's major universities—N.C. State, UNC-CH, Duke, UNC-Greensboro, Wake Forest, and UNC-Charlotte—as well as most of the state's population.

Cocaine users typically are young. The dealers know that. They feed off the youth found in college-oriented towns.

Cocaine, Bernholz says, still is not as widely used as marijuana in the county, but it is "certainly a close second."

Among Orange County residents, 41 percent report using marijuana, more than two-and-a-half-times the rate of cocaine use.

A first-year law student who snorted cocaine on and off for four years says most cocaine users have "underlying emotional and psychological problems.

"Cocaine became popular with the whole 'me' generation," he says. "We don't know where we're going, so we're going to have a good time on the way."

Arthur McBay, chief toxicologist with the state medical examiner's office, blames cocaine's booming popularity for more deaths. A new danger, he says, is the increasing tendency to inject cocaine. Before, most inhaled it, he says.

Mark Worley, a Charlotte truck driver, says injecting cocaine provides a longer and more intense high.

"You come down real fast," he says. "You don't feel like s--- the next day or nothing.

"It's the down side of snorting that makes people go to shooting. When people snort, they can't slow down and can't go to sleep and just want more."

More users and non-users in Orange County agree the drug is not a safe way to get high and should not be legal. Four in five non-users see coke as being dangerous even when used infrequently or in small doses. That awe is not shared among self-reported users. Only two of every five fear small or infrequent doses.

Many of the 17 who died were trying to quit cocaine. Some had been on the drug less than a year. Others vowed they were using cocaine for the last time— until the fatal dose turned that intent to ironic reality.

If a small dose can kill—one expert has likened it to playing Russian roulette—what makes cocaine the high-priced candy for a growing number of Americans?

Some say peer pressure or stress. Others say people use the drug for status and prestige. The most common reason given in the survey by half of those who have tried it is that cocaine makes you feel good.

"It was like the volume was turned up on all my senses," says a local psychologist who tried cocaine once at a party.

He never used cocaine again. Its dark, seductive quality had scared him.

"I can't find the words to describe it," says the law student of the high coke gave him. "It was a feeling of exhilaration, an energy."

A Duke graduate now doing post-graduate work at UNC tried coke at age 18. She says it felt like more oxygen was rushing to her brain.

The drug, she says, was more prevalent at Duke. "It was a party drug," she recalls. "It was the status thing to have."

A 28-year-old journalist who once waited tables in an expensive Greensboro restaurant says he used coke there because of the company he kept.

"You've got a job that does not allow your mind to operate at all," he says. "You can release that frustration on some kind of strong stimulation . . . the same reason Ford Company workers probably come home and drink a case of beer."

Worley, the truck driver, says the work place is where some get drugs.

Susan Cabe, the wife of one of the 17 cocaine victims, says she thought her husband, Clifton, was getting the drug from friends on his job with Duke Power. Another victim, Curly Chavis, probably got started on the fatal road at his job with a Hoke County trucking firm, says his wife, Audrey.

"I know when I was at McGuire there was more than you could shake a stick at," Worley says of drug use at the nuclear power plant near Charlotte. "It's a flea market."

The survey debunked a common myth that people use cocaine to enhance sex. Only one person in 535 gave sex as a reason for using coke.

Robert B. Millman of the New York Hospital-Cornell Medical Center says coke can adversely affect sex.

"Women become non-orgasmic and men impotent," Millman told *The New York Times*. "A little bit of cocaine increases the libido in most men and women, but extended use decreases sensation and ability to perform."

Cocaine use appears to be associated with the use of other drugs.

More than a third of cocaine users also report the use of LSD. About half admit use of amphetamines. Two-fifths say they have used barbiturates. All cocaine users report past or current use of marijuana and alcohol.

Cocaine users think selling cocaine is less serious than do non-users.

The people who were polled were read a list of nine crimes and were asked to tell whether each was more or less serious than selling cocaine.

To people who have tried the drug, the crime of selling it is more serious than selling alcohol to minors. But it is less serious, they say, than car theft or home burglary. For non-users, sale of cocaine ranks above all but drunken driving, selling heroin and armed robbery in seriousness.

"Most people who sell a few grams to support cocaine abuse do not consider this a crime," say Nannette Stone, Marlene Fromme and Daniel Kagan, authors of the book *Cocaine: Seduction and Solution*. "(They) view it as a favor to their friends."

Non-users are more likely than users in the survey to see law enforcement against cocaine in Chapel Hill and Orange County as being inadequate.

But 28 percent of self-reported cocaine users and 60 percent of non-users say they would support a tax increase for more police to enforce drug laws.

"There's a definite correlation between law enforcement priorities and what the public is told and perceives as the major law-enforcement problem of the day," says lawyer Bernholz. "We declare that we have a heroin problem . . . and that we need to prioritize heroin enforcement. Then you pass on to something else sexy . . . you've got a cocaine problem."

Chapel Hill Police Chief Herman L. Stone says the approach to cocaine abuse can't stop at the county line.

Pumping more money into enforcement programs "could make a great impact on what's coming and going and the use of it in this city and Orange County," Stone says.

"But what we do in Chapel Hill has to do with other jurisdictions and has to be done in conjunction with all other operations."

This cooperation is already taking place. Sheriff's deputies in Orange and Durham counties, Chapel Hill and Durham police, and State Bureau of Investigation agents work together in sting operations.

Durham police, not as well-known to dealers in Orange County, make undercover buys here. Chapel Hill police do the same in Durham.

Carolina Poll: key findings

How different drugs relate:

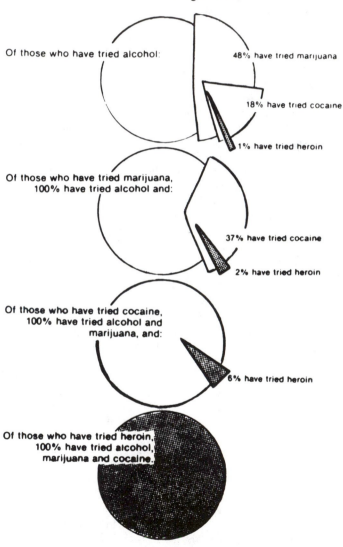

Of those who have tried alcohol:

48% have tried marijuana

18% have tried cocaine

1% have tried heroin

Of those who have tried marijuana, 100% have tried alcohol and:

37% have tried cocaine

2% have tried heroin

Of those who have tried cocaine, 100% have tried alcohol and marijuana, and:

6% have tried heroin

Of those who have tried heroin, 100% have tried alcohol, marijuana and cocaine.

Percent who say they have ever used cocaine

| Men | 20% |
| Women | 12 |

Carrboro	21%
Chapel Hill	19
Hillsborough	4
Elsewhere	6

| Whites | 17% |
| Blacks | 6 |

| Students | 21% |
| All others | 13 |

18-24	21%
25-44	21
45-64	3
65 +	0

| With college | 18% |
| No college | 7 |

How serious a crime is selling cocaine?

	to non-users	to users	
	Drunken driving	Car theft Home burglary Drunken driving	are more serious
	Selling heroin	Selling heroin	
	Armed robbery	Armed robbery	

	Car theft
	Home burglary
	Vandalism
	Selling alcohol to
	  minors
	Shoplifting
	Selling marijuana
		Vandalism
		Selling alcohol to
		  minors
		Shoplifting
		Selling marijuana
			are
			less
			serious

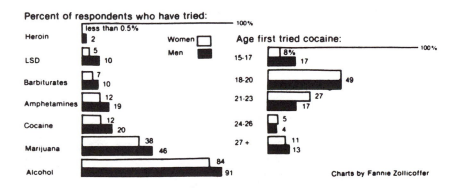

Percent of respondents who have tried:

Heroin — less than 0.5% / 2
LSD — 5 / 10
Barbiturates — 7 / 10
Amphetamines — 12 / 19
Cocaine — 12 / 20
Marijuana — 38 / 46
Alcohol — 84 / 91

Women (white), Men (black), 100%

Age first tried cocaine:

15-17 — 8% / 17
18-20 — 49
21-23 — 27 / 17
24-26 — 5 / 4
27 + — 11 / 13

100%

Charts by Fannie Zollicoffer

Maj. Don Truelove of the Orange County Sheriff's Department says deputies are after dealers, not small-time users.

"There is a lot of money to be made in dealing cocaine," he says. "And that serves to intensify the problem."

Both Herje and Truelove say law enforcement alone won't stop the flow of cocaine.

The survey shows that most of the public supports the view that education and rehabilitation may be the seawall against the wave of abuse.

Nine in 10 of those who have tried the drug say they would support a tax increase for more educational and rehabilitation programs to fight drug abuse. Four of five non-users would support the increase.

"Education is the key," Truelove says. "Information on the problem needs to be out there, and I don't believe law enforcement is meeting those needs."

There's another need 70 percent of non-users in the county see—laws against cocaine use should be made stricter. But only 30 percent of the users thought that the answer to cocaine abuse is tougher laws.

Stone, Chapel Hill's police chief, says existing laws are adequate. It's up to the courts to impose the sentences, he says.

"We need to get away from plea bargains that let them back out and reach the lives they've been reaching," Stone says. "In other words, when you're dealing and you get caught and we've got a good case, we must insist on the maximum punishment."

But Campbell, the small-time seller who knows life outside and inside the prison, says putting more people behind bars is not the answer.

"It's got to be stopped at the top before you can stop it," he says. "As long as you keep filling the prisons up with people off the street, they are going to just keep getting somebody else to sell it."

The following students contributed to the reporting in this story: Richard Boyce, Winfred Cross, Lila Moore, Keith Pritchard, Cindi Ross, James Tomlin and David Wells.

All reports on polls should explain how the poll was taken. In this case, the explanation ran as a sidebar. That technique kept the main story from being overloaded with statistics and at the same time highlighted the information.

How we did the survey

This Carolina Poll, conducted on Feb. 3–5, was designed to represent the attitudes of all adults in Orange County.

It began with a sample of 980 residential telephone numbers drawn from the Orange County Consolidated Directory. The interviewers eliminated 183 nonresidential or non-working numbers. They deleted another 262 numbers on which they repeatedly received no answer or a busy signal, or where people refused to cooperate.

This left a sample of 535 interviews, each about 10 minutes long. To ensure that all adults in a household had an equal chance of being interviewed, students asked to speak to the person at least 18 years old who would next have a birthday.

The error margin is greatest when close to 50 percent said "yes" to a given question. In those cases the error margin is 4.2 percentage points at the 95 percent confidence level. This means that in 95 out of 100 samples, the results would be within 4.2 percentage points of what would have been obtained if every residential listing in the directory had been called.

The error is smaller for the survey's central finding, the 15 percent rate of cocaine use in Orange County. For this question the error margin is three percentage points, meaning that the actual rate of use might be as low as 12 percent or as high as 18 percent.

The cocaine-use question was: "For classification purposes, and in complete confidence, have you yourself ever happened to try any of the things on this list. How about . . . Alcohol? Amphetamines, or uppers? Barbiturates, or downers? Marijuana? Cocaine? LSD? Heroin?"

It's not easy to find someone who will talk with reporters about the sordid death of a relative or friend. But the students got enough people to talk to write profiles on all 17 victims of cocaine use in North Carolina in 1984. The result is riveting reading. Note the capsule profiles of the victims at the beginning of each story. Note also there is no overwhelming pattern among those who died. Generally they were young, but there also were older citizens; there were white-collar and blue-collar workers, men and women, people of means and those with less money, such as students. These human stories show that cocaine is a random killer, striking anywhere, anytime.

THE VICTIMS
Last year, cocaine killed 17 people in North Carolina. Here are their stories.

Bride-to-be

Name: Lisa Dean Johnson
Age: 24   **Occupation:** Waitress
Place of Death: Charlotte

Lisa was forever doing little things—thoughtful things—even picking up a wild bunch of flowers and bringing them to her grandmother.

Virginia Johnson remembers that about her granddaughter Lisa, and she remembers the wedding plans.

Lisa Johnson and Wayne Wilson had just purchased some land and wanted a big house, children and all the rest. The wedding was to be in June.

But the grandmother did not know that the couple's plans for a weekend trip to Charlotte included a cocaine party. The party was to be their last before they settled down and could no longer afford it.

"The last tango; we talked about it and this was it," Wilson says.

That "wild weekend" in February, 1984, as Wilson refers to it, was indeed the last cocaine party. Lisa accidentally spilled a beer into a cocaine packet, then impulsively drank the dissolved cocaine.

She died a few hours later.

Before that weekend, Wilson says, it seemed that nobody ever got hurt with cocaine. "We thought it was harmless. You felt safe around it."

When Johnson was very young, her mother had a nervous breakdown, and she was put into a state orphanage with her two sisters and one brother, according to Lisa's grandmother.

The father, Charles Johnson, was not on good terms with his wife and never contested the children's placement in an orphanage.

Johnson left the orphanage at 15 and moved into a house in Durham where her father and grandparents lived, but she later shared a house with Wilson until she died.

"Lisa was my prize, and I miss her very much," her grandmother says.

Wilson, who was older than his fiancee, met her at a restaurant where she worked as a waitress. They started to date when she was 19.

"When I met her, she was dating a Hell's Angels' leader," says Wilson, a car salesman. "I took her away from a bad scene."

He says that Johnson was a lost person who sincerely wanted to get away from the crowd she was with, but that she still loved to party and get high.

"We loved each other," Wilson says. They argued only about giving up the cocaine.

"Lisa was the most generous person in the world, so it made it hard for me to deny her what she wanted," Wilson says.

"We're talking about a flower—not a briar," says Wilson, "so it's a real tragedy. Cocaine was her only weakness."

His fiancee would want him to talk about what happened, he says.

"If it had happened to me instead of to her, she would have crusaded up and down to tell people how stupid they are to use cocaine and not know it. She would not have let anyone touch the stuff if she had known it was as dangerous as it is, and that's a fact."

— **Genie Lindberg**

Contradictions

Name: Kana Dawn Kessler
Age: 27   **Occupation:** Dancer
Place of Death: Matthews

Her earlier life is a mystery. The police say she was a dancer by profession and had worked in Las Vegas. Her boyfriend says she was a paralegal student in Charlotte. Her father does not want to talk about her.

However, this much is known for sure: She was found curled on the floor of her closet with a 9mm pistol beside her, and her death was caused by cocaine poisoning.

Kana Kessler, 27, died June 22, 1984, in her Matthews home where she had lived for three months. Terry Lankford, her boyfriend, found her at 10 p.m., approximately three hours after her death, according to the medical examiner's report.

Officer C.L. Hutchens of the Matthews Police Department says her arms had needle marks from prior injections. Hutchens says Lankford bought her the pistol for protection because she was living alone.

Officer Hutchens remembers that in the three months Kessler was in Matthews, the police responded to several calls from her. She told them she felt like someone was after her. The responding officers said that Kessler exhibited paranoid behavior and that they thought she was intoxicated.

Lankford says that the police exaggerated; he remembers only one such call that Kessler made to the police.

Lankford and Kessler met through mutual friends. Hutchens says that Kessler hung around with the local body-building crowd. The police found syringes and steroid vials in Kessler's garbage, and while the medical examiner's report did not mention steroids, Lankford says she did use them. The police also found marijuana in Kessler's house.

Kessler was the adopted daughter of John J. Kessler of Raleigh. Lankford describes her as very outgoing and easy to get to know. Lankford says he thinks that Kessler had used cocaine for about three to four years.

— **Amy Anderson**

Conqueror

Name: Melanie Ann Sellers
Age: 22   **Occupation:** Student
Place of Death: Matthews

Melanie Sellers once told her sister, "When you do cocaine, you feel like you can conquer the world." But cocaine conquered Melanie. She was 22.

As a child, she participated in typical little girl activities. She was a Brownie and played softball. She loved nature, especially butterflies and daisies. She would often pick a bunch of flowers to give to her mother.

But Melanie grew up—too fast.

"She was 12 going on 21. . . . She took freedoms a 12-year-old had no business taking," her mother, Carolyn Sellers, remembers.

Melanie's problems began in junior high school. She started keeping company with a group of friends, some of whom lived in an apartment complex near the school. While their parents were at work, the group would cut classes to drink, smoke marijuana and party.

As Melanie's involvement with drugs increased, so did the rift between her and her parents. After running away during her eighth-grade year, she finished junior high living with a close family friend in Florida.

Melanie's high school years followed much the same pattern: skipping school, staying out late, and using the money she made working as a receptionist at her parents' health spa to buy alcohol and marijuana.

She began classes at Central Piedmont Community College with plans to become a nurse, but she lost interest and quit. She enrolled again, considering landscape design. But again, she lost interest and dropped out.

By this time, Melanie had moved into an apartment of her own. Although she had been a problem teen-ager, her parents were unaware of her involvement with cocaine until March of 1984, when a friend told them Melanie was using the drug, and he thought she was addicted.

"I was just not educated enough on drug addiction or cocaine," her mother says. "I just didn't realize how dangerous it was."

Abby Mullis, Melanie's older sister, says, "She had told me she was doing it, but she didn't think she would get hooked on it. . . . We really didn't know cocaine was that addicting. . . . I mean, we just thought nobody gets addicted to cocaine."

Melanie was admitted to the hospital, and she confessed she had a problem, but wanted to straighten out. She moved home with her parents, but after about two months, began to get back into her habit.

"We knew she was getting back into it because things would start being missing from the house," Mrs. Sellers says. "I had to hide my jewelry. I had to take my checkbooks, important papers—everything—out of the house. I couldn't even bring my purse in."

In the final months before her death, she would often go into her room and lock the door. She was extremely secretive about her friends, suspicious of her family—no one could get close to her.

"She seemed at times to be in an emotional shell. She seemed at times like she didn't have any feelings," Mrs. Sellers remembers.

On October 13, 1984, Melanie died of acute cocaine poisoning. She was found on her den floor with almost $2,000 worth of cocaine spread beside her body.

Police found that Melanie's cocaine was 45 percent pure, as opposed to the 10 percent pure street drug. Further investigation revealed a gram scale, with the price tag still attached. Police guessed that she was planning to become a dealer.

— Lauren Brown

Family man

Name: Clifton Harvey Cabe
Age: 31   **Occupation:** Radiographer
Place of Death: Charlotte

Clifton Cabe's life was already over by the time his family realized that it had been touched by cocaine.

"It was so sad that he died, because he had it all: a good job, a $120,000 home and a beautiful little girl," says his widow, Susan N. Cabe.

The Cabes had been married eight years. Clifton, 31, died at home of a heart attack that was induced by cocaine poisoning. As a radiographer for Duke Power Co. in Charlotte, he monitored radiation levels at McGuire Nuclear Station. Susan thinks his drug connection started at work.

While he was alive, she had no knowledge of his drug use and detected no personality changes.

"I disagree strongly with drug use," she says. "He knew that I would have left him if I had known about it."

Her husband had a problem with hardening of the arteries, and she had attributed his death solely to his heart ailments. When the medical examiner's report released about one month after his death revealed that he had died of a cocaine overdose, she searched the entire house and found a small quantity of cocaine, which she flushed down the toilet.

Susan says that she believes her husband's death was accidental, and that he may have tried cocaine for the experience, but "he got hold of something he didn't know about."

She suspects that he was getting the drugs from his friends at work, but they would not tell her anything about her husband's death.

"They all act like they don't know anything."

Joe Coulter, manager of the Assistance Program of Duke Power in Charlotte, says that although the company has an early identification plan, he was unaware of Clifton's involvement with cocaine until two months after his death.

"We try to identify drug users early, before someone is detected actually using drugs on the job," Coulter says. "We want to identify the user in order to get him treatment and help him."

— Keith Pritchard

Sports lover

Name: Larry Keith Adams
Age: 31   **Occupation:** Painter
Place of Death: Burlington

Keith Adams, a self-employed painter and a manager for a local rock 'n' roll band in Burlington, rarely met a stranger because he already knew everyone in town, his brother Wayne Adams remembers.

Keith's friends were always in and out of the small house on Thompson Street. "This place was worse than Grand Central," Wayne says. "There were parties here all the time, and the phone rang constantly."

The house's party atmosphere has changed since Keith's death in July, 1984, from cocaine poisoning. His friends hardly ever stop by anymore, his brother says.

Keith moved to Burlington in 1958 with his parents and two brothers. His father worked for a trucking company, and his mother was a housewife.

He was very athletic when he was growing up, Wayne says. "He'd come home from school, set his books on the TV, pick up a ball that went with that season, and you wouldn't see him again until dinner."

Keith attended Southern Alamance High School, where he played on the football and basketball teams. After high school, Keith attended the Technical College of Alamance for a little over a year and then joined the Navy.

He got food poisoning in the Philippines, which led to a gall bladder operation. He was transferred to Camp Lejeune and discharged with 100 percent disability.

It was then that Wayne noticed a change in Keith. He lost 80 pounds in the hospital, and after that he lost interest in sports. Wayne does not know if this was when Keith started using drugs.

After his discharge, he bought the house on Thompson Street from his father in 1977.

Wayne moved in with Keith last April and lived there with him until the beginning of June. "Keith was not a talker, so I really didn't know that much about his private life," Wayne says. "Sometimes he would ask me to go to the store for a while or something, which was his way of saying get lost, and I wouldn't ask any questions."

The last time Wayne saw Keith alive was the night before Keith's death. They had made plans for the next day to work on the house, which Keith was remodeling.

"No one will really talk and tell us what happened that night," Wayne says. "Most of what we know we read in the newspaper and on the death certificate."

According to newspaper reports, Keith drove his car to Albany Street, got out and knocked on a couple of doors asking for help. At one door, he collapsed. He died soon afterward.

— **Lori R. Nickel**

A normal life

Name: Sharon Goudes Doggett
Age: 21   **Occupation:** Homemaker
Place of Death: Matthews

Sharon Doggett was making some changes in her life when she lost it.

Her father was helping her and her husband Kevin buy a house in Matthews, a small town a few miles south of Charlotte, her hometown. They never moved in.

Doggett, 21, a homemaker and 1981 graduate of Kings Business College, died in Greensboro last Oct. 8 of cocaine poisoning.

"For the most part, I guess her life was fairly normal," Father Phaethon

Constantinides of Holy Trinity Greek Orthodox Cathedral in Charlotte recalls. "They (Doggett and her husband) seemed to be happy from all indications. Her sister said she was looking forward to coming back to . . . Matthews to set up housekeeping."

Doggett's mother, Alma Goudes, doesn't want to talk about her daughter's death. "It's really just too soon, and actually we didn't know until just a short time ago what she had died of," she says. "We had been told she choked to death."

Records at the Chief Medical Examiner's Office verify that. On the bottom of a letter confirming the cocaine death was a hand-written note: "This came as quite a surprise to the family. She was arrested in Raleigh for possession of cocaine."

Records show that Doggett was arrested in January, 1982, and charged with felony possession of cocaine and simple possession of marijuana. She was found guilty of the cocaine charge and given a six-month sentence suspended for three years.

"She was just a little girl trying to enjoy life and got caught up in all that," Constantinides says. "I get the feeling she was pretty much normal—not too much noise, not too introverted, from what the family said."

According to the medical examiner's record, Kevin Doggett reported that he had left the couple's house around 8:30 p.m. Oct. 8 and had returned 45 minutes later to find his wife "unresponsive and gasping for air. He (dragged) her out in the yard to try to revive her."

Doggett was pronounced dead about 10 minutes after she arrived at Moses H. Cone Hospital in Greensboro.

— **Cindi Ross**

Youngest death

Name: Wanda Jean Allison
Age: 19   **Occupation:** Waitress
Place of Death: Hendersonville

Wanda Allison called her brother on a Monday in September to tell him she was going to a party the next night.

Before that night was over, she had become the youngest person to die of a cocaine overdose in North Carolina in 1984.

Two days before her 19th birthday, she had been arrested for possession with intent to sell and deliver a controlled substance as well as selling and delivering a controlled substance. She was placed on probation.

"The only impression I have of Wanda is she was just really bad into drugs," says Allison's Henderson County probation officer, Ragan Hare. She adds that Allison broke probation in August 1984, so she didn't see her after that.

Allison's grandmother, Elizabeth Naylor of Hendersonville, says drugs changed her granddaughter's life.

"I wasn't around her much for the last two or three years of her life," she says. "But before that, her personality seemed to be all right. But, I think after she got on that dope, it ruined her. I have kind of mixed feelings. I loved the kid. I love all my grandchildren. But I wonder sometimes if she was ready to go."

On Sept. 25, 1984, Allison's body was found at the end of Wilson Lake Road in the shallow water of Lake Normal in Iredell County. She was wearing a cut-off white T-shirt with a horse on the front and a blue bathing suit bottom.

Probation Officer Hare says the situation was sad but almost inevitable.

"We all sort of knew she was on a self-destructive course, and we tried to do what we could, but it just wasn't enough."

— **Steve Ferguson**

Mutual friend

Name: Kamba Renee Williams
Age: 24   **Occupation:** Unemployed
Place of Death: Harrisburg

Name: Deborah Wallace DuBose
Age: 25   **Occupation:** Plant clerk
Place of Death: Harrisburg

Kamba Williams and Deborah DuBose didn't know each other. But they had two friends in common: One was cocaine, and the other was the owner of the trailer in which they died.

The two had been recently separated from their husbands. Kamba Williams, from Charlotte, died May 27 in Mark Worley's trailer near the small town of Harrisburg, about seven miles east of Charlotte.

On July 31, Deborah DuBose of Hartsville, S.C., died in the same trailer.

Worley says the deaths and the publicity afterward were tough for him.

The episode "came close to killing me," he says. "They made it out like I was a drug dealer, which I was not. They made it sound . . . like I should have been put away. I was hurt, down, depressed like I almost wanted to die. I finally realized it wasn't my fault."

Kamba Buckner married Buddy Williams in 1976 when she was 17 and he was 22. They lived in Charlotte where Buddy drove a truck for Ashland Chemical Co., and Kamba worked first at a fast-food restaurant and later at a department store. In August of that year their only child, Becky, was born, and in 1978 the couple separated. They were divorced in 1980. Buddy says he thought they had married too young.

He describes his late wife as a talented person who wrote poetry and music, painted ceramics, and played the guitar. She liked cats and had two. She enjoyed camping.

But Buddy Williams says that when they got divorced his wife began using cocaine. He says he does not know if she used it while they were married but blames her friends for influencing her after the divorce.

"She started hanging around with low-life," he says. "She moved in with another girl that used drugs."

One man Kamba Williams was living with ended up in prison for assault. She would visit him. Buddy Williams says he disliked the visits because she would take Becky with her.

In January, 1984, the two decided to get back together, but Buddy says his wife had changed.

"She would walk around the house stomping," he says, "Every other word would be 's---.'"

They would argue, and she would sometimes grab his arm to prevent him from leaving. "One night she wouldn't let me get on my motorcycle," he says. "She went and fell inside the back door of a neighbor and said that I beat her."

Worley says Kamba Williams told him that her husband had hit her sometimes, but she said it was usually because she deserved it. Worley had met Williams and her husband through mutual friends six months before she died.

He says Kamba had been using cocaine for years and had problems with depression.

Buddy Williams and his wife again separated in late March, 1984, and Kamba Williams began living with a friend in Charlotte.

Worley lived in Charlotte at the time but kept a trailer near Highway 29 outside Harrisburg.

When Kamba Williams came to see him May 27, Worley says she looked worse than he had ever seen her. Buddy Williams says she had been on a two-day cocaine binge.

Worley describes her as having the "shakes and she had been losing weight. She was getting down to the bones."

Forty-five minutes after she got there, "She said she needed to get a shot." They went out to Worley's van.

"But before we got in the van, she started shaking and spitting up blood," he says. "I kept hollering 'Kamba,' and she didn't know where she was."

He got her in the van, and she did not say anything, but her eyes were open. Doctors at Cabarrus County Memorial Hospital in Concord pronounced her dead on arrival.

In July another death occured at Worley's trailer.

Worley is a truck driver for Ram Leather Care, a company owned by his father that sells leather, suede and mink coats. For three years he drove a route to Myrtle Beach, S.C., that took him through Hartsville every two weeks.

On one of these trips three years ago, he met Deborah DuBose, who lived in Hartsville with her husband, Rodger, and worked at Sixty Minutes Cleaners. Worley says that he would stop and see Deborah DuBose for a few minutes to break up his trip, and that they had drunk beer together at her house once or twice.

In July, Worley says Deborah DuBose called him.

"She said her husband had beat her, and she had to get the hell away from him." Worley says he told her she could stay in his trailer.

About a week later the Cabarrus County Sheriff's Department got a call to go to the trailer. When no one answered their knock, the two officers kicked the door in and found Deborah DuBose face down on the bed.

The state medical examiner said she probably had been dead for two days. Drug equipment and cocaine were found in the garbage beside the trailer.

Worley says he first knew of DuBose's death when the sheriff's department called him.

He says he was surprised at Deborah DuBose's death because he did not know she used cocaine.

"She would eat a lot of speed at work," he says. "I didn't know her being into anything except speed."

Worley says his life has changed dramatically since the deaths.

In November, he married a woman who had been his childhood sweetheart. He says his attitude has changed.

He says he thinks a lot of people use the drug to have fun and forget their problems.

"It changes your mind and attitude. It makes you happy and you forget about a lot of stuff—till you come down and then you have the same problems."

— **Richard J. Boyce**

A life-saver

Name: Stephen Craig Pryor
Age: 25   **Occupation:** Student
Place of Death: Winston-Salem

On a summer day in 1978, Stephen Pryor saved the life of a 7-year-old boy at the Parkland Senior High School pool in Winston-Salem.

Pryor was 19. He pulled Jamie Freeman from five feet of water after the boy had been underwater for at least a minute.

Immediately Pryor began mouth-to-mouth resuscitation. After 30 seconds, Freeman began to breathe on his own again.

In a congratulatory article the next day in the *Winston-Salem Journal*, Larry McLean, head of the County Drowning Unit, said "Pryor did a real good job. He simply saved that kid's life."

Pryor's reaction: "When I saw that kid breathe, it was one of the greatest sights in the world."

Six years later on April 1, 1984, just 10 days after his 25th birthday, Steve Pryor was found dead at 12:30 p.m. in his Winston-Salem home by his younger brother Brett.

Police estimated that Pryor had died anywhere from five to 12 hours before he was found. Paraphernalia used for preparing and injecting drugs were lying close to the body. An autopsy later showed that Pryor had died from an accidental overdose injection of cocaine.

"I didn't know anything about Steve using cocaine," recalls his grandmother, Myrtle J. Pryor. "It was a big shock to me. He seemed to be the same person he always was until the end.

"Steve would always go out of his way to help someone. That's what I loved him for. He was the light of my day," she says.

According to his 83-year-old grandmother, Pryor had broken his back once falling off a horse at Tanglewood Park in Clemmons. He broke it a second time while working at a bridal show at the Benton Convention Center in Winston-Salem.

Mrs. Pryor last saw her grandson when he had been released from Forsyth Memorial Hospital, only a few days before he died.

"He suffered so much. He could have taken the cocaine to ease his pain, but God only knows. We don't," she says.

— **Richard Craver**

Terrified

Name: Curly Chavis
Age: 32   **Occupation:** Leather worker
Place of Death: Maxton

Curly Chavis of Maxton couldn't hide from the voices. A raucous trip to Baltimore and shooting bullets into his trailer couldn't shield him.

Curly kept "hearing things in the house," says his wife, Audrey. These voices had convinced him someone was trying to kill him.

On a hot day last May after an hour of heart massage, the voices caught Curly. Doctors at Southeastern General Hospital in Lumberton gave up on him. They couldn't restart what cocaine poisoning had stopped.

Curly was a Lumbee Indian with a passion for leather work. His art still adorns his in-laws' home.

But cocaine pulled him down quickly. As far as his wife can tell, Curly started injecting cocaine only three weeks before he died. The seduction probably began on his job with a Hoke County trucking firm.

"I kept finding spoons and little syringe things," Audrey remembers. She has returned to her parents' home in Robeson County's Prospect Community.

"I asked him," she says. "He kept saying 'No.'"

Curly couldn't spend enough time with their young daughter, and he never missed payments on their mobile home, Audrey recalls.

But cocaine changed him. Curly would come home in a rage, and he abused Audrey at least once. He was paranoid, she says, and insisted she was plotting his death. Audrey knew Curly needed help.

Four days in the Southeastern General psychiatric ward didn't help. Doctors never discussed his treatment with Audrey. She says that adds to her frustrations now.

His homecoming was violent. Curly shot up the trailer, then his mother's home.

Audrey gave Curly another chance when he came back from Baltimore. It seemed better at home with their little girl. But Audrey wondered whether the calm would last.

It didn't. Curly was replacing bullet-ridden windows when a friend from Pembroke came over. He wanted Curly to "ride off a piece," Audrey says.

"When he came back . . . he went wild again," she says. "We got in the car. He was driving, I'd say, 80 or 90 miles per hour."

Curly jumped from the moving car at Lumber Bridge. He ran across a field, terrified that someone was trying to kill him. He fought with rescue workers who had come to help. Then, unconscious, Curly went into cardiac arrest.

Confused and tired, Audrey drove home thinking Curly would come back after sobering up. But he never did.

"The doctors said he just gave up," Audrey says.

— **Bob McCarson**

On the edge

Name: John Ralph Nichols
Age: 36   **Occupation:** Welder
Place of Death: Winterville

John Nichols told friends he was going to spend a long weekend fishing in Morehead City. But when the weekend came, he took a different journey.

On June 9, 1984, Nichols was rushed to the emergency room at Pitt Memorial Hospital in Greenville. Richard Young, the medical examiner who admitted Nichols, says Nichols had injected a speedball, a shot of cocaine and amphetamine.

"I understand he was running around, thinking that people were after him; he was trying to crawl up under his house," says Nichols' former employer, John Roberts, owner of Roberts Welding Contractors, Inc., in Winterville.

"Nichols had a long history of drug use," Young says. He had even talked to his parents about killing himself, but Young says he does not believe that Nichols committed suicide.

"His last lucid statement was 'I always do drugs for fun,'" Young says.

Nichols died seven days later.

Nichols had worked as a welder for Roberts on and off for about two years. Roberts says he was aware that Nichols used drugs when he hired him, but they didn't have an adverse effect on his job performance.

"You can tell somebody that's been partying all weekend, because he comes in Monday morning, he's a nervous wreck; he's on edge, eyes are glazed and bloodshot.

"But John, Monday morning he'd come to work, he'd be alert. He was strong and healthy.

"I really felt like he had come back with a goal, whereas before he was just working as a means to an end. He wanted to be the best iron foreman I had, and he was approaching that goal."

Lou Roberts, John's brother and vice president of the company, says he also talked with Nichols and tried to relate to him through his own experience as a drug user.

Roberts says that his experience led him to become a Jehovah's Witness and that he tried to share his faith with Nichols.

"But John was really heavy into space and extraterrestrial life," Roberts says. "I think he felt like Ezekiel's prophecies and visions were actually an out-of-space infiltration into the earth and that these visions were really just a product of a spaceship.

"One of his goals and desires was that he was anticipating someday construction being done in space." Nichols would have volunteered to do construction work in space, given the chance, Roberts says.

— **Margaret Bell**

A talented man

Name: Michael Neal Peyton
Age: 25   **Occupation:** Construction worker
Place of Death: Wake Forest

Michael Peyton kept trying to escape from drugs. He hitchhiked to Iowa to see his grandfather. He later joined the Navy to get away from old friends and old habits. Finally, last September, he landed a new job, moved and told friends that Friday would be his last day of using drugs.

It was. They found his 6-foot-5-inch body slumped in a Ford pickup truck parked on a dirt road in Granville County. He was dead from cocaine poisoning.

Peyton, a minister's son, had a variety of talents, such as playing center on his varsity basketball team and playing a trombone in the band at Wake Forest-Rolesville High School.

His drug use began with marijuana in junior high school.

"He was running with some kids that we were pretty certain were on drugs," recalls his mother, JoAnn Peyton of Wake Forest. "We questioned Mike. At first, he denied it.

"He had always assured me . . . he wasn't going to get into hard drugs; he was smarter than that," Mrs. Peyton says.

Peyton's basketball coach said he had "a lot of potential." Teachers said he was intelligent and well-liked but had poor motivation. He dropped out of high school in January of his senior year.

Then, Mrs. Peyton says, he started searching for stability. He earned a high school equivalency certificate and enlisted in the Navy, where he lasted two months.

Back home, he drifted from job to job. He was arrested for selling marijuana and spent a year in prison. Mrs. Peyton says he felt that going to prison made him realize where his life was heading.

The day of his release from prison, Mrs. Peyton says, he enrolled at Wake Technical College, where he later graduated with A's in every subject. His specialty in electrical repair and maintenance led to a job at Crompton-Pilot Mills in Raleigh. Then the plant closed. Employment was hard to find, but he kept working at various jobs.

In January, 1984, he got a job with a good salary at Burlington Finishing Plant and was able to buy a new Harley-Davidson motorcycle. More money meant drugs were easier to get. By late spring he withdrew more and more from his family. They thought it was because of a girlfriend.

By summer's end, the increased use of cocaine took its toll: He lost his job. Then he was ready to start over.

He sold his mobile home and got a new job and a place to live away from his friends. For the first time, he told some friends that he had a drug problem.

The job started on Saturday, Sept. 29. That left Friday as the last day for him to use drugs. The cocaine overdose that killed him, according to the medical examiner, was an accident.

— **Cindi Ross**

Workaholic

Name: Frank Edward Ippolito Jr.
Age: 48 **Occupation:** Carpenter
Place of Death: Kill Devil Hills

On Sunday night, Frank Ippolito seemed relaxed, his housemates recall.

"I said goodnight about 9:30, and that was the last time I saw him alive," says Marty Glidden, Ippolito's housemate and closest friend.

Ippolito, a construction worker, didn't show up for work that Monday morning, Nov. 26, 1984. Ben Buotot, Ippolito's boss and the owner of B&B Construction, Inc., went to Ippolito's house to find him. Buotot asked Glidden whether he had seen Ippolito that morning. He hadn't. Together, they entered Ippolito's room.

Glidden says that they could immediately tell that something was wrong. Ippolito's skin was discolored, and he was cold, Glidden says. He had been dead for several hours.

The medical examiner thought at first that Ippolito had died from natural causes, probably a heart attack, says Kill Devil Hills Police Chief Jim Gradeless.

But Gradeless says police found hypodermic needles and less than a gram of cocaine in the room. An autopsy confirmed that Ippolito had died from a heart attack triggered by a cocaine overdose.

Ippolito had been steadily regaining strength after multiple bypass heart surgery in the summer of 1983. Three or four weeks after his surgery, he had started back to work and had taken up golf. He had become a regular at Sea Scape Golf Course in Kitty Hawk.

"He loved to watch sports on TV and loved to play golf, and he loved to sit around and bull---- with his friends," Marty Glidden says. "He was a crazy, happy guy."

"He got a hold of some stuff that hadn't been stepped on," Glidden says, meaning that it hadn't been diluted.

Ippolito specialized in framing and woodworking. Mike Riddick, owner of Riddick Homes Corp. in Kitty Hawk, says that Ippolito did very good work at times. Riddick employed Ippolito on and off for about 14 years.

Riddick says Ippolito was a workaholic when they first met, working seven days a week, every week. His other friends say they never remember him taking off more than three or four days at a time.

"That's the one thing I always admired about him," Riddick says.

"But he always handled working hours better than idle time. Then he abused his body, and he knew he was abusing his body."

— **Margaret Bell**

A good-timer

Name: Jack Stanford Dickerson
Age: 35   **Occupation:** Tobacco worker
Place of Death: Greensboro

Jack Dickerson of Greensboro could not stay away from friends and good times.

He was having a good time the night before his death on March 3, 1984.

Dickerson had gone out that night with a female friend, recalls his mother, Margie Dickerson. The friend and Dickerson had been out playing cards and drinking. Afterward they returned to his apartment.

Mrs. Dickerson says her son collapsed there and could not be revived. The friend tried shaking Dickerson and pouring water on him. The friend then went to a neighbor's house, where she phoned Mrs. Dickerson and then an ambulance.

"They had been drinking too much," Mrs. Dickerson says. "The autopsy report said he had gotten hold of some poisonous substance. It was too much for him."

The autopsy report revealed that Dickerson died from cocaine and morphine poisoning.

Dickerson, who was 35, was the only black in North Carolina to die from cocaine abuse last year.

Mrs. Dickerson says the only drug she was aware of her son using was marijuana. She says she is sure her son's continued dealings with drugs may have stemmed from peer pressure.

"His doctor had him write a little paper not to be mixed up with people that were on drugs—to stay away from them. He just couldn't stay away from old friends."

Dickerson was born in Durham, and his family later moved to Greensboro, where he attended high school.

After high school, he joined the Army and left for New York. It was while in New York, during the late 1960s, that he met and married his wife, Libby. Dickerson left New York and moved back to Greensboro in the mid-1970s without his wife and two sons.

He lived with his parents for about a year and then moved into an apartment with his younger brother, Kenneth.

During the time Dickerson spent at his family's home, his mother became aware of his drug use. She says she believes her son started using drugs while he was in New York.

"I would find marijuana in a bag in his room," she says. "I didn't know what it was, and I would throw it in the trash. He would get so angry about it. He would go out to the trash and get it out."

Dickerson had worked at P. Lorillard Tobacco Co. for five years. He enjoyed fishing and playing golf in his spare time. He also liked to go to church, his mother says.

"His favorite church was where they got up and shouted and displayed emotions," she says.

— **Cheryl Williams**

Family favorite

Name: Richard Stephen Thompson
Age: 31   **Occupation:** General contractor
Place of Death: Kernersville

The boy held a small, furry object in his hands.

"Mom," he said. "Look what I found in the storm cellar."

As the boy's mother looked at his prize, she saw the blood.

"I'm sorry, son," she said. "But I'm afraid the kitten is going to die."

"No!" he said. "I'm not going to let it die."

Fifteen years later, the cat did die at a ripe old age. But its owner, Richard Thompson of Greensboro, wasn't that lucky. At age 31, he died alone in his car parked in a Kernersville driveway. The cause of death: intravenous cocaine poisoning.

Thompson's mother, Mary Lou Thompson, also of Greensboro, recounts the story nearly a year after he died on April 8, 1984.

"Richard was always the family darling," she says.

As a child, he was interested in animals and music, she says. Among the musical instruments he could play were the piano, cornet and drums.

Thompson's drug use began in high school with marijuana, his mother says. When he became involved with more serious drugs, his parents began noticing a change in him.

A psychiatrist at North Carolina Memorial Hospital in Chapel Hill prescribed a complete change in environment for Thompson, his mother says. But he refused to leave his home and his old friends.

After high school, he became a builder. He worked for several area contractors, and he taught carpentry classes at Guildford Technical Institute for a year.

In 1975 he married Debbie Gabriel, a Greensboro resident. Together, in 1979, they formed the Thompson company, which specialized in home improvement, custom carpentry, building and remodeling.

A 1982 feature story in the *Greensboro News and Record* described their marriage as "a partnership in every way." Said Thompson: "Debbie's good enough that we can trade off. We both get to be boss. It's pleasing to me that she can do as well, if not better, than I can."

Two years later, Thompson's name appeared once again in the publication. Instead of in a feature story, however, this time it was part of an obituary.

"I wish I had some words of wisdom," his mother says. "But I don't. As a way of warning others, drugs could and did ruin a fine young man with a family who loved him."

— **Susan G. Oakley**

Con artist

Name: Joseph Clyde Biggerstaff
Age: 48   **Occupation:** Salesman
Place of Death: Charlotte

Clyde Biggerstaff died of natural causes. But the cocaine that he used probably speeded the process, adding to the load on his thickening arteries and enlarged heart, according to the Mecklenburg County Medical Examiner. And so authorities count him as one of North Carolina's 17 cocaine victims of 1984.

He was a big man, a former high school football player. His 300-pound body on a 6-foot-4-inch frame made him seem less vulnerable than he was. "He was well-liked by everyone," recalls Ann Pressley, his former wife.

Police, however, can think of some exceptions—such as victims of Biggerstaff's swindles during his days as a con artist.

Biggerstaff and Pressley were married shortly after graduating from Harding High School in Charlotte where Biggerstaff played defensive guard for the Harding Rams. They had two children and then separated while the children were still young.

Biggerstaff had circulation problems. They were evidently getting worse, and the cocaine had made him lose considerable weight.

Capt. Wade Stroud of the Charlotte Police Department, who knew Biggerstaff for 29 years, says, "I never knew him to hang out with anybody but flimflammers."

"He was a confidence man. One of the better known games that he was involved in was to get a businessman or someone with a little money to invest in a liquor still. But the still never existed."

Stroud says Biggerstaff was arrested and charged with running that con game in Horry County, S.C., but he was never convicted.

Biggerstaff was convicted in Federal District Court in Greensboro of conspiring to smuggle cigarettes. He spent three years in prison during the early '70s for this crime.

"But he wasn't that bad a dude," Stroud says. "I can't think of a time that he tried to hurt anybody intentionally."

Biggerstaff was taken from his home in Charlotte to Memorial Hospital at 7:30 p.m. on August 24, 1984. He died an hour later of heart disease. Blood and urine tests revealed cocaine.

"It's a natural disease. The cocaine didn't cause it, but it probably didn't help," a representative for the Mecklenburg County Medical Examiner said.

— **Jim Hoffman**

By including an interview with a defense attorney, the high cost of a criminal defense and the high odds against winning acquittal are made clear.

The law takes a heavy toll in fees, fines, prison sentences

By Lee Bollinger

If you are caught dealing in cocaine, be prepared to pay the price.

That price includes court costs, expensive lawyers, stiff fines and high bonds. After that, be prepared to serve time in prison.

Possession of even small amounts of cocaine can be costly. With a misdemeanor charge, bond will be $500 to $1,000. A conviction will result in court costs and fines of up to $2,500.

Possession of a gram or more of cocaine means a felony charge. Legal fees range from $15,000 to $100,000. Bond can be more than $100,000. Court costs and fines may run as high as $25,000.

And if you are a smuggler, be ready to pay even more. The best defense lawyers can cost $100,000 to $250,000. Bond is usually $1 million to $5 million, and a conviction can mean court costs and fines of up to $500,000.

Attorney Martin Bernholz of Chapel Hill, who has handled drug cases throughout the country, says that the laws against cocaine are not fair to the defendant.

"My best defense in drug cases is begging for mercy from the court. In our heyday, we could win about 1 percent of our cases on technicalities. Now, technical victories in court happen next to never."

Bernholz says that the average sentence for trafficking in cocaine is three to six years if the people cooperate, 10 to 20 years if they don't. There is a minimum fine of $250,000 for anyone convicted of cocaine trafficking, he says.

Federal courts hand down stiffer penalties than state courts. The state courts have no mandatory sentences. Federal courts begin mandatory sentencing in cases involving 28 grams or more of cocaine, according to Bernholz.

He says that a typical mandatory sentence for smuggling is 35 years in prison. Smugglers can expect to serve at least half that time.

Other elements make North Carolina law harsh. Bernholz says that defendants usually are charged with multiple crimes, so sentences must be served consecutively.

If you can afford a good defense, you have another handicap.

"A poor man has a better chance in court with a drug charge than a rich man," Bernholz says, because a rich drug dealer makes the court angry.

Clearly, the series needed to explain the effects of cocaine on its users. This reporter turned to several professional sources for a scientific report.

Body pays the price of abuse

By Cindy Partridge

Cocaine has been called today's "drug of choice." But many who choose it ignore the medical consequences.

Joel L. Phillips and Dr. Ronald D. Wynne, authors of *Cocaine: The Mystique and the Reality*, say that coca leaves have long been used by natives of South America as a religious symbol, a medium of exchange, a means of keeping warm, and even as a substitute for food and sex.

Phillips and Wynne say many in our society use cocaine to escape the pressures of daily life, while others like the feeling of confidence and power the drug gives. Still others depend on cocaine for weight loss or as a sexual stimulant.

Research shows that the drug can be addicting. Dr. Joseph M. Cools of Durham, who specializes in treating cocaine addicts, says, "Cocaine is so positively rewarding that people keep going back to it." Cocaine is not addictive in the same way as drugs such as heroin because there are no withdrawal symptoms, Cools says.

Professor Steven D. Wyrick of the UNC-CH School of Pharmacy calls cocaine a "non-physically addicting, but severely psychologically addictive drug." He says that while cocaine affects the central nervous system, the cause of the euphoria is not understood.

Cocaine's effect is similar to amphetamines, Cools says. "It speeds up all the systems of the body." Many users like the boost of endurance or confidence that gets them through the day. But this boost can be damaging. Cocaine's immediate effect is a numbing of tissues touched by the drug. When cocaine is snorted, mucous membranes become inflamed, and the user has a continual runny nose. Over a long period, the nose cartilage may be eaten away, causing a need for plastic surgery.

Rubbing cocaine on the gums causes users to ignore tooth decay, and blood vessels can be constricted if cocaine is injected.

Free-basing cocaine involves smoking it in a water pipe after it has been heated in a mixture of sodium hydrochloride and ether and then dried to resemble pure cocaine. Inhaling the purified vapors can cause lung function to deteriorate.

Cocaine causes the heart rate to increase, so that even small amounts of cocaine can lead to a heart attack.

While cocaine gives a feeling of euphoria, this is followed by depression, loss of weight, appetite, productivity and energy. In *Cocaine: Seduction and Solution*, Nannette Stone, Marlene Fromme and Daniel Kagan write that more cocaine is used after the first high begins to wear off to prolong the euphoria and avoid this "crash." They say this practice can lead to overdose, seizures and death.

The stimulant effects also can cause stroke, irregular heartbeats or embolism, especially in users who have high blood pressure or heart disease.

Death can result when cocaine is injected with another drug, such as heroin—a combination known as a "speedball." Comedian John Belushi died from a speedball injection in 1982.

Orange County, like other counties, has professionals who deal daily with victims of drug abuse. Their comments illustrate an important aspect of the drug problem.

Agencies help rebuild desperate lives

By David Wells

The high rate of cocaine use in Orange County is old news to the people who run counseling and rehabilitation centers in the Triangle area.

"Cocaine use here is wide-open," says Jack Sayre, a substance abuse treatment therapist at the Orange-Person-Chatham Mental Health Center in Chapel Hill. "About 60 percent of the people I work with are cocaine abusers.

"Most of the people who come here are in serious trouble. They're either in debt, or they've lost a wife or girlfriend, or they're having legal difficulties."

Cocaine use and abuse is just as serious at UNC-CH. "Carolina is an affluent campus, and cocaine is an affluent drug," says Sue Gray, the Director of Health Education at UNC-CH's Student Health Service. "You would be naive to believe that cocaine isn't big here.

"We help cocaine users look at risk management. . . . Psychologically, it's addictive."

At the mental health center, Sayre says that problem users are placed in primary-care groups that meet once a week for 10 weeks. Members must agree to attend each meeting. They also must agree to abstain from taking any substance or drug, including alcohol, during treatment.

"We try to teach them the impact of addiction, that it's a disease that needs to be treated," Sayre says. "We help them formulate a pattern for their lives that will incorporate this knowledge."

Gray and the Health Education Department at UNC-CH counsel both problem users and those who may be in the process of developing a problem.

"Students are adults, and they make up their own minds about cocaine," Gray says. "They need to know the facts, but not from the dealer. He's only after money."

Sexual enhancement is a major reason students use cocaine, Gray says.

"I've spoken with some people who do not want to have sex without it. They say it's like intensifying an orgasm. But in the end, it takes away from your sexual performance.

"When you can't sexually perform, when you'd rather get high alone than be with your friends, when you can't seem to keep enough cocaine on hand—that's when cocaine has become more important to you than anything else."

Cocaine abusers can also seek help from the Charter Northridge Hospital in Raleigh, which has detoxification programs.

Dr. Tom English, a psychologist at the for-profit hospital, says the response to the programs has exceeded the staff's expectations. The hospital has a two-step process for addicts—a detoxification and an education program.

"We help them get over their anxieties from the drug," English says, "whether they have the shakes, or they're agitated, or in a depressed state. We use mild tranquilizers as needed, like Librium or Valium. It depends on the patient."

The education program, English says, helps clarify the patient's values. "We try and help them see why they started using the drug," he says.

"We focus on the life-style of cocaine users. Cocaine is exciting, exotic, it hypes you up and gives you a false energy and sense of confidence. But it's a seductive drug. I know someone who became addicted between four and six weeks."

Although 15 of the 17 cocaine victims in North Carolina last year were white, English says the hospital has treated nearly as many blacks as whites. "They're usually young adults, well-educated, generally with a financial means and a high value for being on top of things. Sometimes they're perfectionists and high achievers."

The hospital can be quite costly. With insurance, treatment can cost from $15 to $75 a day. But without insurance, treatment can cost as much as $1,000 a day.

Why would a medical student turn into a drug seller? Here, a reporter overcame reticence in the student and his friends to explore that question.

Arrest ruins a student's medical career

By Winfred Cross

Frederick Patton Moore had a lot going for him. He was intelligent, well-liked and had a good sense of humor, according to his friends. He was also a medical student at the University of North Carolina at Chapel Hill.

He was on his way up. So why did he feel the need to use and sell cocaine and heroin?

That question may never be answered. Moore, 27, from Winston-Salem, was arrested April 26, 1984, on charges of possession with intent to sell and deliver cocaine and heroin. He pleaded guilty to three counts of selling and possessing heroin and to one count of selling and possessing cocaine. He was sentenced Sept. 10 to eight years in the State Department of Corrections. He is serving his sentence at the Southern Correctional Center in Troy, N.C., and he plans to do so without talking to reporters.

"I have other projects that I'm working on," Moore said in a brief telephone interview. "I don't think it would be a good idea to talk to you."

Moore, a 5-foot-5-inch, slender black man known to his friends as Rick, is not the only one who won't talk. Most people who know him suddenly become silent when his arrest is brought up.

There are, however, a few of Moore's former classmates who will speak candidly about him. Although all of the students were surprised that he had been using and selling hard drugs, they all suspected that Moore had had a problem with drugs and alcohol.

"We knew he drank a lot of beer and smoked some dope, but we didn't know he was into anything like cocaine," says Michael L. Zollicoffer, a fourth-year medical student from Baltimore. "He gave the impression that he just wanted to have fun and escape the pressures of reality."

A medical student who wishes to remain anonymous says it was common for Moore to smoke marijuana while at the medical school. "I knew he smoked dope; that was widely known," says the fourth-year student. "Rick would go into the bathroom between classes and get lit."

"I sat down and talked with him about some of my own experiences with drugs to get him to talk about his," says another fourth-year student who wants his identity protected.

Although his friends thought of him as an intelligent student, he had problems with his course work. At the end of his second year, he decided to repeat the year instead of taking the final exam. After repeating the year, he again did not take the final exam.

Michael A. Smith, a fourth-year student from Selma, says he didn't know Moore had academic problems until it was too late. "I thought he knew how to balance academic and social things pretty well."

Moore participated in the Medical Educational Development program in 1980. The MED program helps minority students prepare for medical school. Evelyn McCarthy, director of the MED program, says Moore was in the program in 1980 and performed "competently."

"The sad thing about this whole situation is that it ruins his medical career completely," McCarthy says. "He worked very hard for his career."

Moore graduated from Hampton Institue in Hampton, Va., in the late '70s where he majored in biology. After graduation he worked for a while before he applied to the MED program. He was accepted into the UNC-CH medical program in 1981.

Moore was arrested in April of last year at his girlfriend's home on Grant Street, according to Master Officer Marvin Clark of the Chapel Hill Police Department. Clark says the warrant for Moore's arrest was issued by a magistrate after information had been gathered by undercover agents. Moore sold cocaine and heroin to these agents on two occasions. Moore did not have any cocaine on him when he was arrested, Clark says. "He told me had gotten himself into an alcohol and drug abuse program to straighten himself out."

This next carefully written story explains how a business operator diligently strives to remain within the law.

Shopkeeper sticks by the law

By Kurt Rosenberg

The sign on the wall is impossible to miss. Clearly and unmistakably, it spells out the rules under the heading of "PUBLIC NOTICE." The notice says that

PUBLIC NOTICE

All Merchandise sold in this Store is intended for LEGAL Use by the Customer. Any person attempting to buy Merchandise for Illegal Purposes, or implying Illegal Use, will be denied Service, and asked to Immediately Leave the Premises.

You must be 18 years or older to purchase Tobacco and Snuff Products and Accessories.

We require a valid Photo I.D. Driver's License for Proof of Age, upon request.

Thank You

Hoffman's warning to buyers

anyone attempting to buy merchandise for illegal (i.e., drug) use will be denied service and asked to leave the store.

George's Catalog and Shop, at 117½ East Franklin St., will be a decade old next month, and George Hoffman says he has had no problems with police since he opened the store. He feels accepted by the community, by fellow businessmen on Franklin Street and by law officers. And when North Carolina's Drug Paraphernalia Act became effective over three years ago, Hoffman says it did not in the least bit affect the way he ran his business.

"The law has no reason to change me," he says. "I was doing what they said for a long time. I think that I'm good for the community and the community is good for me. I've never had any troubles with the community. I've had one or two people walk by that have said, 'Oh, that's a head shop.' But I don't like that term."

The store is one of three smoking accessories shops owned by Hoffman. Another, which opened in 1983, is located not far from the original one, on North Columbia Street. The third one opened in Raleigh in 1982.

Hoffman sells a variety of items at a variety of prices. There are hand-held pipes for as low as $3 each and scales selling for as high as $200. There are water pipes, snuff grinders, rolling papers, spoons and straws. And all of them, Hoffman says, are intended to be used with legal substances. That is why he has posted his "Public Notice."

"It just lets people know if they intend to buy an item for an illegal purpose, I'd rather not have them buy it," he says. "If they come in with a druggie-type attitude, I'll ask them to leave. There's all different kinds of ways you can use an item, and as long as there's a law on the books, I have to discriminate."

The alternative is not pleasant. The North Carolina law is based on the federal Model Drug Paraphernalia Act prepared by the Drug Enforcement Administration and is similar to legislation enacted by at least 20 other states. It defines "drug paraphernalia" broadly, including all equipment, products and materials of any kind that are used to, or are intended or designed to, facilitate violations of the Controlled Substances Act. Many of the items on the long list have legal uses and when used legally, are not considered drug paraphernalia. Consequently, the Drug Paraphernalia Act specifies a number of factors that, along with additional evidence, can be considered in determining whether or not an item is legal.

The act consists of three separate sections. The first covers the intentional possession or use of drug paraphernalia for illegal purposes. A violation is a misdemeanor, punishable by a fine of no more than $500, imprisonment for no more than a year, or both.

The second part concerns the delivery and manufacture with intent to deliver drug paraphernalia to be used illegally. This also is a misdemeanor and is punishable by a fine of no less than $1,000, a maximum of two years in prison, or both.

The final section prohibits the advertising of drug paraphernalia. A violation is a misdemeanor punishable by a fine of no more than $500, imprisonment for no more than six months, or both.

Though he says the controversial law has had no impact on his store, Hoffman is strongly against it. He contends that while it has some merits, in general the law is discriminatory.

"It's cut down a tremendous amount on the bad apples that were beginning to creep into the industry," Hoffman says. "But the law should be made in such a way that every merchant should be responsible for the things he sells. Why not do it to all merchants? Have they checked out any of the convenience stores to find out how they're selling their products? That's selective enforcement. It should be the same for all shops."

Furthermore, he says, the law is extremely difficult to enforce. "At what point does the merchant know it's going to be used for an illegal purpose?" Hoffman asks. "The only way they could enforce the law would be to have somebody come in and say they're going to buy something for (use with) a controlled substance."

Obviously, that will rarely, if ever, happen. But Hoffman says it would be naive to think no patrons of any stores buy items to use illegally.

"I imagine that sometimes people have come in here and have not said they are going to use (an item) in an illegal manner who have done that," he says. "No merchant can say that none of his items have ever been used illegally and be truthful about it."

Even serious topics can sometimes lend themselves to a light touch. Witness this next report on a drug sting.

Trapping a local supplier in 5 easy steps

By Lila Moore

How easy is it to sting a sitting duck?

"It was one of the easiest cases we've had," police Detective Don Tripp says about setting up Ted Bartlette for arrest.

Bartlette, who's been in prison since May, was one of the biggest cocaine suppliers in Orange County, Tripp says.

The sting on Bartlette followed a model that Chapel Hill police say they use often:

1. Find the trail. An undercover officer buys cocaine several times from a street-level pusher. That's anyone who sells in small quantities, whether he's actually on the street or in the country club.

Then, police trail this seller to his supplier.

From this tracking, Detective Tripp and his force knew their pusher was going to Bartlette to get the small amounts of cocaine.

In an attempt to engage Bartlette face to face, the undercover officer asked his pusher to take him to his source. Predictably, the pusher did not want to cut himself out of the profits, and refused.

2. Send a decoy. The undercover officer asks for more cocaine than his friend has on hand. The request will force the pusher to go to his source. The pusher has only a given time frame to pick up the goods, since he and the undercover officer agree on the time to meet again.

This was the next step in trapping Bartlette.

3. Watch and wait. From a room at the top of Granville Towers, a highrise private dorm on Franklin Street, the detectives hardly needed binoculars. To look down on Bartlette's Colony Court home, they could just raise the shades, talk on their radios and take photographs.

4. Have the search papers ready. As soon as the pusher left Bartlette's home, police moved in with a search warrant. They charged Bartlette with possession, intent to sell and deliver cocaine, trafficking cocaine, and possession and manufacture of marijuana.

"You don't just keep seven or eight ounces around the house," Tripp says. At the current street value of $1,800 to $2,300 per ounce, Bartlette's stash was worth more than $12,000.

5. Tidy up. Police retrieved the sting money and the rest of the cocaine. They arrested the pusher, too.

From start to finish, the whole operation had taken about two months.

But how did it all start, anyway?

Informants. Police often use them. Their motives might be revenge or money, and for good information, police will pay as much as $1,000.

Why not go after Bartlette's supplier?

That one is not so easy. Tripp, city police, county agents, and the State Bureau of Investigation suspect that Bartlette's source comes from out of town and makes more than one "drop" when he does.

Bartlette's refusal to reveal his source was a mistake, Tripp says. He does not believe that cooperation would have put Bartlette's life in danger.

Not revealing names is just a policy dealers have, Tripp says.

The victim has his or her own viewpoint about his or her arrest. It's only one element in this wide-ranging interview.

In prison, there's time to study, reflect

By Lila Moore

From the guard gate, he walks past the mess hall, the bunk house and the inmates talking in twos and threes, silhouetted against Sunday's early dusk.

In another place, this sandy-haired, soft-spoken man, dressed in collegiate plaids, would be everybody's favorite nephew, the clean-cut boy-next-door.

But now, Ted Bartlette, 30, is in prison. In a small cabin on the compound, he seats himself deferentially on the opposite side of the table and asks, "Have you ever done it?"

He's talking about cocaine. A positive answer means you share a certain fellowship with him. Cocaine researchers might say it means sharing the prolonged state of molecular excitement which comes when coke users get high.

"Cocaine is very subtle," Bartlette says, as he talks about how he became a con. "I didn't do it that much. I was working 10 and 12 hours a day."

A troubleshooter for printed circuit boards at Vicker's Audio in Chapel Hill, Bartlette was also building a satellite disk installation business when he was arrested last spring.

"A toot might keep me awake, and I could work okay, but if I went back to the truck a second or a third time, I wouldn't want to do any more work when I came back. I'd pack up and go home. I really couldn't snort on the job."

Cocaine users who begin to sell often do it as a favor to friends, analysts say. Bartlette, also, did someone a favor. He delivered cocaine for a friend. The friend turned out to be an undercover cop.

The sting lit up his middle-class Colony Court neighborhood about 500 feet from the UNC-CH campus.

"The cops were yelling out the windows, 'Whoopee—we got a big' un!' There must have been seven cops," he says. "They raced around Hardee's leaning on their horns."

In May, 1984, Bartlette was convicted in Orange County Superior Court of intent to sell cocaine. He was sentenced to three years. Employers' testimonies secured him work release as "an accomplished electronics technician."

In Durham County Prison, the 39 others in his work release unit call him the "whiz kid." They leave him alone.

Through the work-release program, he demonstrates spread sheets, word processing, color graphics, and video games at a local micro-computer center six days a week. He catches his ride from Durham to Carrboro around 6 a.m. and returns to the prison by 8 p.m. each weeknight.

He spends his Sundays outside prison with his sponsor, an aerospace engineer.

At night in prison he studies gemology—gemstone cutting, brokerage and appraisal. He has a 97 average in his correspondence course and hopes within five years to be a master gemologist.

After his mother died when he was three, he was raised by his grandmother and his aunt and uncle.

He was an honors student at a small, elite boarding school. He canoed and hiked at summer camp in upstate New York.

In the '70s he left home and settled in New Mexico, where he apprenticed himself to a goldsmith. She made $1,000 a day, he says, and he designed and set jewelry for her several years.

"I like to design things that are not like anything else, like inlay inside a piece," he opens his palm and touches his gold wedding ring, "where only you can see it—things that are, you know, personal."

Later on, still in Hopi and Navaho country, he sold natural cosmetics, opened a restaurant and, finally, established a graphics business for TV, video, and print advertising.

"I care about real quality. I care about helping people. I don't understand why people cut corners.

"At the trial, they brought out that the cocaine I sold was 85 percent pure. I wouldn't cut it. I mean, it's not good for you anyway, but the stuff they cut it with is really not good for you."

No, he won't sell cocaine again. Not because he thinks there's anything wrong with it, he says. And not exactly for fear of punishment. "You can't fear what you don't know, and there's no way anyone could know what it's like to be in prison. You're nothing here."

He turns his ring. "Sometimes I feel so bad I just hold my book and stare, and I can't read anything.

"I'm fortunate," Bartlette says. "I'm learning about engineering and about aerospace design and gemology, and being in jail has given me the chance to learn about computers."

Among the mementos Bartlette keeps in a briefcase is a response letter from a person who has influenced his life. It reads in part:

"Your letter was one of the most moving that I have ever received. You obviously have excellent reasons to hate me, but apparently you do not. . . . To my amazement, you are looking at your present situation as an opportunity to learn and to improve yourself. . . . I do not hesitate to tell you that your letter goes a very long way toward justifying my existence."

It is signed by the judge who sentenced him, James H. Pou Bailey.

Here, we explain how the section was done. Also, we provide information that serious readers need—and credit that participants deserve.

A look at the story behind the section

The cocaine report represents three months' work by students at the UNC-CH School of Journalism.

Students in the advanced reporting class of Philip Meyer, William Rand Kenan Jr. Professor, and Associate Professor Jane Brown's media research methods class began planning the investigation in January. While the reporting class conducted interviews with cocaine victims' families and with officials, the research class considered theoretical aspects of the survey.

In February, the students conducted a Carolina Poll of Orange County residents, using a central telephone bank in the School's Knight Advertising Center.

Students analyzed the results using a statistical computer program and terminals at the UNC-CH Institute for Research in Social Science.

Students in Assistant Professor Bill Cloud's advanced editing class revised the stories and created the layout and design for the section.

Students in Lecturer Rich Beckman's photojournalism class provided the photographs.

Gina Hart and Andy Miller supervised the editing, and Margaret Ryan was in charge of production.

Tables and graphs were prepared by Fannie Zollicoffer as part of an independent study.

Phyllis Rich served as photography editor.

Advanced reporting students: Amy Anderson, Margaret H. Bell, Lee Bollinger, Richard Boyce, Lauren Brown, Richard Craver, Winfred B. Cross, Steve Ferguson, Jim Hoffman, Genie Lindberg, Bob McCarson, Marty Minner, Lila Moore, Lori Nickel, Susan Oakley, Cindy Partridge, Cassandra Poteat, W. Keith Pritchard, Kurt Rosenberg, Cindi Ross, Jimmy Tomlin, David E. Wells and Cheryl Williams.
Media research methods students: Tom Anderson, Mary Ann Arim, Liz Clark, Jamal El-Hindi, Keith Fishburne, Craig Fisher-LaMay, Bonnie Foust, Nick Henry, Kathy Keller, Rita Lauria, Lorraine Marca, Jim McDuffie, Jo Ellen Meekins, Kevin Meredith, Andy Miller, Leslie Purcell, Olivia Ross and Amy Styers.
Advanced editing students: Diane Beatty, Clarice Bickford, Nicole Broom, Phillip Brown, Richard Burnett, Caroline Compton, Tom Corrigan, Jamal El-Hindi, Chris Fields, Bonnie Foust, Pattie Harris, Lane Harvey, Jeff Hiday, Sherry Johnson, Susan Lalik, Liz Lucas, Jean Moore, Glenn Peterson, Mary Alice Resch, Lee Roberts, Bill Rose, Kelly Simmons, Allison Smoak, Doug Tate and Carolyn Wilson.
Photography students: Jeff Van Dyke, Kelli Coggins, Karla Sleeper, Gretchen Gass and Nancy Good.

The Questionnaire Used by Students

Editorial Note: This is the questionnaire used by students to interview 535 Orange County residents by telephone in February 1985. You will see how the questionnaire is designed to keep students on track while eliciting some "private" information from respondents. Drug use questions are sometimes buried, especially early in the approximately ten-minute interview. See if you can spot how these student journalists tried to work up to the hard questions about drug use.

School of Journalism   Feb. 3, 4, 5

Time dialed phone: _____ p.m.

Time respondent on phone: _____ p.m.

Time last question answered: _____ p.m.

Hello. My name is _____ from the School of Journalism at UNC. We do the Carolina Poll, we're doing one today, and it is completely confidential. I need to know what county you live in right now, either as a student or as a fulltime resident.

IF NOT ORANGE, TERMI-NATE.

And how many persons 18 and older are at this number?

NUMBER OF PERSONS: _____ persons

IF MORE THAN ONE: Okay. And their ages?

WRITE DOWN AGES:

Okay, let's see now. That's _____ persons, and their ages are _____ and _____. Is that right? IF NO, CORRECT. IF YES, CON-TINUE.

Now we need to choose one person to interview, and the way we do that is to choose the one with the next birthday. Which of the _____ of you will be the next one to have a birthday?

WRITE DOWN IDENTITY (AGE OR RELATIONSHIP OR FIRST NAME):

IF IT IS THIS PERSON, PROCEED WITH INTERVIEW. IF NOT, GET THE CHOSEN PERSON ON THE LINE OR MAKE AN APPOINTMENT FOR CALLBACK.

---

1. The first thing I need to know is what city or town do you live in?

1. Chapel Hill
2. Carrboro
3. Hillsborough
4. Other, none

2. Are you a student? (IF YES) Where?

1. UNC
2. Duke
3. Durham Tech
4. Other

3. I'm going to read a short list of problems facing the people of Orange County. For each one, please tell me whether you think it is a very serious problem in Orange County, somewhat serious, not too serious, or not serious at all.

	VS	SS	NT	NA	DK
Alcohol abuse....................	1	2	3	4	9
Child abuse......................	1	2	3	4	9
Use of illegal drugs.............	1	2	3	4	9
Speeding in school zones	1	2	3	4	9
Poor upkeep of roads	1	2	3	4	9
Unleashed dogs	1	2	3	4	9
Light sentences for convicted criminals	1	2	3	4	9

---

4. Do you think the use of illegal drugs is more or less of a problem in Orange County than in the rest of the United States?

More............... 1
Same 2
Less 3
DK................. 9

5. (IF YES) Why do you think drug abuse is more of a problem in Orange County than in the rest of the United States? (PROBE)

Students 1
Other 2
DK 9

6. Okay. We've been talking about some specific problems here in Orange County, including the use of illegal drugs. Now I would like to ask you a few questions about cocaine. Do you think cocaine use in Orange County is higher or lower than it is in the United States as a whole?

Higher 1
About same 2
Lower 3
DK 9

7. Why do you think people use cocaine? DO NOT READ LIST. PROBE. CIRCLE AS MANY AS APPLY.

	Cited	Not Cited
Fun and recreation..............	1	2
Get high, feel good	1	2
Curiosity, experimentation.....	1	2
Boredom, nothing else to do...	1	2
Status, prestige	1	2
Everyone else is doing it.......	1	2
To increase one's energy level	1	2
Addiction or dependence	1	2
Enhancement of sex	1	2
Relief of stress...................	1	2
Feeling of power and control.	1	2
Some other reason	1	2

8. As I read you a list of types of people, please tell me if you think each uses cocaine more or less than the average person.

	More	Same	Less	DK
University students	1	2	3	9
Professional people, such as lawyers or doctors..............	1	2	3	9
Visitors to Orange County	1	2	3	9

	More	Same	Less	DK
Professional athletes............	1	2	3	9
College athletes.................	1	2	3	9
People who live in Chapel Hill................................	1	2	3	9
High school students	1	2	3	9
People who live in Carrboro ..	1	2	3	9
Law enforcement officers	1	2	3	9
People who live in Hillsborough.....................	1	2	3	9

9. Do you know anyone who uses or has used cocaine?

Yes.................. 1
No 2
Refused 3
DK.................. 9

10. We would like to know how you feel about cocaine use. As I read you a list of statements, please tell me how much you agree or disagree. Do you strongly agree, agree somewhat, disagree somewhat, or strongly disagree?

	SA	A	D	SD	DK
Cocaine is a safe way to get high................................	1	2	3	4	9
Cocaine use should be legal...	1	2	3	4	9
Cocaine is dangerous even when used a little bit...........	1	2	3	4	9
People in Chapel Hill are more tolerant of cocaine than people in most of the U.S.	1	2	3	4	9
Laws against the use of cocaine should be made more severe ..	1	2	3	4	9
Law enforcement against cocaine in Chapel Hill and Orange County is not adequate..	1	2	3	4	9

11. In general, when you see references to cocaine on television, is it portrayed as very dangerous, dangerous, acceptable or very acceptable?

Very danger 1
Dangerous 2
Acceptable........ 3
Very accep........ 4
DK, not port 9

12. Would you support or oppose a tax increase to pay for more police officers to enforce drug laws in Orange County?

Support 1
Oppose........... 2
DK................ 9

13. Would you support or oppose a tax increase to pay for more educational and rehabilitation programs to fight drug abuse?

Support 1
Oppose........... 2
DK................ 9

14. Here's another list. Please tell me whether you think each item is more or less serious than *selling* cocaine.

	More	Less	DK
Home burglary	1	2	9
Car theft.........................	1	2	9
Vandalism.......................	1	2	9
Drunken driving	1	2	9
Armed robbery	1	2	9
Sale of heroin...................	1	2	9
Sale of marijuana...............	1	2	9
Selling alcohol to 17-year-olds	1	2	9
Shoplifting	1	2	9

Now these questions are for classification purposes.

13. What is your age?   _____

14. What is the last year or grade of school that you have completed?

0–8 1
9–11 2
12................. 4
13–15............. 5
16 6
17+............... 7

15. And what is your race?

White.............. 1
Black 2
Other............. 3

16. I have just one more list. Again, for classification purposes and in complete confidence, have you yourself ever happened to try any of the things on this list. How about . . . READ LIST

	Yes	No	DK
Alcohol	1	2	9
Amphetamines or uppers	1	2	9
Barbituates or downers.........	1	2	9
Marijuana	1	2	9
Cocaine...........................	1	2	9
LSD................................	1	2	9
Heroin............................	1	2	9

17. IF COCAINE TRIED ABOVE, ASK:

	Yes	No	DK
a. Have you used cocaine in the past month?	1	2	9

b. About how often do you use cocaine?

More than once a week.............. 1
Weekly........... 2
Several times a month 3
About once a month 4
Several times a year............... 5
Once or twice a year 6
Less often........ 7
DK, refused 9

c. And how old were you the first time that you tried cocaine? _____

That's all of the questions. This study has been done for a class in reporting at the UNC School of Journalism. Would you be willing to talk to a student reporter to discuss the issue of illegal drugs in greater detail?

Thank you for your time and co-operation.

RECORD SEX WITHOUT ASKING:	Male...............	1
	Female............	2
RECORD SERIAL NUMBER FOR EVERYONE:		_____

Index